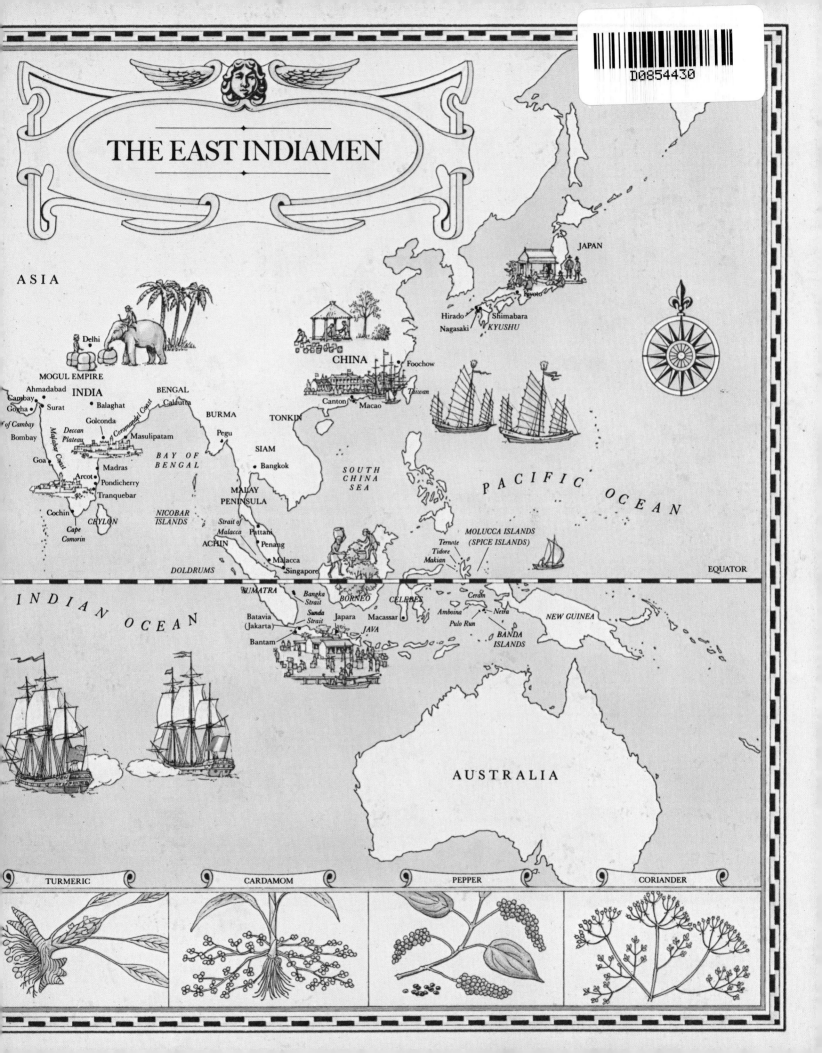

THE EAST INDIAMEN

ASIA

Delhi

MOGUL EMPIRE

Ahmadabad
INDIA
Cambay
Gogha   Surat   Balaghat
of Cambay   Golconda
Bombay   *Deccan Plateau*   *Coromandel Coast*   Masulipatam
Goa
Arcot   Madras
Pondicherry
Tranquebar
Cochin
CEYLON
Cape Comorin

BENGAL
Calcutta

BURMA

Pegu

SIAM
Bangkok

MALAY PENINSULA

NICOBAR ISLANDS

Strait of Malacca   Pattani
ACHIN   Penang
Malacca
Singapore

DOLDRUMS

BAY OF BENGAL

TONKIN

SOUTH CHINA SEA

CHINA
Foochow
Canton   Macao
Taiwan

JAPAN
Hirado   Shimabara
Nagasaki   *KYUSHU*   Kyoto

PACIFIC OCEAN

MOLUCCA ISLANDS (SPICE ISLANDS)
Ternate
Tidore
Makian

EQUATOR

INDIAN OCEAN

SUMATRA   *Bangka Strait*
Batavia (Jakarta)   *Sunda Strait*   Japara   Macassar
Bantam   *JAVA*

BORNEO   *CELEBES*

Ceram
Amboina   Netra
Pulo Run
BANDA ISLANDS

NEW GUINEA

AUSTRALIA

TURMERIC   CARDAMOM   PEPPER   CORIANDER

The Seafarers THE EAST
INDIAMEN

TIME
LIFE
BOOKS

The Cover: Off the coast of China, the British East Indiaman *Asia* runs under full sail in this early-19th Century oil painting by W. J. Huggins. In his youth Huggins served on Indiamen as an ordinary seaman; returning to England around 1815, he became one of the most popular marine painters of his day.

The Title Page: As depicted on a plate by a Chinese craftsman in 1756, the Dutch Indiaman *Vryburg* rides upon a stylized sea. Many 18th Century sea captains commissioned Cantonese artisans to portray their vessels on porcelain while they awaited loading for the passage home.

The Seafarers

THE EAST INDIAMEN

by Russell Miller

AND THE EDITORS OF TIME-LIFE BOOKS

TIME-LIFE BOOKS, AMSTERDAM

The Seafarers
Editorial Staff for *The East Indiamen*:
Editor: Jim Hicks
Designer: Herbert H. Quarmby
Chief Researcher: W. Mark Hamilton
Picture Editor: Peggy L. Sawyer
Text Editors: Anne Horan, Stuart Gannes, Gus Hedberg,
Lydia Preston, David Thiemann
Staff Writers: Kathleen M. Burke,
Donald Davison Cantlay
Researchers: Cécile Ablack, Carol A. Enquist,
Adrienne George, Fran Glennon, Sheila M. Green,
Ann Dusel Kuhns, James R. Stengel, Jean Strong
Art Assistant: Michelle René Clay
Editorial Assistant: Ellen Keir

Special Contributors
Bryce Walker (essay); Barbara Hicks (research)

Correspondents: Elisabeth Kraemer (Bonn);
Margot Hapgood, Dorothy Bacon, Lesley Coleman
(London); Susan Jonas, Lucy T. Voulgaris (New York);
Maria Vincenza Aloisi, Josephine du Brusle (Paris);
Ann Natanson (Rome).
Valuable assistance was provided by Nakanori Tashiro,
Asia Editor, Tokyo. The editors also wish to thank:
Janny Hovinga (Amsterdam); Enid Farmer (Boston);
Katrina Van Duyn (Copenhagen); Bing Wong
(Hong Kong); Peter Hawthorne (Johannesburg);
Martha de la Cal (Lisbon); Judy Aspinall, Karin B. Pearce
(London); John Dunn (Melbourne); Carolyn T. Chubet,
Miriam Hsia, Christina Lieberman (New York);
Marie-Thérèse Hirschkoff (Paris); Mimi Murphy (Rome);
Mary Johnson (Stockholm); Peter Allen (Sydney);
Katsuko Yamazaki (Tokyo).

ISBN 7054 0635 0

TIME-LIFE is a trademark of Time Incorporated U.S.A.

The Author:
Russell Miller is a British journalist and
author whose work has appeared regularly
in *The Sunday Times* and is syndicated
throughout the world. During the course of
extensive travels in Europe and the Orient,
he has visited many of the port cities whose
harbors were once filled with East Indiamen. He is the author of *The Resistance* in
the Time-Life Books' World War II series.

The Consultants:
John Horace Parry, Gardiner Professor of
Oceanic History and Affairs at Harvard
University, holds a Ph.D. from Cambridge
University. Among his historical studies
are *The Discovery of the Sea, Europe and a
Wider World* and *Trade and Dominion*.

Peter Marsden, a staff member of the Museum of London, is a specialist in nautical
archeology and an authority on 17th and
18th Century Eastern trade. His extensive
writings include *The Wreck of the Amsterdam*, an account of a Dutch East Indiaman
lost off the coast of England in 1749.

William Avery Baker was curator of the
Hart Nautical Museum at the Massachusetts Institute of Technology, and was a
distinguished naval architect. He wrote
numerous studies on maritime history,
and designed reproductions of many
vessels of the 17th and 18th Centuries.

Contents

Chapter 1

An all-out race for the Orient's wealth

Welcoming spice-laden Indiamen home from the East, fishing smacks crowd Amsterdam harbor in 1599—the dawn of an era of quickening trade.

andemonium broke loose in England's Dartmouth harbor one soft summer afternoon in 1592 when the *Madre de Deus,* a Portuguese carrack captured while homeward bound from India, dropped anchor near the town's dock. She was the biggest ship anyone in Elizabethan England had ever seen, a floating castle that dwarfed the little fishermen's cottages fronting the quay. She stretched to 165 feet in length, and had a beam of 47 feet and a burden of nearly 1,600 tons—about three times the capacity of the largest English ships. Her seven decks, towering one above the other, were studded with 32 brass guns and a multitude of secondary ordnance. The gilded wood and bright paint work of her decorations and emblems glistened in the sun.

It was not the ship's size and majesty, however, that attracted the crowds of people that soon flocked into Dartmouth. It was her cargo. The *Madre de Deus* was packed with a fortune in Oriental riches, and every merchant, huckster and thief within riding distance was intent on getting part of the treasure. In fact, the looting of the carrack had really begun weeks earlier, right after she was surprised by a squadron of six English warships off the Azores. The squadron, under the command of Sir John Burrough, was waiting to ambush Spanish ships from the Caribbean, but a Portuguese carrack from the Indies was not a prize the British were prepared to let slip by.

When, after a brief but bloody engagement, the victorious English sailors clambered aboard the giant vessel and lifted her hatches, they could hardly believe their eyes. Chests were crammed with gold and silver coins, flawless pearls, amber, jewelry set with large diamonds, and vials of precious musk. Costly tapestries and bolts of calico lay below. And deeper in her hold they found cargo of even greater value: 425 tons of pepper, 45 tons of cloves, 35 tons of cinnamon, 25 tons of a dyestuff called cochineal, three tons of mace, three tons of nutmeg, two and a half tons of benjamin (a highly aromatic substance used in perfumes and medicines) and 15 tons of ebony. Before Sir John could take charge of the prize for the return voyage to England, his sailors had stuffed their pockets with all the Portuguese booty they could carry.

At Dartmouth the pillaging continued as the light-fingered sailors trafficked with the greedy throng that flooded the town. Jewelers rode down from London in search of bargains, and privateers from nearby ports sailed round to the harbor to join the free-for-all. Fishermen ferried customers between quay and carrack, and the local taverns were crowded with drunken sailors trading chunks of amber for tankards of ale. A large share of the captured treasure was owed to Queen Elizabeth; when she heard what was happening, she sent Sir Walter Raleigh down from London to retrieve her share of the booty and discipline the looters. "If I meet any of them coming up," Raleigh swore, "if it be upon the wildest heath in all the way, I mean to strip them as naked as ever they were born, for Her Majesty has been robbed and that of the most rare things."

And robbed she was. Sir John Hawkins, Treasurer and Controller of the Navy, estimated that the complete cargo of the *Madre de Deus* had been worth about half a million pounds—or nearly 50 per cent of all the money then in the English Exchequer. When what was left of it finally

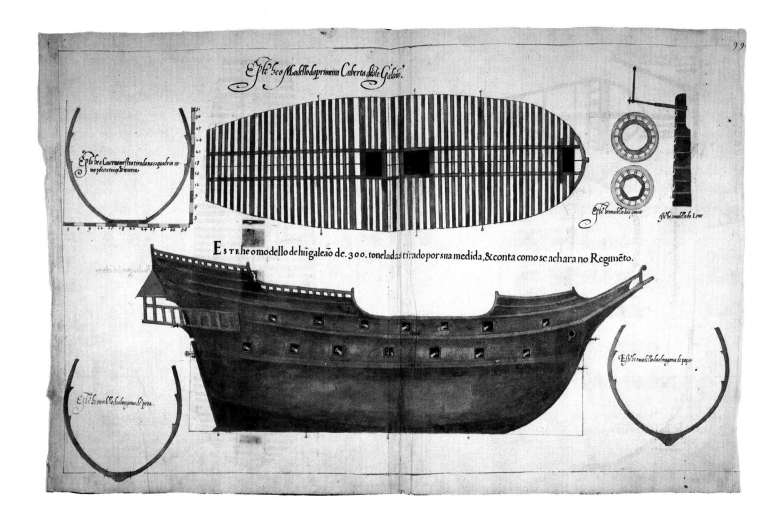

This carpenter's plan from a 1616 shipbuilding manual dissects a 300-ton galleon of the kind the Portuguese sailed in the Indies trade. The drawing features a bird's-eye view of the main-deck beams (top center) and a broadside view of the hull. In the corners are a rudder, two fighting-top platforms (upper right) and (clockwise from lower right) three cross sections of the hull at the afterdeck, the foredeck and amidships.

arrived in London, carried round the coast in 10 freighters, its value was put at about £140,000. Even so, it was a fabulous haul, and for the merchants of London it offered a tantalizing glimpse of the cargoes they might regularly enjoy if they could break what was then a Portuguese monopoly of Eastern trade.

As it happened, a small British fleet was on its way to the East Indies at that very moment. It had been dispatched with some misgivings as to the value of such a dangerous and costly venture, but the wealth found aboard the *Madre de Deus* guaranteed that other English expeditions would follow, whatever the outcome of the pioneering voyage. Within a decade British merchants and seafarers inspired by the Portuguese carrack's treasure would be developing a rewarding trade with the East and laying the foundations for what was to become the most powerful commercial organization the world had ever known.

The Honourable East India Company would establish a mercantile fleet of gigantic proportions and with it reap the riches of the Orient. The Netherlands and France, too, would form companies to compete for the trade of China and the region then known as the East Indies—an area encompassing the Indian subcontinent, the Malay Peninsula, Sumatra, Java and the countless islands scattered east of the South China Sea. In time a substantial portion of the world's population would come under the sway of the rival enterprises. The English East India Company, the most powerful of them all, would eventually control great areas of Asia with its own army and rule over hundreds of millions of people.

Yet trade was the primary concern of the companies, and homeward-bound East Indiamen—as their vessels were called—carried cargoes that altered European life in fundamental ways. The arrival of cotton from India, for example, provided many Europeans for the first time with comfortable and relatively cheap undergarments to wear beneath their woolen clothing, while coffee and Chinese tea virtually revolutionized the drinking habits of Europe.

But spices made up the great bulk of the cargo brought from the East. Meat spoiled quickly during warm weather; spices both preserved the meat and masked its taste. Spices were also the basis of many medicines. Such was their value in the 16th and 17th Centuries that men were prepared to die for them—and indeed many had died long before the British became interested in the market.

The key to trading with the East by sea was Vasco da Gama's discovery of the route round the Cape of Good Hope in 1497. By 1515 the Portuguese had established fortified trading posts in East Africa, at Hormuz in the Persian Gulf, at Cochin and Goa in western India, at Malacca, and in the Moluccas—the fabled Spice Islands. By jealously guarding the Cape route and the secrets of how to navigate its passages, the Portuguese monopolized the trade while doubling Europe's supply of pepper and other spices. Beginning in the middle of the 16th Century, both the English and the Dutch separately sought to break the Portuguese corner on the spice market by finding a new route to the East. Geographers offered two promising alternatives—a northeast passage over the top of Europe and Asia, or a northwest passage through the frozen islands north of the American continent. Both routes, as it turned out, were for all practical purposes navigational dead ends.

To many onlookers in Europe, England's ambitions to traverse the arctic seas or challenge the Portuguese along their established routes seemed almost laughable. The English were considered rough diamonds—uncouth, ill-mannered ruffians for the most part, with not much talent for trade. They had no colonies and could not even claim dominion over the Scottish peoples who inhabited the northern part of their island. Moreover, they had very few ships, and most of those were of insufficient size to cross the oceans. But during the penultimate decade of the 16th Century, two events greatly enhanced England's status as a maritime power and her interest in the East.

In 1580 Sir Francis Drake completed his triumphant voyage round the world. Eight years later a loose assemblage of English warships defeated the Armada, a great fleet Spain had sent to launch an invasion of Britain. English confidence ran higher than ever before. The merchants of London began to seriously consider the possibility of opening trade with the East via the Cape of Good Hope. Drake had shown that the journey was feasible in an English ship, and war with Spain had removed any political problems that might have been involved in challenging the Portuguese monopoly (in 1580 Portugal had become a Spanish province).

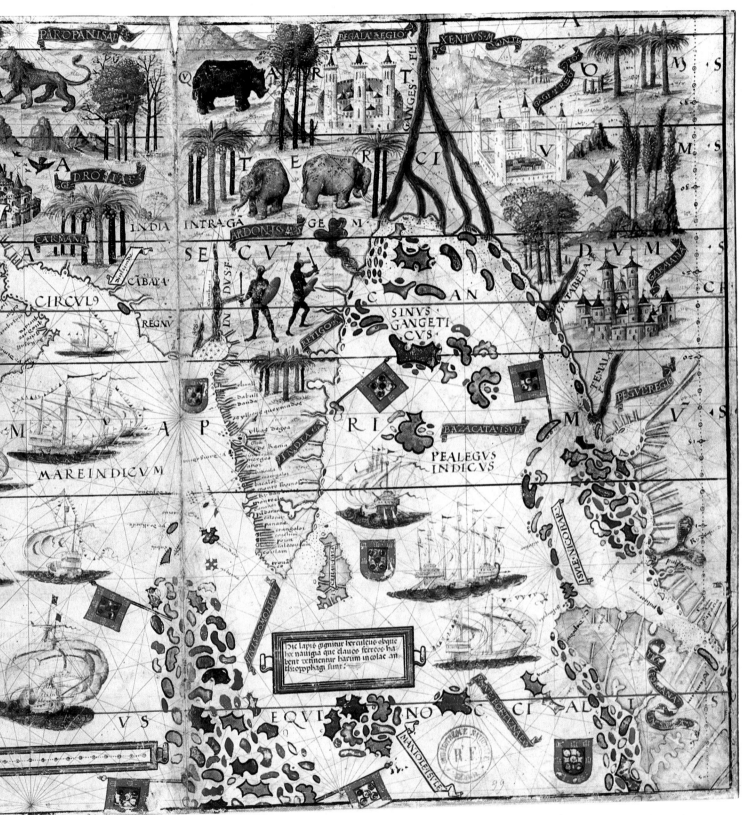

Fortresses, mosques, warriors and indigenous beasts decorate
a 16th Century map of lands bordering the Indian Ocean. The red-
and-blue flags indicate Portuguese settlements; crosses
and crescents respectively mark Portuguese and Muslim ships.

In October 1589 Queen Elizabeth was handed a petition from a group of London merchants seeking permission to send a fleet of ships around the Cape of Good Hope. "Great Benefitte," they said, "will redound to our countree, as well as for the anoyinge of the Spaniards and Portingalls (nowe our enemyes) as also for the ventinge of oure comodities."

The Queen vacillated, perhaps out of a reluctance to release good ships for some far-flung venture at a time when Spain might attempt another attack, or perhaps because of doubt about the "Benefitte" to be obtained (this was nearly three years before the capture of the *Madre de Deus*). But the merchants persevered and eventually received the royal blessing. Three ships, none exceeding 350 tons, were fitted out for the voyage: the *Penelope*, the *Edward Bonaventure* and the *Merchant Royal*. George Raymond, a veteran seafarer who had distinguished himself in the battle against the Spanish Armada, was appointed to command the expedition in the *Penelope*. James Lancaster, a London merchant, was master of the *Edward Bonaventure*, in which ship he, also, had fought the Armada; a mariner named Samuel Foxcroft was captain of the *Merchant Royal*. The little fleet left Plymouth on April 10, 1591 and, veering out into the open Atlantic, struck south.

At first, with the help of a fresh northeast wind, the ships made good progress, but shortly after they had passed the Canary Islands scurvy broke out aboard all three vessels, and two men died from it before the fleet reached the Equator. Edmund Barker, a sailor aboard the *Edward Bonaventure*, diagnosed the affliction as being the result of the weather, which, as he put it, was "wonderful unholesome from 8 degrees of northerly latitude unto the Line at that time of the yeere; for we had nothing but ternados, with such thunder, lightning, and raine, that we could not keep our men drie 3 houres together; which was an occasion of the infection among them."

Delayed by contrary winds, the ships did not reach the Cape of Good Hope until July 28. Raymond ordered them into the shelter of Table Bay to rest and reprovision. A landing party went ashore to trade with a group of Hottentots who had gathered on the beach, but before any exchange was made the Africans suddenly bolted. Thereafter, the only fresh food the Englishmen could find for nearly three weeks was "muskles and other shel-fish" that they gathered from the rocks around the bay, and the few geese they were able to bring down with their muskets. Then one day the Hottentots unexpectedly reappeared at the shoreline with a herd of oxen, bullocks and sheep. Trade was brisk: Two knives bought an ox, a single knife a sheep or a young bullock.

After about a month at Table Bay, it being "thought good rather to proceed with two ships wel manned then with three evill manned," as Edmund Barker wrote, the *Merchant Royal* was sent home with 50 men, and the rest of her crew was distributed between the other two vessels. The *Penelope* and the *Edward Bonaventure* continued together, doubled the Cape easily and set a course up the southeast coast of Africa.

Then, off Mozambique's Cape Correntes, the two ships ran into a "mighty storme and extreeme gusts of wind" that sank one of them. Lancaster's purser, Henry May, who watched in horror from the deck of the *Edward Bonaventure*, later recalled: "We saw a great sea breake over our admirall, the *Penelope*, and their light strooke out; and after that we never saw them any more."

Command of the expedition now fell to James Lancaster. The weather cleared within three days, and after satisfying himself that the *Penelope* had indeed gone down, Lancaster decided to press on up the African coast. His troubles, though, were far from over. Four days later the *Edward Bonaventure* was hit by a bolt of lightning. Edmund Barker described what happened: "In the morning, toward ten of the clocke, we had a terrible clap of thunder, which slew foure of our men outright, their necks being wrung in sonder without speaking any word, and of 94 men there was not one untouched; whereof some were stricken blind, others were bruised in their legs and armes, and others in their brests, so that they voided blood two days after; others were drawen out at length, as though they had been racked. But (God be thanked) they all recovered, saving onely the foure which were slaine outright. Also with the same thunder our mainmaste was torne very grievously from the heade to the decke, and some of the spikes, that were ten inches into the timber, were melted with the extreme heate theereof."

By early October the Englishmen were approaching the densely populated stretch of the coast that lay above Mozambique. Bargelike, barksided vessels known as pangaras began to appear, and at the end of November Lancaster anchored in the fabled port of Zanzibar, where he hoped to spend most of the coming winter. There the expedition learned that the Portuguese were already taking steps to protect their trade monopoly against possible competition. They had told the Africans that the English were violent, cannibalistic people and warned them to avoid English ships at all cost. But the merchants of Zanzibar largely ignored these stories, and by the time Lancaster was ready to sail on three months later he had established friendly relations with the people of the town— including the Portuguese factor, who apparently was glad of European company even if it was the competition.

From Zanzibar, Lancaster headed for Cape Comorin on the southernmost tip of India. But because of a combination of navigational errors and unfavorable winds and currents, the *Edward Bonaventure* ended up 800 miles to the east of the Indian subcontinent at the island of Gomes, off Sumatra, at the beginning of June. With the summer monsoons coming on, Lancaster hurried on to the port of Penang, off the west coast of the Malay Peninsula, where he planned to wait out the bad weather. Sickness took a terrible toll while the ship lolled at anchor off Penang. By August the 97 men who had left the Cape had been reduced to 34, only two thirds of them fit enough to work the ship.

Nevertheless, Lancaster was determined not to return home empty-handed, and he knew none of his backers would object if he obtained a return cargo by means other than trade. Thus, during September, the Englishmen did their best to live up to at least part of the reputation the Portuguese had invented for them in Zanzibar. They stopped and boarded four local merchant ships in the Strait of Malacca, relieving one of them of a cargo of pepper belonging to the Portuguese. Then they attacked a large Portuguese ship, homeward bound from Goa, plundered it and marooned the Portuguese crew on the nearest shore.

On December 3 the *Edward Bonaventure* arrived off Ceylon, where Lancaster hoped to take more Portuguese shipping. But he himself had fallen ill, and his men, disheartened by the many fatalities, were growing weary of the long voyage. They demanded that the ship make for home, and Lancaster, lying in his cabin "more like to die then to live," gave way. On December 8, 1592, the *Edward Bonaventure* set sail for England. She neared the coast of Africa in February 1593, doubled the Cape a few weeks later and on April 3 arrived at St. Helena, where Lancaster hoped to reprovision.

The leg from the little mid-Atlantic island to home was insignificant compared with the distances they had just traveled—but this last phase of the journey proved an utter nightmare. After leaving St. Helena, the *Edward Bonaventure* stalled in the doldrums for over a month. Lancaster then attempted to reach Trinidad, missed the island and was buffeted about the Caribbean by a series of vicious storms. He eventually lost his ship when her cables were mysteriously cut while she was stopped at a small island near Puerto Rico; she drifted off with five men and a boy aboard, never to be seen again.

Lancaster, who was rescued from the island by a French ship, reached England on May 24, 1594, with a mere handful of his men; the rest had died or deserted since leaving St. Helena.

Financially, the expedition had been a disaster. Only one ship, the *Merchant Royal,* had returned, and she brought home nothing but sick men. However, Lancaster had penetrated the Indian seas as far as the Malay Peninsula without effective hindrance by the Portuguese. To the London merchants who had lost money on the expedition, that achievement was no consolation, but it did bode well for future ventures.

Moreover, while Lancaster was away, the *Madre de Deus* had been captured, and her incredible treasure had been working its powerful magic on British ambitions. In 1596 Sir Robert Dudley, son of the Earl of Leicester, one of the Queen's favorites, proposed financing a voyage to Cathay via the Strait of Magellan. Three ships—the *Bear,* the *Bear's Whelp* and the *Benjamin*—were fitted out, and command was given to Benjamin Wood, a veteran of several expeditions to the West Indies. The fleet sailed in July 1596 with a letter from the Queen in Latin to be delivered to "the Great Emperor of China." None of the ships was ever seen again. This disaster, following close on the failure of Lancaster's voyage, might have spelled an end to English mercantile aspirations in the East, had not events across the Channel renewed the determination of London merchants to try again.

It was inevitable that the Dutch would join the competition for Oriental commerce. Intrepid mariners and excellent shipbuilders, they owned a huge merchant fleet and controlled much of the trade along the coast of Europe, from Spain in the south to the Baltic in the north. Their maritime strength was due in part to the scarcity and high price of land in the Netherlands. In other countries people with money to invest put it into real estate, but in Holland they invested their savings in shipping and short-term trading ventures.

The Dutch knew a great deal about Portuguese trading operations in

The Gallion of Mallacca

The St. Christopher Admirall

conception of

The holy Crosse

*Portuguese Indiamen replenish
their stores at the South Atlantic island of
St. Helena, the only revictualing post
between Cape Town and the Cape Verde
Islands. The spring water, wild goats
and citrus fruits were so welcome that the
pilot who drew this chart in 1589
called the island "an earthly paradise."*

the East, mainly from Dutchmen recruited into the Portuguese service. The most influential of these was the geographer Jan Huyghen van Linschoten *(pages 26-31)*, who in the mid-1590s published two major works that, taken together, added up to a virtual blueprint for anyone who wished to dismantle the Portuguese monopoly. One was a book of sailing directions for Eastern waters and the other was his journal, which included a complete catalogue of Portuguese possessions in the East, showing the hollowness of Portugal's claim to be lord of the "conquest, navigation, and commerce of Ethiopia, India, Arabia and Persia." The Portuguese had indeed established themselves in these countries, but their presence there, Linschoten revealed, consisted merely of several far-flung trading stations tolerated by the local governments. His writings were quickly translated into Latin, English, German and French, and were instrumental in persuading many European merchants to consider risking money on an adventure in the East.

In March 1594 nine Dutch merchants set up a Company of Far Lands at Amsterdam to finance a voyage to the East Indies for spices. A fleet of four ships, commanded by one of the merchant's cousins, a mariner named Cornelis Houtman, left in the spring of 1595. The expedition took nearly 15 months to reach Bantam on the northwest coast of Java, by which time many men had died from scurvy and those still alive were brawling among themselves. After much negotiation Houtman eventually secured a trading agreement with the King of Bantam, but the Dutch merchant was arrogant and highhanded with the local inhabitants, and that attitude, plus his refusal to pay the going price for spices, created bad feelings and delays. Nearly two and a half years had elapsed before the fleet got back to Amsterdam, and only 89 of the original 249 men had survived. But the cargoes—245 bags of pepper, 45 tons of nutmeg and 30 bales of mace—more than covered the cost of the expedition, and the trade agreement opened the lid of the Oriental treasure chest.

During the next year five separate trading companies were set up in different Dutch towns, and no fewer than 22 ships were fitted out and dispatched to the East. Only 14 returned. By far the most successful of these voyages was a second venture mounted by the Company of Far Lands. Eight ships under the merchant-mariner Jacob van Neck sailed on May 1, 1598. The fleet rounded the Cape after only three months at sea, but then was split up by heavy storms. Van Neck, with three ships, arrived at Bantam on November 25 to a cordial welcome from the inhabitants. Trading was brisk, and by New Year's Eve all three ships were fully laden. The Dutch sailors were celebrating their success when the other five ships of the fleet hove into view and were "joyously received."

Van Neck headed home with four loaded ships while the rest of the expedition made its way farther east to the Spice Islands to buy cloves, nutmeg and mace. After an absence of less than 15 months, van Neck's four vessels returned to Amsterdam and were greeted with ecstasy. As the city's church bells rang out in celebration, the ships' officers and merchants were treated to a civic reception. "So long as Holland has been Holland," an eyewitness wrote, "such richly laden ships have never been seen." The 300 tons of pepper and 125 tons of cloves brought back by van Neck not only paid for the entire expedition but yielded its investors a profit of 100 per cent. When the other ships returned home safely the following year, heavily laden with spices, the profits of the venture rose to 400 per cent, and the church bells were ringing again.

In London, merchants were dismayed by these Dutch triumphs. Their only established trading link with the East was through the Levant Company, a consortium of English merchants who had arranged to have silk, indigo and spices carried overland from India and Persia through Turkey to the eastern Mediterranean ports. Now this cumbersome and expensive connection was mortally threatened by the Dutch adventurers, who could sell their sea-transported Eastern goods at far lower prices than those the Levant Company charged.

Rumors that the impudent Dutch were planning to buy ships in English ports to supplement their East India fleets finally prompted the London merchants to act. On September 22, 1599, a meeting was held in London to raise funds for a "voiage to the Easte Indias, (the whiche it maie please the Lorde to prosper)." There was no shortage of subscribers. Even many of the investors who had lost money backing Lancaster wanted to join in. In all, 101 men put their names and "the Somes that they will adventure" to the subscription list. Although the enterprise was headed by Sir Stephen Soame, Lord Mayor of London, most investors were ordinary city tradesmen willing to take a gamble, as a sampling of the list shows: Nicholas Leatt, ironmonger, £200; Ralfe Buzbie, grocer, £200; Edwarde Collins, clothworker, £200; William Garwaye, draper, £500; Francis Cherie, vintner, £200; Henrye Bridgeman, leather seller, £200. The total subscription was 30,133 pounds 6 shillings 8 pence, a very considerable sum in 1599. But within the lifetimes of most of its first subscribers, the value of the East India Company—the name the backers gave to their venture—would multiply 50 times over.

At a meeting two days later, the subscribers resolved to petition the Queen for permission to send a trading fleet to the East, and to solicit from her a grant of "sole privilege for soe manie yeres as can be obteyned and for such freedomes of Custome and other tollerations and favors as may be gotten." Elizabeth was known to be in favor of the venture, but talks with Spain to end the long war were imminent, and she had no wish to disrupt them by a direct challenge to Spanish and Portuguese trade in the East; she wanted to assert British trading rights through negotiation. A deputation of subscribers was summoned to the Privy Council on October 17 and informed of the Queen's decision: She would withhold approval.

Peace negotiations opened in Boulogne in the spring of 1600, and the question of trade in the East figured prominently. The Spanish quoted the papal bull of 1493, which divided the non-European world between Spain and Portugal, as Spain's authority for exclusive trade in the Orient. The English commissioners countered with documents that listed all the areas in the East not under effective Spanish or Portuguese control, and claimed the right to trade in those areas if they so desired. In June 1600 the English diplomats at Boulogne were instructed not to yield to Spanish demands for the restriction of English voyages to the East Indies. The next month, negotiations broke down.

Back in London the Privy Council let it be known that a new petition

Queen Elizabeth's air of command in this portrayal reflects her assessment that "I have the heart and stomach of a king." The doughty monarch officially launched her country's seagoing commerce with the Orient by chartering the East India Company in 1600.

Warrior-merchant James Lancaster rests his hands on his sword and a globe in this stern portrait. He fought for England against the Spanish Armada in 1588 (alluded to in the Latin verses above his shoulder) and commanded the East India Company's first fleet in 1601.

from the merchants might be approved. An urgent meeting of the original subscribers was called, and on September 23 they unanimously agreed to "goe forward in the said viage" if the Queen would give her permission. This time she did so; on December 31 she signed the charter of "the Governor and Company of Merchants of London Trading into the East Indies," granting the company a monopoly of trade for 15 years.

Not wanting to lose even a day of their 15-year charter, the merchants had begun preparations for the voyage immediately after the September 23 meeting. By the end of September they had purchased three ships: the *Hector*, 300 tons, the *Susan*, 240 tons, and the *Ascension*, 260 tons. All of them were former Levant Company vessels with capacious holds. A fourth ship, a 600-ton warship with the unbecoming name of *Malice Scourge*, was purchased for the grand sum of £3,700 after protracted bargaining with her owner, the Earl of Cumberland. All four ships were put into dockyards along the Thames for refitting. Time was short and winter was coming on. To prevent the men from leaving their work to "Runne to the Alehouse," the company had a barrel of beer rolled out to each yard every day.

Meanwhile, the company directors attended to the task of working out the complicated financial arrangements for the voyage. Twenty-four thousand Spanish reals of eight—silver coins that were accepted currency in the Orient—were acquired from France to buy return cargoes, it being realized that English merchandise, mainly manufactured woolens, iron, tin and lead, would not attract a sufficient market in the East to fill four ships by barter. The sailors were to be paid two months' wages in advance, and included among their provisions were "Beare for 4 monethes at a pottle per man per day, Syder for 8 monethes at a quart per man per day and Wine for 8 monethes at a pint per man per day."

The problem of what presents should be taken along to give to Eastern kings and princes received great consideration. European merchants who ventured to the Orient at that time were dealing with major, long-established empires. By comparison with the Mogul Empire that ruled most of India, for example, Europe was a collection of petty principalities. Offering an Eastern potentate colored beads and glass trinkets would never do. Europeans arrived in the Orient as supplicants, and they had to bring appropriate gifts. The items finally selected for this expedition included silver ewers, plumes, spectacles, a case of pistols, helmets, looking glasses and embroidered belts.

To command the fleet, no man was better qualified than James Lancaster. Five months after returning from his first disastrous voyage to the East Indies, Lancaster had gone back to sea, leading five ships in a successful raid against Portuguese possessions in Brazil. The directors of the new East India Company unanimously agreed that he should be offered command of their first voyage. There had been a suggestion from the Queen's Lord High Treasurer that the position should go to a soldier, Sir Edward Michelborne, a friend of the Earl of Essex. But the merchants wanted nothing to do with Michelborne, begging to be allowed to "sort ther busines with men of ther owne qualety." Sir Edward was an aristocrat and, as the company spelled it out, "Wee purpose nott to ymploy anie gent in anie playse of charge, lest the suspition of the imployment of gents do dryve a great number of the adventurers to withdrawe ther contributions." The job of pilot major went to John Davis, veteran of several expeditions to find a northwest passage and recently returned from the East Indies with the Dutchman Cornelis Houtman.

The fleet assembled on the Thames at Woolwich during the first few days of February 1601. Lancaster and Davis were to sail in the *Malice Scourge*, now renamed the *Red Dragon*. William Brand, a "grave and discreet merchaunt and one which hath the Arabyann, Spanish and Portugall languages," was captain of the *Ascension*, and John Heyward and John Middleton, two experienced seamen, were given command, respectively, of the *Susan* and the *Hector*. A 120-ton pinnace, the *Gift*, was to carry additional stores for the first part of the voyage.

In a stroke of ingeniously pragmatic diplomacy, Lancaster was provided with six identical letters of royal greetings signed by the Queen—each with a blank space to be filled in with the name of the ruler to whom it was to be presented. "Elizabeth by the grace of God," the letters began, "Queen of England, France and Ireland, Defendresse of the Christian Faith and Religion. To the great and mightie"—here the ruler's name was to be inserted—"our loving brother, greeting." Three merchants were appointed to travel with each ship to handle the actual commercial business in the East. Including these supercargoes, as they came to be known, the total complement of the fleet was 480 men.

On the cold, gray morning of February 13, a small crowd of investors and well-wishers gathered on the riverbanks to watch the fleet set sail. It was not an auspicious departure. Adverse winds kept the five ships in the Thames estuary for weeks. On April 20 they finally cleared the English Channel, and a week later the little ships were bucking and rolling through Atlantic swells before a fair wind. After passing the Canaries, the fleet set a course that took them too close to the coast of Africa; as a result, they spent a month becalmed in the doldrums.

Off the coast of Guinea the wind picked up, and on the morning of June 21 a single sail appeared on the horizon. Lancaster's privateering reflexes came into play, and he ordered the fleet to give chase. By 2 o'clock in the afternoon, English sailors were boarding a lone Portuguese carrack, outward-bound from Lisbon. They helped themselves to 164 butts of wine, 12 barrels and 176 jars of oil, and 55 hogsheads and vats of meal, which, one of the merchants on the *Red Dragon* reported—hoping, perhaps, to mitigate this most unmercantile behavior—were "a greate helpe to us in the whole voyage after." The booty was divided equally among the ships, and the fleet continued on its way, crossing the Equator at midnight on the last day of June.

On the 20th of July, Lancaster halted the fleet in order to rid himself of one of his own ships. The little victualer *Gift*, which had been supplying the other ships with provisions since they had left England, was now nearly empty, and she was slowing down the progress of the expedition. Her crew was divided up among the other ships, and her masts and sails were taken down and stowed away as spares. Her deck cabins were then broken up for firewood and, according to plan, she was left adrift.

Holding a southerly course toward the tip of Africa, the rest of the ships made excellent progress. But they now had been at sea without

A company that survived by shipping spices east

Persians guard a caravan to the Levant. Camels, called "ships of the desert," had been transporting cargo for thousands of years.

While most Englishmen cheered Captain James Lancaster's inauguration of maritime commerce with the Orient in 1603, one bloc of merchants thought the achievement was bad news indeed. They were men with investments in the Levant Company, a trading concern that had been established in 1581 in the Syrian city of Aleppo, where ancient overland routes from Turkey, Arabia, Mesopotamia and Persia converged. Here, Arab merchants had dealt in spices long before Europeans reached the Indies by sea. And here, British merchants of the Levant Company bought spices (together with such Mediterranean delicacies as wine, oil, honey and currants) and shipped them back to England by way of the Mediterranean.

The English East India Company, which emerged quickly on the heels of Captain Lancaster's voyage, proved able to purchase a consignment of spices in the Far East for about a third of the price that the Levant Company had to pay for the same quantity in Aleppo. The higher cost to the Levant Company was a reflection of the markups that were taken by the Eastern merchants in return for their services in transporting the spices all the way from the Orient—first by ship across the Indian Ocean and through the Persian Gulf, then by caravan across the deserts of Persia and Mesopotamia.

In addition to paying the cost of the spices, the Levant Company spent heavily to maintain good relations with the vast corps of Ottoman officials who ruled more than three million square miles of the Near East. The largess that was dispensed to the Sultan and his minions ranged from cash payments in gold coins to presents of jewel-studded clocks, silver pitchers and a pack of 13 well-bred dogs. This overhead, which the Levant Company naturally included in its own markup when selling spices in London, further widened the discrepancy between its prices and those charged by the East India Company.

But the Levant Company merchants soon discovered that inexpensive spices in London represented a windfall for themselves no less than for the public; the company could buy the spices in England instead of in Aleppo, and then ship them back through the Mediterranean for resale to merchants in the Middle East. By 1626 the value of the Levant Company exports to Turkey alone came to a total of £250,000, and the company was making bigger profits than it had during the years when its trading traffic flowed in the other direction.

fresh food for six months and, at least on the three smaller vessels, telltale signs of scurvy—bleeding from the nose and gums—were evident among the men. The health of sailors aboard the *Red Dragon* was better because Lancaster had laid in a stock of bottled lemon juice on that ship and prescribed three spoonfuls daily to every man.

So many men were stricken on one of the other ships that the merchants serving as supercargoes were obliged to take turns at the helm and even to go aloft to help furl the topsails. By the time the fleet arrived at Table Bay, on September 9, Lancaster had to send parties from his own crew onto the other ships to help them maneuver into the anchorage, for "the state of the other three was such that they were hardly able to let fall an anchor to save themselves." The reckoning was dismal: 105 of the 480 men in the squadron had died.

At Table Bay the sick were put ashore in tents made from the ships' sails. Nourished by fresh meat and vegetables bought from the Hottentots, most of them recovered. After seven weeks the fleet put to sea again, and on the morning of November 1 the four ships rounded the Cape.

But scurvy forced Lancaster to seek fresh rations once more, and the fleet put into Antongil Bay, on the northeast coast of Madagascar, on Christmas Day, 1601. There the men learned from a message scratched on a rock that five Dutch ships had been there two months before, losing, during their visit, 150 to 200 men to tropical fever.

When the Englishmen went ashore to bargain for fresh fruit and meat, they discovered the inhabitants of Madagascar to be "very subtill and craftie in their bartering, buying, and selling." As one of the English merchants said: "They will sift you continually to give a little more, and then no man wil sell without that price." Lancaster tried to settle the matter by laying down a fixed number of glass beads to be paid for different provisions. Still, extensive bargaining sessions were necessary before the Englishmen finally bought 15 tons of rice, 40 bushels of peas and beans, eight oxen, and a large number of chickens.

Bartering was not the only problem Lancaster faced at Antongil Bay. On January 17, Christopher Newchurch, the surgeon aboard the *Ascension*, became depressed and tried to poison himself. He failed and, after three or four days of agony, recovered sufficiently to be stripped of his rank. Then 13 men from the *Red Dragon*, including the master's mate, the preacher and the surgeon, died of dysentery. At their funeral an absurd accident compounded the loss. It is best told in the words of the anonymous author of "A True and Large Discourse of the Voyage," a narrative description of the whole adventure by someone who sailed aboard the *Ascension*: "Saterday, the lamentablest accident happened. The maisters mate of the admiral died, and the rest of the captaines went to his burial; and according to the order of the sea, there was 2 or 3 great ordinances discharged. But the gunner, being not so carfull as he should have beene, unfortunately killed the captaine of the *Ascension* and the boatswaines mate of the same ship. Many others were hurt and besprinkled with the bloud of these massacred men, who, going to the burial of another, were themselves carryed to their owne graves."

No one was sorry to bid farewell to Antongil Bay when the fleet sailed on March 6, 1602, and directed its course toward Sumatra.

Sir Thomas Smythe, who became the first governor of the English East India Company in 1600, holds a map of far-flung lands—a symbol of the trading monopoly's global reach. The Latin inscription framing the portrait aptly styles him the "Golden Knight": In 21 years as governor, he parlayed the company's initial capital of some £30,000 into well over £1.5 million.

Three months later, on June 5, the four ships arrived off Achin, their first trading port of call, at the northern end of the island of Sumatra. Achin, the present-day city of Kutaraja, Indonesia, was a major Asian trading center, and the sails of many different nations—Gujarat, Bengal and Malabar in India; Pegu in Burma; and Pattani on the Malay Peninsula—were already anchored in the roadstead.

Two Dutch factors, left behind by one of the Dutch fleets that had preceded the Englishmen, were first on board to greet the English visitors. No doubt they were only too pleased to see other European faces; the intense hatred that was to be generated by the rivalry between the Dutch and the English had not yet developed. Lancaster was astonished to learn that the Queen of England was well known in Achin, by reason of "the warres and great victories which she had gotten against the king of Spaine," and the Dutchmen assured him he would receive a warm welcome from Ala-uddin Riayat Shah, the King.

But perhaps even the imperturbable Lancaster was not prepared for what greeted him when some of Ala-uddin's retainers were sent to pick up the English captain for his interview with the potentate. Six great elephants appeared on the foreshore, surrounded by trumpeters, drummers and a troop of 20 men carrying silk streamers. On the back of the biggest elephant, some 14 feet high, was a richly decorated pavilion-like structure, lined with crimson velvet and containing a gold basin. The letter from Queen Elizabeth (with Ala-uddin's name hurriedly entered in the appropriate space) was reverently placed in the basin and covered by richly embroidered silk. Then Lancaster heaved himself uneasily onto the back of another elephant, and the whole procession, led by the trumpets and drums, moved off to the palace.

Before being ushered into the presence of the King, the visitors were instructed by court officials in the necessary obeisance to be made: With shoes and stockings removed, they had to hold their palms together above their heads, bend forward at the waist and say "doulat" (prosperity), after which the King would return the salute and invite them to be seated cross-legged on the ground.

Ala-uddin turned out to be an aged man, grossly fat, who had succeeded to the throne by the time-honored method of murdering two previous occupants; nevertheless, his hospitality was first-class. Lancaster first delivered the Queen's letter and then a selection of suitable presents—a large silver basin and cup, a looking glass, a headpiece with a plume, a case of pistols, an embroidered sword belt and a fan of feathers. All of these were received by a court nobleman on behalf of the King, except the fan, which the King particularly liked and took with his own hands and "caused one of his women to fanne him therewithall."

After everyone was seated, the King ordered a banquet to be served. More than 200 gold and brass dishes of cooked meats were carried in, along with brimming gold cups of rice wine. During the feast the King asked Lancaster questions about Queen Elizabeth. How long had she reigned? Was she married? Then, according to another Englishman who was present, "the King told Lancaster, if the words in Her Majesties letter came from the hart, he had cause to thinke well thereof."

"Dinner being ended," the chronicler went on, "the king caused his

damsels to daunce and his women to play musicke unto them; who were
richly adorned with bracelets and jewels, and this was a great favour, for
hee dooth not usually let them be seene to any." Before the visitors
departed, Ala-uddin presented Lancaster with a white calico robe embroidered in gold, an ornate girdle and two fine daggers, all of which he
was obliged to wear as he left the palace.

As a result of the Queen's letter and the amiable carousing that followed its presentation, the King granted his English guests freedom to
trade and immunity from the payment of customs. For Lancaster it was a
significant achievement: the first treaty between an Eastern monarch
and the English East India Company. But permission to trade was one
thing, actual trade another. The previous year's harvest had been poor,
and pepper was both scarce and expensive. After several weeks at Achin,
it became clear to Lancaster that he was not going to be able to find return
cargoes for his fleet, so he sent the *Susan* to Priaman, a Sumatran city 450
miles to the south, said to be a source of cheaper and more plentiful

*In the Strait of Malacca, the Portuguese
carrack Santo Antônio fights off encircling
English and Dutch vessels. Captain
Joris van Speilbergen of the Schaep (bottom
left) was unable to resist a patriotic
exaggeration in this scene from his journal:
Though three ships are shown flying
Dutch colors, only the Schaep was Dutch.*

spices. Then he turned his thoughts to other ways of filling his ships.

Privateering was second nature to Elizabethan sailors, particularly if the victim was a Spanish or Portuguese ship, and Lancaster knew he could rely on the ferocity and enthusiasm of his men in a fight at sea, even against superior odds. It could not have been a difficult decision to put out into the Strait of Malacca to lie in wait for the enemy merchantmen he knew plied those seas.

There was just one problem: The Portuguese envoy to the court of Ala-uddin would surely raise the alarm if the fleet set sail. But Lancaster and the King were now fast friends. When the Englishman suggested that the King might detain the Portuguese envoy on some pretext to prevent him from warning his countrymen in Malacca that the English ships were preparing to sail, Ala-uddin slyly agreed, provided Lancaster brought him a "faire Portugall maiden" as his share of the prize.

On September 11, 1602, the *Red Dragon*, the *Hector* and the *Ascension* hoisted their anchors and headed out to sea, while the fuming Portuguese envoy daily petitioned the King for permission to leave Achin and was daily refused. On October 3 in the Strait of Malacca, the crew of the *Hector* sighted a distant sail. As night was falling, the stranger fell in with the *Hector*. She was a large, well-armed Portuguese carrack of about 700 tons. At first she put up a valiant fight against the *Hector* and the *Ascension*, but Lancaster, arriving on the scene in the *Red Dragon*, discharged six of his bow guns in one volley. The carrack, dismasted by the salvo, promptly struck her colors.

For the rest of the night the Portuguese merchantman drifted with her unwelcome escort close by. At dawn the Portuguese captain clambered into a boat and was rowed across to the *Hector* to formally surrender his ship. It took the unfortunate Portuguese crew nearly six days to transfer 950 packs of calico and numerous chests of other merchandise from their vessel to the victor's ships. Lancaster would not let the English sailors help because he knew they would steal the pick of the booty.

By October 24 the English fleet was back at Achin. Lancaster selected presents for the King from the prize cargo and side-stepped his inquiry about the "faire Portugall maiden" by saying he could find "none so worthy that merited to be so presented." At Achin the *Ascension* completed her lading with pepper and spices procured by two English merchants left behind while the fleet was in the Strait of Malacca.

On November 9, carrying a letter and presents from the King for his "cousin" Queen Elizabeth, the three ships finally left Achin. The *Ascension* set a course for England. The *Red Dragon* and the *Hector* made their way to Priaman, where they found the *Susan* still taking on pepper and spices. She was instructed to complete her cargo as quickly as possible and follow the *Ascension* home, while the two remaining ships headed for Bantam, where Lancaster hoped to find further trade.

Bantam was a prosperous commercial center used by all the trading nations of the East and a regular port of call for junks from China. The *Red Dragon* and the *Hector* dropped anchor in the roadstead on December 16, both ships announcing their arrival with "a very great peale of ordnance, such an one as had never beene rung there before that day." The next day Lancaster was conducted to the court of the King, who turned out to be a small boy, 10 years old. After delivering another of the Queen's letters and the usual presents, Lancaster soon secured a trade agreement. The English merchants found a ready sale for their wares and were able to buy 276 bags of pepper, each weighing 62 pounds. By February 10, 1603, both ships were fully laden and ready to depart.

Anxious that his expedition should establish permanent trading links with the East, Lancaster designated eight sailors and three merchants to remain in Bantam and establish a factory, as trading posts were called. They would trade what was left of the British wares to put together return cargoes for subsequent English fleets. In addition, a 40-ton pinnace was acquired and sent to the Moluccas with a crew of 10 men and two merchants to seek more trade there. On February 20, "with thankes to God and glad hearts," the *Red Dragon* and the *Hector* again rocked Bantam harbor with a blast from their guns and left for home.

At first they made good progress, but at the end of April, somewhere south of Madagascar, they ran into a "very great and a furious storme that continued a day and a night, with an exceeding great and raging sea. Our ships were so shaken that they were leakie all the voyage after." A week later, catastrophe struck the *Red Dragon*. "Wee had another very sore storme, which continued all the night," wrote one of the merchants, "and the seas did so beate upon the ships quarter that it shooke all the ironworke of her rudder, and the next day, in the morning, our rudder brake cleane from the sterne of our shippe, and presently sunke into the sea. This strooke a present feare into the hearts of all men."

They had good cause to be afraid. With no rudder in such bad weather, they could not steer the *Red Dragon* to meet the waves head on, and thus she was likely to capsize in a trough between two of the mountainous undulations. "Our ship," said the merchant, "drave up and downe in the sea like a wracke, which way soever the wind carried her."

Lancaster, calm and resourceful as ever, ordered the mizzenmast taken down and put over the stern to see if the ship could be steered with it, but the heavy seas smashed it against the hull with such force that it was hastily brought back on board. When the weather improved a little, a diver went over the side to investigate what remained of the iron eyebolts, or gudgeons, on which the rudder had been hung. His report offered little hope: Just three of the original five were left, one of them broken. Yet the *Red Dragon's* only chance of getting back to England was by improvising a new rudder of some kind, and the ship's carpenter was already sawing the mizzenmast into planks to create an acceptable replacement. With great difficulty, the crew managed to affix the new rudder, but after three hours in the sea it broke off, taking with it one more of the precious gudgeons.

All this time the *Hector* was loyally standing nearby. Now the despairing crew on the *Red Dragon* gathered round Lancaster to demand that he abandon ship. He refused and, to prevent any men from deserting to the *Hector*, he secretly decided to send that ship back to England immediately. In the privacy of his cabin, he wrote to his employers, the directors of the East India Company:

"Right Worshipfull, What hath passed in this voyage, and what trades I have settled for this Companie, and what other events have befallen us,

Carrying parasols to shade themselves from the tropical sun, Dutchmen mingle with merchants from many Eastern lands at the busy port of Bantam in Java. Among the goods pictured in this commercial scene are spices dispensed from dozens of individual stalls, foodstuffs ranging from rice to fish, and a selection of spears and scimitars in a corner of the marketplace at upper left.

you shall understand by the bearers hereof. I will strive with all diligence to save my ship and her goods, as you may perceive by the course I take in venturing mine owne life and those that are with mee. I cannot tell where you should looke for mee, if you send out any pinnace to seeke mee; because I live at the devotion of the winds and seas. And thus fare you well; desiring God to send us a merrie meeting in this world, if it be His good will and pleasure.

> "Your very loving friend,
> James Lancaster."

He sent the letter across to the *Hector* by boat, with instructions that she should "depart and leave him there." But her master was loath to leave his commander under such conditions, and at daylight the following morning Lancaster was surprised to see the *Hector* still at her station, a few miles away across the heaving sea. "These men regard no commission," he muttered, but made no further attempt to persuade her to leave.

Two days later the weather turned fair and the sea calmed enough for Lancaster to try once again to hang the makeshift rudder, which fortunately had been fished from the sea after it had come loose. The best swimmers from the *Hector* were sent to help. This time they succeeded in attaching the enormous blade so that it held, and finally the two ships got under way again.

It was the end of their misfortunes. On the morning of June 16, they sighted St. Helena, where they stopped for fresh food and water. On September 11, 1603, they anchored in the Downs, an anchorage off the Southeast coast of England. "Thanked be Almightie God," wrote the merchant, "who hath delivered us from infinite perils and dangers in this long and tedious navigation."

The four ships—the *Ascension* and the *Susan* had already arrived home safely—brought back 1,030,000 pounds of pepper, the sale of which eventually showed a 95 per cent profit for the subscribers to the voyage. But more important was the fact that England at last had established sea trade with the East. For his significant role in this achievement, Lancaster was knighted by King James I, who had succeeded to the throne on the death of Elizabeth while the mariner was in the East.

Subsequent voyages, in 1604 and 1607, showed even bigger profits. It must have appeared to those fortunate merchant-adventurers in the City of London that now nothing could stop their exploitation of this new-found gold mine in the Orient. But if they expected success to come without a struggle, they were deceiving themselves. In 1602 Dutch merchants, realizing there was no point in competing among themselves, had formed the United East India Company with a massive capital investment of £540,000, an investment they were more than ready to protect with their enormous fighting fleet. The Portuguese, too, were willing to fight to retain their influence in the East. And the rulers of the diverse, scattered and warring kingdoms that made up the Orient owed no allegiance to anyone, least of all the latecoming English.

Ambition, greed, fear, danger and disease: These were the ingredients stirred by the opening of trade between Europe and the East. Many factions were involved, and they agreed on almost nothing except their desire for more profits. It was an explosive mixture.

The man who told Portugal's secrets to the world

Dutch author Jan Huyghen van
Linschoten is surrounded by scenes of
his travels in this engraving from his
journal. The inset at upper left depicts the
Portuguese colony of Goa. At upper
right is the East African port of
Mozambique, where Portuguese ships
put in for resupply; the two lower scenes
show the Atlantic island of St. Helena.

"I stayed in India to learn the manners and customs of the land. I will in truth set these down as I have seen." So wrote the Dutch traveler Jan Huyghen van Linschoten as he began an account of the five years he spent in Portuguese-occupied western India. His illustrated journal, sampled here and on the following pages, created a sensation throughout Europe. Until its publication in 1596, information about the Orient had been sparse and details of Portuguese trade there a well-kept secret.

The son of a Dutch innkeeper, Linschoten at an early age had evinced a fascination with the exotic. As a child, he recalled, he "took no small delight in reading histories and strange adventures." In 1580, at the age of 17, he traveled to Lisbon and found work with a merchant. Three years later he secured an appointment as clerk to a Portuguese prelate who was bound for India and a position as Archbishop of Goa.

Soon after arriving in India, Linschoten made a start on what would become his compendium of Eastern lore. He marveled at the devotion of Hindu pilgrims who flocked to bathe in the Ganges, a river said to "have its source in an earthly paradise." And he carefully documented the practices of Jainism, a religion whose followers refused to eat animal flesh and "have hospitals to heal all birds and beasts that ail."

In order to write about Eastern curiosities that he could not observe firsthand, Linschoten interrogated travelers passing through the port of Goa. From these visitors he culled intriguing descriptions of such far-off realms as Japan, where the "sharp-witted" inhabitants "go very well appareled in silk," and China, a "country all enclosed by a wall," where "there are oranges sweeter than sugar" and "books printed five or six hundred years before there was printing in Europe."

After the Archbishop of Goa died in 1587, Linschoten set out on a meandering, four-year return journey to Holland. Once at home, he organized his notes into a polished text, translated his on-the-spot sketches into illustrations that were rich in authentic detail despite their incongruous classicism, and compiled a catalogue of sea routes and sailing directions for the Orient. Much to the dismay of the secretive Portuguese, his report immediately aroused the envious greed of the rest of Europe.

Astride an elephant, the King of the Indian principality of Cochin rides in state, surrounded by his retinue of warriors. The royal guards announced the approach of the monarch, Linschoten noted, by "making a great knocking with the hilt of the rapier on their shields."

In this sketch of local inhabitants, Linschoten depicts (from left) a family from a farming district near Goa, a sword-carrying warrior from the Balaghat region, and a professional dancing maiden.

"They step forward with a great pride and vainglorious majesty, with a slave to keep the sun and rain from them," observed Linschoten of these typical Portuguese gentlemen in Goa. Most of the Portuguese households, he added, relied on "six, 10, 20 or even more" slaves to maintain their life of ease.

A life of sumptuous ease in far-off Goa

The Portuguese haven of Goa, reported Linschoten, "is green in both winter and summer and always has some fruit in season." His description of this "chief city of India," nearly the size of London in the late 16th Century, presented a tantalizing vision of wealth and leisure.

Many of the Portuguese lived in villas outside the city, where, he observed, "they have many pleasant gardens in which they dally." Attended by scores of servants and carried through the streets like Indian nobility, the Portuguese enjoyed an intoxicating round of concerts, picnics, dances and boating expeditions. Portuguese Jesuits had established a major university and a hospital in Goa, both funded by the Crown with profits amassed in trade.

Life was made all the more felicitous by a climate of racial and religious tolerance. Portuguese policies allowed Indians and Europeans to intermarry, and Catholic priests used no coercion to win converts. In Goa, wrote Linschoten, "every man holds his own religion."

A Portuguese lady, reclining in a palanquin, is borne by her slaves along a footpath outside Goa—a rare outing for a European woman. "Christian women in India are not often seen abroad," noted Linschoten, "seldom venturing out unless it be to church or to visit friends."

In Goa's crowded main square, parasol-shaded Portuguese mingle with people from every rank of Indian society at the daily auction. In the left foreground, water vendors shoulder a large urn slung from a pole, and an amah, or Indian nursemaid, holds an infant while talking to a slave girl. Before the table in the center of the square, an auctioneer asks for bids on a cloak.

A Portuguese galley rowed by prisoners of war patrols against local pirates and smugglers along the western Indian coast.

A port full of ships—with holds full of riches

No aspect of the Portuguese presence in India more astonished Linschoten—or his readers—than the volume and opulence of the trade in Goa. He studied and sketched a variety of vessels crowding the city's harbor, from Portuguese merchant ships to Indian fishing boats.

African gold, ivory, ebony and slaves, Indian pepper and textiles, and Ceylonese cinnamon passed through Portuguese brokers in Goa. Every year Portuguese fleets left for Malacca, where they took on spices for the European market, and Macao, where the ships picked up silks that were bartered in Japan for silver.

Linschoten's account also contained a startling military revelation: The once-formidable Portuguese Navy had deteriorated into a poorly armed fleet, unable to maintain control of a Far Eastern trading empire. This testimony led British and Dutch adventurers—carrying precious maps of Portuguese trade routes published by Linschoten—to set off in unprecedented numbers to grab their share of Asia's riches.

Small Indian craft—some made from planks lashed together with coconut roping (foreground), and others hewn from tree trunks (background)—ply the waters off western India.

Linschoten was fascinated by Chinese junks like this one, with its rattan sails and wooden anchor. Although he never reached China, the Dutchman eagerly transmitted reports of that country's vast maritime traffic. "In Canton," he reported, "there are said to be more ships than in the whole of Spain."

Chapter 2

"No trade without war, no war without trade"

F rom the deck of the *Dragon*, an English East Indiaman riding at anchor off the northwest coast of India on the muggy night of November 29, 1612, the lights of four great Portuguese galleons could easily be seen across the silky black sea. Alone in his cabin, Captain Thomas Best contemplated his chances for victory in the morning, when his two merchantmen—the *Dragon* and a pinnace called the *Hosiander*—would take on the Portuguese warships. Best had inspected his armament earlier that day, when the enemy fleet was approaching, and he had appealed to his crews, as one participant later wrote, to put their faith in God and "shew ourselves trew Englishmen, famoussed over all the world for trew vallour." Now there was little more he could do.

Confrontations between the British and the Portuguese in Oriental waters were not unusual in the early 17th Century. Although the rulers of the two countries had signed a truce in 1604, it did not recognize England's claim to commerce in the Eastern seas, where Portugal had dominated European trade for nearly a century. Portuguese commanders, operating from naval strongholds at Hormuz on the Persian Gulf, Goa on India's west coast and Malacca on the Malay Peninsula, felt free to defend their interests by attacking all intruders, including the English.

Best's arrival 10 weeks earlier at the port of Surat represented the third attempt by an English East India Company fleet to open trade with the Mogul Empire, the largest, richest and most powerful of India's kingdoms. On both previous occasions, the Portuguese had persuaded Surat officials, by bribing and intimidating them, to refuse the English permanent trade concessions, and Portuguese coastal vessels had attacked English boats ferrying goods out to the Indiamen. The Portuguese had also prevented the Dutch from establishing permanent trade at Surat, going so far as to hang two Dutch merchants who had tried to open a factory there in 1602. Nevertheless, these actions did not produce complacency: The Portuguese expected their competitors would try again.

The English and Dutch were interested in India initially because they wanted to obtain cheap Indian cloth to barter for pepper and other spices in the Malay Archipelago. The two East India Companies had found little market for European goods in those islands, but there was an enormous demand for Indian cottons, especially the calicoes made on the Coromandel Coast of southeast India. Despite opposition from the Portuguese, the Dutch in 1606 and the English in 1611 had obtained permission from the rulers of the eastern Indian kingdom of Golconda—an independent state just to the south of Mogul territory—to open trade

Dutch invaders assault the spice-rich Moluccan island of Tidore in 1604, blowing up two Portuguese ships (foreground, center) and storming the Portuguese fortress. Although the attack was successful, the Dutch lost the island back to the Portuguese two years later, and then spent half a century vainly trying to reclaim their prize.

at Masulipatam and Petapoli, the most important Coromandel ports.

But the Golconda concessions, as useful as they were to the spice trade, did not begin to exploit the rich opportunities for commerce that existed in India. The Mogul Empire, which stretched across the northern half of the country from the Arabian Sea to the Bay of Bengal, had far greater potential as a market for European goods. In exchange it could offer cheap cotton, Eastern luxury goods that flowed overland into northern India from throughout the Orient, and saltpeter—needed in Europe for the manufacture of gunpowder.

The key to sea trade with the Mogul Empire was Surat, a major emporium that lay just inside the Gulf of Cambay, close to the mouth of the Tapti River. Besides having a well-protected harbor, Surat offered access to Mogul marketplaces in the interior. The Portuguese, stung by their failure to prevent the interlopers from opening trade on India's southeast coast, were determined to stand fast at Surat.

Now a real test was at hand. Admiral Nuño da Cunha, in charge of the fleet that had been dispatched from Goa to deal with Thomas Best, had made a public vow to destroy every one of the intruders. He had reason to feel confident. In addition to the galleons, he had a fleet of 25 armed vessels that the Portuguese called frigates, but that were actually small coastal craft. His total force numbered some 2,000 men. Opposing him were the mere 200 English sailors aboard the *Dragon* and the *Hosiander*.

But the odds against the English were not as hopeless as the figures indicated. True, the Portuguese galleons were huge and heavily armed, but they were less maneuverable than the English ships. More important, the Portuguese force included many Portuguese soldiers, who were of little value in a naval battle except at close quarters, and large numbers of Indian sailors, called lascars, who were not trained for combat. The English, on the other hand, were all fine seamen and skilled gunners.

Best, a capable commander with 30 years' service at sea, knew that if he allowed the galleons to get close enough to put boarding parties on his ships, his men would be overwhelmed by sheer weight of numbers. To avoid being trapped in the narrow confines of Swally Hole, the Surat anchorage, he had sailed boldly out to meet the Portuguese fleet as soon as it was sighted on the afternoon of November 29. A few ineffectual shots had been exchanged before darkness intervened.

At dawn on November 30, Best's two ships weighed anchor and sailed into the heart of the enemy fleet. The English gunners were stripped to the waist and ready for action. The *Dragon* immediately took on the Portuguese flagship, loosing a broadside that caused carnage on her crowded deck. Portuguese soldiers gamely returned the fire, but their marksmanship was no match for that of the English gunners, and their shots struck mainly sails and rigging. The English ships then wove in and out among the galleons, pouring shot into the great vessels and sustaining little damage themselves. "Yf myne eyes had not seene," the disdainful Best wrote to the company, "I could not beleved ther basenes and couardlynes. Than thease 4 gallions thay have no better in all thease countryes. In burden thease 4 ar from 700 to 900 and 1,000 tonns; good ordnance (better than we have any), but so small use thay make of them, with so little skill, that a man would never desier a better an enymy."

Fashionable 18th Century English merchants from the Indian port of Surat (background) enjoy a leisurely stroll on the banks of the Tapti River. Life there a century earlier was less idyllic. "I could not peep out of doors," wrote one Englishman in 1608, "for fear of the Portugals, who in troops lay lurking in the byways to murther me."

Although they were poor gunners, the Portuguese were not actually behaving in so cowardly a fashion as Best described. They had moved their ships directly into the English fire in an effort to close with the *Dragon* and *Hosiander* and board them. This proved an unwise course, however, when Best fell back and the Portuguese captains—whose galleons drew considerably more water than either English vessel—followed him into the shallows at the mouth of the Tapti River on an ebb tide. First one galleon went aground, then a second, then a third. They were now easy targets for the English gunners and suffered severe punishment until the flood tide refloated them several hours later. Despite their wounds, the galleons promptly resumed their lumbering pursuit of the British ships in a running battle that continued until dusk, when both sides anchored for the night. Incredibly, only two English sailors had been killed and one wounded in the fighting, while Portuguese casualties numbered some 150 dead and many more wounded.

The English put out to sea the next day, hoping the galleons would follow, but the battered Portuguese refused the bait. After waiting offshore for two days, Best impudently returned on December 3 and anchored within taunting distance of the enemy. But still Nuño da Cunha showed little inclination to resume the fight. In disgust, Best sailed west across the Gulf of Cambay to reprovision at Mahuva, a Mogul port.

Three weeks later, on December 23, the fleets met again, this time off Mahuva. Ralphe Standish, surgeon on the *Hosiander*, described the rout: "The *Dragon* steered from one to another, and gave them such banges as maid ther verie sides crack; for we neyther of us never shott butt were so neere we could nott misse. We steered after the *Dragon*, and when she was with one we weere with another. And the truth is we did so teare them thatt some of them weere glad to cutt cables and be gone."

The drubbing continued for two days, from sunrise to sunset. On the second afternoon an incendiary shell was hurled into the Portuguese flagship, setting her deck ablaze. "This day we tore them most cruellie," Standish wrote. "We see swimming by our shipp peecces of tymber, boords, and ould hatts and clothes. Ther sailles weere allmost torne from yards, some of them, and ther tackleing cutt in peecces." It was the end of the affray. Christmas Day found the Portuguese ships limping home.

News of the English victory soon reached the Mogul court at Agra, where it caused considerable stir. Jahangir, the Mogul Emperor, could barely conceal his delight in the humiliating public defeat that had been handed the arrogant Portuguese. He promptly granted the English company permission to open trade at Surat, at two other ports on the Gulf of Cambay—Cambay and Gogha—and at the huge inland marketplace of Ahmadabad. Under the terms of the royal grant, the English were allowed to leave a small group of merchants at Surat to prepare cargoes for subsequent fleets. Meanwhile the *Dragon* and the *Hosiander* were loaded with Indian cotton, and on January 17 they weighed anchor and headed for Sumatra, where Best hoped to negotiate more trade treaties and fill his ships with pepper for the voyage home.

Less than a year after his departure, the Portuguese in India made another clumsy attempt to rid themselves of their rivals. In September 1613, Portuguese galleons captured a large Mogul trading vessel returning from the Red Sea. They apparently intended to hold her hostage until the English were thrown out of India, but the plan misfired disastrously. Jahangir was enraged by the Portuguese effrontery, and his umbrage was increased by the fact that his mother held a big stake in the captured ship's cargo. In a fit of temper the Mogul Emperor declared war on the Portuguese in his domain, ordering their Jesuit churches closed, their fortresses destroyed and all Portuguese nationals arrested.

The war quickly bogged down: The Moguls lacked the heavy artillery needed to conquer the Portuguese, and the Portuguese had too few troops to do more than defend their forts. Months dragged by and neither side gained the upper hand. For the English merchants left at Surat, the ongoing hostilities meant little except that, with trade suspended between Surat and Portuguese Goa, some 400 miles down the coast, the market was suddenly glutted with cheap cotton and indigo. Businessmen first, they set about amassing cargoes for the next English fleet.

In October 1614 four English East Indiamen sailed into Swally Hole with broadcloth, lead, quicksilver, tin, pewter, iron, looking glasses, shirts, shoes and sword blades for trade. The ships also carried many presents for Jahangir (among them an oil portrait of the Emperor, which, because it had been painted from a verbal description and did not resemble him, was not well received).

The Moguls were glad to see the English fleet. At Surat the Emperor's Viceroy immediately tried to enlist the aid of the visitors against the Portuguese. The fleet commander, Nicholas Downton, refused: At home James I was trying to cultivate ties with Spain and Portugal—both ruled by Philip III—and the East India Company had been told to avoid unprovoked attacks on the Portuguese. Downton's response so angered the Viceroy that he forbade the fleet to trade. Then, speculating that the embargo might incite the English to join the Portuguese against him, he changed his mind and allowed the ships to land their cargoes.

In Goa the news that another English fleet had arrived at Surat reopened all the wounds Best had inflicted on Portuguese pride two years earlier. The Portuguese Viceroy, Dom Hieronymo de Azevedo, was intent on revenge and decided to take personal command of an expedition to teach the insufferable English a lesson.

On January 18, 1615, sailors on board the four Indiamen in Swally Hole crowded onto the top decks and, with some trepidation, watched the approach of a magnificent Portuguese fleet: six massive galleons mounting a total of 114 guns, two 200-ton ships, a 120-ton pinnace and some 60 small Portuguese frigates. As the fleet drew near, Downton considered following Best's example and sailing out to confront the enemy; however, he decided to take his chances in the anchorage, whose shallowness would deter the biggest Portuguese galleons. Azevedo, meanwhile, signaled his ships to heave to.

For two days the Portuguese and English ships rode at anchor. Finally, on January 20, Dom Hieronymo de Azevedo made his move. As the tide rose, he ordered his three smallest ships and a number of the frigates to attack the *Hope*, a 300-ton Indiaman moored some distance from the rest of the English fleet. Downton was in his cabin on the 650-ton *Gift*, writing a report, when he received word that Portuguese swordsmen were

Dom Hieronymo de Azevedo, the Portuguese Viceroy of Goa when the English arrived in India, adopts a martial stance in this portrayal. An English officer who battled and beat him near Surat in 1615 had nothing but praise for his leadership. "I never see menn fight," he reported to the East India Company directors in London, "with greater resolution than the Portugales."

swarming onto the *Hope's* deck. Instantly he ordered the rest of his ships to cut their anchor cables and join the battle.

On the *Hope* sparks flew as English cutlasses clashed with Portuguese swords. Three times it seemed as if the Portuguese had won control, and three times they were beaten back. Then the other English ships arrived within range and began bombarding the Portuguese vessels.

From the topmost deck of his galleon, unable to intervene because of the vessel's deep draft, Azevedo saw first one, then another and still another of his ships catch fire under the merciless barrage of the English guns. The *Hope,* too, caught fire, and the Portuguese aboard her, daunted by the flames around them and the determination of the English sailors, threw themselves into the sea and swam for the nearest frigates. The three blazing Portuguese ships, abandoned by their crews, drifted toward the sandbanks, where they stuck and burned to the water line. The blaze on the *Hope* was soon extinguished by her crew, although not before her mainmast was largely destroyed. At the end of the day the English counted only five men dead; Portuguese bodies littered the beach. It was said that 350 men were later carried away for burial.

Azevedo had not given up. Early in February he twice tried to destroy his enemy with fire ships, sending two blazing vessels loaded with powder and smeared with pitch into the English fleet; both ships drifted harmlessly past the Indiamen. All the while, English merchants were busily trading at Surat. On March 3, having completed their business under the very noses of the Portuguese, the English sailed for Bantam. Azevedo made a show of pursuing, but when the English rounded and prepared to engage his fleet, he ordered his squadron back to Surat.

Azevedo's failure dealt Portuguese power in the Indian Ocean a devastating blow. Jahangir regarded the English as his deliverers and thereafter treated them as allies. In 1618 Sir Thomas Roe, the new English Ambassador to the Mogul court, negotiated an agreement for widespread trading privileges in return for protecting Mogul ships from Portugal's galleons. Although the Portuguese continued to trade with the Moguls, their commercial position in India was irreparably damaged.

In the spice-rich islands of the East Indies, too, the Portuguese were suffering serious setbacks—this time at the hands of the Dutch, undoubtedly the most aggressive of the contenders for the riches of the Orient. In 1604 one of the Dutch East India Company's first fleets—13 heavily armed Indiamen—drove the Portuguese from the islands of Tidore and Amboina in the Moluccas and established a trading factory at Banda. In 1605 another fleet sailed to the Malay Peninsula and attacked the Portuguese fortress at Malacca. The city was on the verge of surrendering when a Portuguese armada of 43 ships manned by 3,000 men arrived and repulsed the Dutch. Two years later yet another Dutch fleet attacked Makian, the most important clove port in the Moluccas, and was deterred from victory only by the sudden arrival of a squadron of Spanish ships. By then there was little doubt about how the Dutch intended to conduct their business affairs in the East.

The Dutch company's charter gave it explicit authority to wage war and to build and maintain fortresses. Ambitious company officials, sent

A fanciful map by French navigator-cartographer Guillaume Le Testu depicts East Indian laborers collecting and dispersing Javan spices while horned monsters lurk about. Testu never visited the Spice Islands, but compiled a nautical atlas in 1556 that was based on accounts by European traders.

east with these broad powers, considered themselves as much warriors as merchants. "Your Honors should know that trade in Asia must be maintained under the protection and favor of Your Honors' own weapons," one company officer wrote home to his superiors. "We cannot carry on trade without war nor war without trade."

The Dutch followed a two-step plan to monopolize the spice business: first oust the Portuguese from their island strongholds, then oblige local potentates to grant the Dutch sole trading rights in return for protection. When island rulers demurred, their cooperation was secured by force.

These coercive methods were demonstrated with typical efficiency in March 1609, when a powerful Dutch fleet arrived at the island of Neira, in the nutmeg- and mace-producing Bandas. The Dutch demanded the right to build a fort commanding the anchorage, but the islanders refused, fearing that a Dutch presence would mean the loss of their independence. The Dutch immediately landed an army of 1,200 men, crushed local opposition and proceeded to build their stronghold. Pursuing the same tactics elsewhere, the Dutch soon had factories and forts spread throughout the East Indies—from Achin on the western tip of Sumatra to Ternate and Tidore in the Moluccas.

At home the Dutch professed friendship toward the English, but their officials in the Orient did everything possible to exclude their rivals from the spice trade. The English company's only East Indies factory at the time was the one James Lancaster had started at Bantam in 1603. English East Indiamen calling at other ports invariably met Dutch factors warning them off. "The broad-beamed Hollanders daily persecute us," reported one merchant to his superiors, "making us long for vengeance." Another complained: "Those rascals the Dutch will not let us trade, notwithstanding our rights here are equal to theirs." In November 1611 the English company appealed to the government, sending a petition that set out the wrongs company servants had suffered at the hands of the Dutch, and asking for help to secure freedom of trade. The English Ambassador at The Hague made representations on the matter, but nothing was achieved. The Dutch insisted that commerce in the territories they had wrested from the Portuguese was their exclusive right.

While diplomatic negotiations dragged on in Europe, the English East India Company took action on its own. It declared its intention to ignore Dutch treaties and to trade wherever islanders were willing to do business. The move was shrewd, since the local spice growers were already thoroughly disenchanted with the new monopolists. Once the Dutch had obtained exclusive trading rights, they beat down prices to about half the rates prevalent under the Portuguese, causing deep resentment. Thus English ships were welcomed. In March 1613 English merchants could be found at the Moluccan island of Ceram—"out of sight of the Hollenders," gloated an English official—buying cloves at a much higher price than offered by the Dutch. That same year Thomas Best, fresh from his victory over the Portuguese at Surat, opened trade at four pepper ports in Sumatra. Within a few years, factories were established on the Malay Peninsula, at Achin in Sumatra, at Jacatra in Java, and at Macassar, a clove port on Celebes, a large island west of the Moluccas.

The English merchants' strengthened position in the Indies only rein-

Tranquil little Tranquebar: an unprofitable but long-lived outpost

This letter from the Nayak of Tanjore, written on solid gold in April 1620, authorized Danes

The Portuguese, English and Dutch were not the only Europeans vying for Oriental trade: Almost every Western nation of any importance—including France *(pages 104-105)*, Sweden, Denmark, Austria and Prussia—sent out Indiamen to look for Eastern riches. Among the least successful of these aspirants were the Danes, yet they managed to maintain a presence in India longer than did most of their rivals.

King Christian IV chartered the Danish East India Company in 1616. Four years later the company leased the sleepy port of Tranquebar on India's Coromandel Coast from its overlord, the Nayak of Tanjore. The Danes built a fortress there to protect their trade, but soon found—mainly because of a long, expensive war that tied up Danish capital and ships in Europe—that they had little trade to protect.

Far from paying out handsome dividends, the Danish company at times actually assessed its stockholders in order to stay in business. After 1639 not a single Danish ship arrived at Tranquebar for some three decades. Meanwhile, Christian IV died, and his successor, Frederick III, tried in vain to

King Christian IV, champion of Danish sea trade for half a century, stands beside the crown he wore at his 1596 coronation.

In this 17th Century view, Tranquebar is dominated by the fort built in the 1620s. The wall that later protected the town is not shown. Mosques (I), pagodas (H) and a Catholic church (E) testify to the diversity of the colony's populace.

to settle, build a fortress and buy pepper in Tranquebar—all in exchange for 18 iron cannon.

peddle the fort to other European rulers. King Frederick sent letters to Tranquebar occasionally, telling the 200 or so Danes there to hold on, that relief would be on its way any year now.

Surviving on local trade, they did hold on. In the 1660s they erected a wall to protect the town against the current Nayak of Tanjore, who was trying to raise the rent by force. The ramparts staved off the greedy landlord and gave the settlement a new purpose. It became a refuge for people fleeing India's constant wars, including English, Dutch and French merchants trying to escape one another's armies. Offering safety and a neutral port, the Danish factory had its best years when other nations fought.

But after British conquest of most of the subcontinent brought a degree of stability to India, the Danish outpost again fell on hard times. By 1800 it was little more than a retirement town for aged Danish officials who preferred not to return to a Denmark they no longer knew. In 1845 the Danes sold Tranquebar to the British, lowering their white-crossed red flag for the last time, 225 years after first raising it.

forced the Dutch determination to expel them. On March 13, 1616, an English fleet of four Indiamen and a pinnace, sent to trade at the island of Wai in the Bandas, was met by a Dutch fleet of nine Indiamen that had orders to drive off the intruders at all costs. Both sides cleared for battle, but the English commander, Samuel Castleton, finally chose to negotiate. The Dutch dictated the terms, essentially decreeing that the English should not attempt to trade at Wai until the Dutch assented. From Wai, Castleton sailed to Luhu on Ceram, where he was shooed away by a Dutch squadron guarding the port. He went on to Ternate and Tidore, only to discover the islanders were too afraid of the Dutch to risk selling their cloves to an English fleet. The luckless Castleton died before his ships returned, holds empty, to the main English factory at Bantam.

The English were finding such ignominious treatment increasingly intolerable, and events rapidly slid toward open war. In October 1616 two English Indiamen, the *Defence* and the *Swan*, sailed east from Bantam with orders to occupy the Banda island of Pulo Run. The commander of the expedition, Nathaniel Courthope, was to resist any Dutch attempts to land on the island once the English colors had been hoisted.

Two days before Christmas the *Defence* and the *Swan* anchored off Pulo Run. Courthope was welcomed by the inhabitants, who professed themselves perfectly willing to be placed under British protection. During the next few days the English landed guns from the ships and erected batteries on the beach of an islet just offshore. The inevitable Dutch response came on January 3, 1617, when three Dutch Indiamen from Neira arrived at Pulo Run with a strong landing force. But to the surprise of the Dutch commander, Cornelis Dedel, hundreds of warlike islanders swarmed onto the beach, ready to resist the invaders. Faced with hostile local forces as well as Courthope's batteries, Dedel decided to return to Neira for reinforcements. A week later a Dutch pinnace taking soundings near the English anchorage was driven off by gunfire from shore.

For a time the English at Pulo Run seemed safe from further Dutch attention, but early in February the *Swan*, returning from a trip to Ceram, was attacked by a Dutch ship crammed with soldiers from Neira. During the brief engagement the *Swan* lost more than half her crew. She was then overpowered by a boarding party and towed into Neira, the Hollanders "much glorying in their victorie and showing the Bandanese their exploit, saying that the King of England might not compare with their great King of Holland," an English eyewitness reported.

The loss of the *Swan* was a major blow to Courthope, but he was soon to face more trouble, this time from his own men. One night during the third week of March, the *Defence* disappeared. Some of her crew, tired of languishing at Pulo Run, had cut her cables and sailed to Neira, where they surrendered to the Dutch. Then Dutch ships blockaded the island to cut off any assistance to the English merchants and mariners.

The British refused to be intimidated. In November 1617, Laurens Reael, Governor General of the Dutch Indies, wrote to his English counterpart at Bantam, demanding the immediate evacuation of Pulo Run. The Englishman replied that the island and its people would be defended to the last. In March 1618 two English ships, the *Solomon* and the *Attendant*, were sent to relieve Courthope, but they were captured by

The Banda Islands, ridged with mountains that yielded prized nutmeg and cloves, were the most richly endowed group in the Moluccas. But the blessings of nature brought upon them a bloody curse: The Portuguese, Dutch and English fought over them from 1600 to 1810.

four Dutch Indiamen within sight of Pulo Run. Rumors quickly spread that the Dutch had treated their English prisoners savagely. Relations between the Dutch and the English were now strained to the breaking point throughout the islands. At Bantam the situation had deteriorated to the extent that English and Dutch sailors were fighting in the streets.

In March 1619 Reael was replaced as governor general by Jan Pieterszoon Coen, a young, ruthless, single-minded company official. In November an equally single-minded English captain, 46-year-old John Jourdain, arrived at Bantam to take charge as president of the English company's entire East Indies operations.

Jourdain and Coen were already bitter foes as well as outspoken proponents of strong-arm tactics in defense of their respective companies' interests. They had verbally crossed swords in 1613, when Jourdain, then captain of the Indiaman *Darling,* had attempted to trade at Ceram, where Coen was in charge of the Dutch factory. Coen had warned the Englishman in a "chollericke manner," wrote Jourdain, that he would be prevented by any means from buying cloves there, and Jourdain had asserted that the "countrye was as free for us as for them." He then defiantly bought cloves from a local chief, until Dutch threats to punish any islanders dealing with the English dried up the supply. Now, five years later, the two men were to settle their differences by force of arms.

The English were in a strong position. Jourdain had come out in a fleet of five ships, which joined the six English East Indiamen already anchored in the roads at Bantam. Most of the Dutch fleet had gathered in the Moluccas, where Coen anticipated that hostilities with the English would soon break out. On November 28, Jourdain called a meeting at the Bantam factory, where it was "with one consent resolved to lay hold upon all occasions to redeem the disgraces and losses done to our Kinge and countrie." An unsuspecting Dutch ship, the *Zwarte Leeuw*, was then seized in Bantam harbor and held hostage for the redress of English grievances. Coen responded by burning down the English factory at Jacatra. The two nations were now effectively at war in the East.

A few days after the capture of the *Zwarte Leeuw*, English sailors rummaging through her hold for liquor dropped a lighted candle into a barrel of arrack and set the ship on fire. The *Zwarte Leeuw* was destroyed, along with a £14,000 cargo of rice and pepper. From that moment on, little went right for the English. Shortly before Christmas the rival fleets met off Jacatra and fought to a draw, even though the English had 11 Indiamen to the Dutch seven. Both sides claimed victory, and Coen withdrew to the Moluccas to assemble reinforcements.

As soon as Coen departed, the King of Jacatra laid siege to the Dutch fort, which had been built in his city without his permission. Then Sir Thomas Dale, commander of the English fleet, joined forces with the King's army, and by February the Dutch garrison was near surrender. At that critical juncture, however, the *pangaran* (protector) of nearby Bantam, who claimed suzerainty over both ports, entered the fray. He arrived with an army and threatened to attack the English factory at Bantam unless the Jacatra fort, once captured, was turned over to him instead of to the local ruler. Dale capitulated to his demand, then decided to give up the siege himself, and returned to Bantam. The English withdrawal enabled the Dutch garrison at Jacatra to hold out. Coen arrived with a huge fleet, relieved his beleaguered countrymen and renamed the town Batavia, "as Holland was called in days of old." Later he would make it the site of the Dutch company's Eastern headquarters.

Thus far in the war, the English had achieved nothing except the capture of a single Dutch ship, which they had accidentally destroyed. Meanwhile the relationship between Jourdain and Dale had degenerated into constant quarreling. Their responsibilities overlapped, and they could not reach an agreement on what their strategy against Coen should be. In the end, Jourdain set out from Bantam with two ships to visit English factories on the Malay Peninsula. Dale sailed to India with the remainder of the fleet to refit at Masulipatam on the Coromandel Coast. Leaving Bantam unguarded was a disastrous mistake. Coen immediately sailed his fleet into the harbor and destroyed the English factory. He then dispatched three strongly manned ships in pursuit of Jourdain. On the evening of July 16, 1619, the Dutch squadron found Jourdain's ships,

Dr. Laurens Reael radiates the gentle good humor and intelligence that made him a distinguished poet, a correspondent of Galileo's—and, from 1615 to 1619, an uncommonly candid governor general of the Dutch East Indies. Reael was constantly criticizing his countrymen for being "grasping" and contemptuous of the islanders.

the *Hound* and the *Sampson,* anchored at Pattani in the Gulf of Siam.

When lookouts first spotted the Dutch ships approaching Pattani, the English officers urged Jourdain to weigh anchor, stand out to sea and make a running fight of it. But Jourdain, thinking that such a move might be interpreted as flight, stubbornly refused to budge. He declared, according to one of his men, that "it should never be reported that he would run away from a Fleming." His pride was to cost him dear.

That night two of the Dutch ships maneuvered into positions from which they could present their broadsides to the *Sampson's* bow and stern, and the third moved alongside the smaller *Hound.* At daybreak the battle began with a thunderous roar. Soon the sultry morning air was filled with smoke and deafening noises: bellowed commands in Dutch and English, the shrieks of dying men, the crackle of muskets, the boom of cannon and the sound of splintering wood.

The wind had died during the night, and the English ships could neither sail away from the Dutch nor maneuver into better positions to fight them. Only five of the *Sampson's* guns could be brought to bear on the enemy. After two and a half hours of ferocious combat, even Jourdain saw the situation as hopeless: 11 men lay dead on the *Sampson's* deck, and 35 others were seriously wounded. He ordered a white flag of truce hung out, and then clambered onto a boom to hail the Dutch commander and propose that they negotiate a surrender. A sudden volley of musket fire burst from one of the Dutch ships, and the Englishman fell dead, shot through the chest. The *Sampson* was taken at once; the *Hound* struggled for another half hour or so before she too surrendered.

The remainder of the English fleet fared no better. Sir Thomas Dale was desperately ill with malaria by the time he arrived at Masulipatam. He was carried ashore to the English factory, where he died on August 9, 1619. His second-in-command, Martin Pring, took charge but could not decide what to do—and so did nothing. Meanwhile Coen rounded up other English ships scattered about the East Indies. In August his forces captured one English Indiaman in the Sunda Strait between Java and Sumatra, and in October they surprised and took four more off Tiku in Sumatra, bringing to 11 the number of English vessels lost to the Dutch since the British first occupied Pulo Run, nearly three years earlier.

In March 1620 Pring was reinforced by three English ships from Surat, and he at last decided to act. His combined fleet sailed for Bantam intending to hit back at the Dutch, but on April 8 in the Sunda Strait, it met a ship bringing word from England that the Dutch and the English East India Companies had agreed to halt hostilities. Under the new accord, the English were to have a third of the Moluccan spice trade and half the pepper trade of Java. In return, they were to share expenses for maintaining Dutch forts and to act as allies against the Portuguese and Spanish, who still clung to a handful of fortresses in the archipelago and remained a sporadic threat to Dutch and English shipping. Ironically, the agreement had been signed 10 days before John Jourdain was killed.

News of the accord did not reach the stranded English sailors on Pulo Run until November 1620—just one month after their commander, Nathaniel Courthope, had died in a skirmish with the Dutch while returning from a nearby island in a small boat.

Jan Pieterszoon Coen's expression betrays the cruel pleasure he took, as chief architect of Dutch East Indian supremacy, in riding "the natives with a sharp spur." The two-time governor general had all 15,000 inhabitants of the Banda Islands either killed or enslaved.

The struggle for the wealth of the East now shifted to the other side of the Indian Ocean, where ambitious English merchants were again incurring Portuguese resentment. At Hormuz, an island at the mouth of the Persian Gulf, the Portuguese had built a fortress that gave them control of shipping in the gulf and a monopoly of sea traffic in Persian silk. The only other silk route to Europe was overland through Asia Minor, then in the domain of the Ottoman Turks, Persia's hereditary enemies.

The first English East Indiaman to visit Persia arrived at Jask, a seaport on the southern coast, in December 1616. She was the *James*, from Surat, carrying an enthusiastic merchant named Edward Connock. Connock was cordially received at the court of the Persian ruler, Shah Abbas, where he delivered an eloquent dissertation on the advantages of competition. The Shah, heartily sick of Portuguese and Ottoman domination of his silk traffic and eager to expand his trade with Europe, needed little convincing. He offered at once to supply Connock with 3,000 bales of silk on credit. He also grandly proclaimed the English King to be his brother and gave the English permission to trade in any Persian port they chose—without having to pay customs duties.

Alarmed by this erosion of his Eastern trade, King Philip of Spain and Portugal dispatched a special envoy, Don Garcia de Silva y Figueroa, to the Shah's court in 1618 to argue the case for excluding other Europeans. It was a hopeless and humiliating mission. Figueroa had to listen in silence while the Shah publicly lavished praise on the English. As a delighted English factor wrote to the company in London, the Shah "would sometymes openly proclayme the valour of our nation, soe farre extolling us above the Portingalls that hee woulde tell those forraigne ambassadores then present that he would, despite all the Portingalls forces, have free trade in all his portes; and sometymes he would secretlie whisper unto us that he had a resolution to tayke Hormuz from the Kinge of Spane's hold and deliver it unto the English nation."

At a final audience the hapless Figueroa presented the Shah with letters from King Philip arrogantly demanding exclusive rights to the seaborne silk trade. The letters so enraged the Persian ruler that he tore them to shreds in the envoy's presence and immediately granted the English sole sea-trading rights in silk.

Thwarted in their clumsy attempt at diplomacy, the Portuguese unhesitatingly turned to violence as a means of achieving their aims. A fleet of five men-of-war was fitted out in Lisbon and placed under the command of a national hero, the brave and able Ruy Freire de Andrade, who had a spectacular string of naval successes in India to his credit and was known throughout his homeland as the "Pride of Portugal." Ruy Freire's orders were to sweep the Persian Gulf clear of foreign shipping. His fleet reached Hormuz in the middle of June 1620.

Dutch East India Company yachts and merchantmen crowd Chinese junks in the roadstead off Batavia in Java. The Dutch chose Batavia as their Eastern headquarters because of its deep and capacious harbor; they built it into a cosmopolitan city laced with canals and equipped with two 3,800-foot piers that could accommodate dozens of Indiamen at a time.

At that moment four English East Indiamen—the *London*, the *Roe-buck*, the *Eagle* and the *Hart*—were wallowing up the east coast of Africa. They had left England in late February under the command of Captain Andrew Shilling. Unaware of the danger presented by Ruy Freire's squadron, the *Eagle* and the *Hart* sailed to Jask while the other two ships continued on to Surat. As soon as Shilling's ships dropped anchor at Swally Hole on November 9, the president of the English factory at Surat, Thomas Kerridge, hurried on board the *London*. Kerridge had heard of the Portuguese arrival at Hormuz from the crews of Mogul trading ships, and he warned Shilling of the grave risk to the *Eagle* and the *Hart*. At a hastily convened meeting, the senior officers of the *London* and the *Roebuck* agreed to unload part of their cargoes, take on provisions and head for the Persian Gulf to help their sister ships.

Ten days later the *London* and the *Roebuck* filled their sails and set a course for Jask. On December 5 the *Hart* and the *Eagle* were sighted 240 miles east of Jask. Both ships had arrived safely at the port, learned of Ruy Freire's presence in the gulf and immediately left to seek assistance. With the four Indiamen reunited, Shilling decided to press on to Jask to complete the company's business there, even at the risk of an encounter with the Portuguese.

On the morning of December 16, the four Indiamen approached Jask and found Ruy Freire's squadron anchored in the roadstead, awaiting them. During the morning, the wind fell, and both fleets were becalmed.

The next day a gentle westerly wind enabled the Portuguese to weigh anchor and move out toward the Indiamen. On the *London* a red flag was hoisted at the maintop, signaling the English crews to prepare for action. At 9 o'clock the battle began, with both sides firing furiously while maneuvering for the wind advantage. At 3 o'clock that afternoon the Indiamen were to windward and Shilling ordered a fire ship sent in, but it was abandoned too soon by its volunteer crew and harmlessly passed the Portuguese fleet, trailing thick black smoke. After nine hours' fighting, dusk brought the first phase of the battle to an inconclusive end.

The next day found the Portuguese anchored some 10 miles east of the English, but despite a favorable wind Ruy Freire did not rejoin the fight, so Shilling fell back to Jask to land his cargoes. While the broadcloth and chests of money to buy silk were being unloaded, the Portuguese fleet offshore was reinforced with men and munitions from Hormuz.

The Indiamen had unloaded their cargoes by Christmas, but rain and contrary winds kept them from sailing out to meet the enemy. Superstitious crewmen on the English ships, reported Richard Swan, master of the *Roebuck*, "were perswaded that the Portingalls had brought with them from Hormuz a witch to bring them continuallie a faire winde."

And so it seemed, until the morning of December 28, when "the Lord gave us a prettie easterlie gale" and the English were able to maneuver themselves into a position where they could bring their guns to bear on the galleons. "The grete ordnance from our whole fleete plaied so faste upon them," Swan wrote of the rout, "that doubtlesse not one of these galliounes, unless their sydes had become impenetrable, had escaped us. About three of the clocke in the afternoon, unwilling after so hot a dinner to receive the like supper, they cutt their cables, and drove with

A Dutch flotilla parades past an island in this 1608 canvas by Adam Willaerts. Merchantmen usually traveled from Amsterdam to the Bay of Biscay in convoy. From there, some of the ships headed out for the West Indies, others for the Mediterranean; the Indiamen sailed on around the Cape of Good Hope and to the Orient.

the tyde untill they were without range of our gunnes. And then theyre frigatts came and towed them awaie wonderfully mangled and torne."

No longer harassed by the Pride of Portugal, the English ships returned to Jask, took on 520 bales of silk and departed on January 14.

The next English fleet to visit Jask arrived a year later, on December 14, 1621. It immediately became embroiled in a war that had broken out between the Persians and the Portuguese. During the preceding months the Portuguese had plundered and burned a string of towns along the coast. In retaliation the Shah's army had laid siege to a Portuguese fort on the island of Qishm, some 10 miles from Hormuz. Shah Abbas hoped to evict the Portuguese from both Qishm and Hormuz, but could not do it without naval support. Seizing on the arrival of the five English East Indiamen and four pinnaces as the solution to his problems, he immediately demanded that the commander of the fleet, Captain John Weddell, supply assistance in attacking the Portuguese forts. His demand was accompanied by a dark threat that failure to respond would result in the cancellation of all trading concessions.

Weddell was in a difficult spot. Despite the frequent Portuguese attacks on English shipping in the East, the two countries had remained at peace in Europe. If the English captain helped the Shah, he risked censure at home for assisting a "heathen" against a supposedly friendly European state. If he refused, the English East India Company might lose the promising silk trade. At a conference on board the *London*, Edward Monnox, the English factor in Persia, argued strongly that unless Portuguese power in the Persian Gulf was broken, trade by the English company would be forever at risk. After much anxious debate among his officers, Weddell agreed to support the Shah in return for half the plunder from the forts and a half share in the customs revenue at Hormuz. It was not the first, and certainly not the last, time the company involved itself in a war with little regard for the government at home; in conflicts between company profits and government policy, the latter rarely won.

On January 22, 1622, the English fleet approached to within 150 yards of the Portuguese fort at Qishm, where the defense was being conducted personally by Ruy Freire de Andrade. The next day the ships began to bombard the fort with all the guns they could bring into play. On February 1 the fort surrendered. More than 200 Portuguese prisoners, including Ruy Freire, were sent to Surat in an Indiaman and two pinnaces while the remainder of the fleet embarked 3,000 Persian soldiers in preparation for the assault on Hormuz. The English Indiamen landed the Persian army at Hormuz on February 9. The city was quickly overrun, and the Portuguese garrison withdrew into the fort.

English gunners aboard the Indiamen set to work, firing steadily at the fort and at the five Portuguese galleons moored below the fortress walls. After two galleons had been destroyed, the Portuguese dragged the brass guns from the remaining ships into the fort to reinforce the garrison's armament. The cannon were moved just in time. That evening, when the tide was at its lowest point and the Portuguese ships were aground, a small boat from one of the Indiamen sailed boldly into the harbor and discharged a single shot into the biggest galleon, the 1,500-ton *Todos los Santos*, below her water line. As the tide rose, the galleon's hold filled with water and as it ebbed again she slowly toppled over, breaking the cables and hawsers that moored her to the harbor wall.

On March 17 the Persian army breached the fortress walls with mines and launched an attack that was repulsed only after stiff fighting. When it was clear that the Persians would make another attempt, the Portuguese commander, fearing wholesale massacre at their hands, opened negotiations with the English, offering to surrender provided Portuguese lives were spared. On April 23, 1622, the Portuguese flag at Hormuz was hauled down. The loss of the strategic fort knocked the last major prop from Portugal's once-great commercial empire in the East.

The capture of Hormuz created a sensation in Europe, but at English East India Company headquarters in London excitement over securing trade with Persia was soon overshadowed by news of the rapidly deteriorating situation in the East Indies. The Anglo-Dutch trading accord negotiated in Europe in 1619 had not relieved the friction between the two companies. Jan Pieterszoon Coen was furious because he believed that the treaty had snatched victory from his grasp. "The English owe Your

In this primitive mid-16th Century sketch of the good life at the strategic Persian Gulf entrepôt of Hormuz, Portuguese merchants and their wives relax over a meal of fish, eggs, fruit and wine as one of the many servants in attendance (top right) empties a jug of water onto the flooded floor to cool his masters' tender European feet.

Excellencies a great debt of gratitude," he wrote angrily to his directors in Amsterdam in May 1620, "for they had assisted themselves straight out of the Indies, and you have put them right back in the middle again." Despite the agreement, Coen issued strict instructions that Dutch authority was to be maintained throughout the East Indies.

Letters from the English company's servants were soon full of complaints about the vindictive behavior of the Dutch and the heavy burden of sharing expenses with them. At Batavia the Dutch grudgingly allowed the English to build a factory on a remote site where trade was virtually impossible. An Englishman there who had refused to accept Dutch authority was flogged. And local traders were so terrified of the Dutch that they refused to deal with English merchants until the Dutch had first been satisfied. In 1622 the president of the English company's East Indies operation wrote home that, without more support, his merchants would be "quite tired out with living in this kind of slavery."

Under the terms of the treaty, the English had been allowed to establish a factory on Amboina, one of the centers of the clove and nutmeg trade. Typically, the English factory was a ramshackle wooden building with an adjoining warehouse, whereas the Dutch at Amboina occupied a large and impressive fort garrisoned by 200 soldiers. Gabriel Towerson, the amiable English factor, had under him 18 men and six boys; the total armament of the factory comprised a couple of muskets, half a pound of gunpowder and three swords. The English thus represented little threat to Dutch security on Amboina. But on the morning of February 15, 1623, Towerson was summoned before the Dutch Governor, Herman van Speult, and accused of plotting to overthrow the fort. The bewildered Towerson was arrested, and the other Englishmen on the island were quickly rounded up and put in irons.

Until that moment Towerson had considered himself a friend of the Dutch governor. He had often been invited to dinner at the fort, and only a few days before had written to Batavia asking that van Speult be sent "some beer or a case of strong waters, which will be very acceptable to him." At the same time, van Speult was writing to Coen, assuring the governor general that his orders to preserve Dutch authority would be carried out and "that our sovereignty shall not be diminished or injured in any way by English encroachments, and if we may hear of any conspiracies of theirs against the sovereignty, we shall, with your sanction, do justice to them suitably, unhesitatingly and immediately."

The zealous van Speult soon uncovered a conspiracy. A Japanese mercenary employed by the Dutch was accused of being a spy after chatting one evening with a Dutch guard on the fort's walls and asking too many questions about the defenses. A spell on the rack and the application of red-hot irons to the soles of his feet persuaded him to admit to a plot to seize the stronghold. Other Japanese were arrested and, after similar persuasion, also confessed. Then a drunken Englishman, detained in the fortress prison after threatening to set a Dutchman's house on fire, was put on the rack. In agony, he was willing to affirm whatever the Dutch chose to put in his mouth. What they chose to put there was that the English were implicated in the conspiracy. This was all van Speult needed as an excuse to arrest the lot.

Early on Sunday morning, February 16, the Dutch began to deal with the rival merchants. One by one they were dragged into the torture chamber, where their protestations of innocence soon became blood-curdling screams. Each man was spread-eagled on a huge door and bound hand and foot to iron staples. Then a cloth was wrapped tightly round his face and neck and slowly soaked with water. At the point of suffocation, he was taken down, forced to vomit, then hoisted back up for more punishment. If this failed to yield a confession, lighted candles were applied to his armpits, genitals and feet. Some men broke sooner than others, but all of them broke. One, John Clark, endured so much torment that his body swelled to twice its normal size and water poured from his ears and his staring eyes. Only after suffering terrible burns from the candles did he grunt "yea" to the questions put to him. On February 27, Clark, Towerson and eight other Englishmen, nine Japanese mercenaries and a Portuguese overseer were publicly beheaded.

Three of those who died contrived to leave pathetic scribbled testimony of what had passed. One wrote on the flyleaf of his prayer book: "Then was I obliged to Confess what I Never Knew, or else go to the Torments which rather than I would suffer I did Confess that which as I

53

A 17th Century map—with north lying to the right—shows the mouth of the Persian Gulf. In 1622 English ships and Persian soldiers drove the Portuguese from the region by seizing the forts on Qishm (top left) and the bell-shaped island of Hormuz. In 1625 Portugal tried to recapture Hormuz—losing this time to an Anglo-Dutch alliance.

shall be saved before the Almighty is Not True." In an account book another scrawled: "Through Torment we were constrained to speak that which we meant not, nor ever once imagined, which we do all take upon our salvation. They tortured us with Extream Torment of Fire and Water that Flesh and Blood could not endure it, and we again take it upon our Salvation that they have put us to Death Guiltless of Our Accusations." Towerson penned his own epitaph on a bill of debt: "Gabriel Towerson now appointed to die Guiltless of anything that can be Laid to my Charge. God Forgive them this Sin, and Receive me into his Mercy."

News of these gruesome events did not reach England until May 1624. It aroused a storm of public fury that raged for years. But the English East India Company had already given up hope of expanding trade in the East Indies against the intransigent opposition of the Dutch: Even before the atrocity the English company had decided to withdraw from its factories in the Moluccas and the Bandas. In 1628 the company abandoned its factory at Batavia and centered its drastically diminished East Indies spice trade—now only with Macassar and Sumatra—at Bantam. The Indian subcontinent looked far more promising.

In the years that had passed since the English had established themselves at Surat, they had expanded their trade steadily throughout the Mogul Empire. Subfactories in Mogul provinces became conduits for the riches of northern India: fine cottons, dyes, calicoes and carpets from the interior, and sugar, saltpeter and silk from faraway Bengal on the northeast coast. From Surat the British extended their influence south, down to the Malabar coast, where pepper, cardamom and cassia lignea (a coarse variety of cinnamon) were grown and where the chief Indian marts for cloves and nutmegs from the Malay Archipelago were located.

The English also expanded their commerce on India's east coast. The factory opened at Masulipatam in 1611 proved to be a superb halfway port between the West and the Far East. It was also the center of Golconda's textile trade and a market for the rubies and diamonds of Golconda's famed mines. Additional English factories in cities to the north and south of the port brought increased trade with India's southern interior, whose riches included forests of teak and ebony, and fields of wheat, millet and cotton. In 1639 the company opened a factory at Madras and built a large stronghold, Fort St. George, to protect the British position in that port. The following year Madras superseded Masulipatam as the company's Coromandel Coast headquarters, and a decade later the Madras office took over from Bantam control of all British trade in the East Indies. Working its way north, the company also established factories on the coast of Bengal and up into the Ganges Valley.

Despite its spreading influence in India, the English company was unable to secure the economic stability and maritime might of its Dutch counterpart, which all the while was tightening its grip on the East Indian islands. At home the English East India Company was plagued by financial troubles and political disruption. Throughout India it still faced stiff competition from European rivals, and the dangers and uncertainties caused by turbulent local politics. Nonetheless, by the third quarter of the 17th Century, enterprising English factors had laid the foundation for the British Empire that would rise in the next century.

A priestly foothold in fabled Japan

Francis Xavier, canonized for his evangelical work in the Orient, charts the course of his mission as allegorical figures of East and West look on and a gem-filled cornucopia spills earthly riches onto the ground. The engraving faces the title page of a history of the Jesuits published in Rome in 1653.

In the year 1543 a small vessel manned by Portuguese was caught in a violent typhoon while prospecting for trade along the Chinese coast. Driven far to the east, the voyagers found themselves, when the winds and rains subsided, off a craggy and unfamiliar island. The local lord received the Europeans hospitably. Moreover, he proved an eager customer for the hides and other commodities they carried, paying for the goods with silver ingots. With mounting excitement, the traders realized that they had stumbled upon Japan, a fabled island kingdom sought by Europeans ever since the Venetian traveler Marco Polo had reported its existence two centuries earlier.

The Portuguese had every intention of adding it to the long list of Eastern lands in which they did business, but they were seeking more than riches. Wherever Portuguese merchants went, missionaries accompanied them and attempted to convert the heathen—not always successfully. This time the effort, led by an aristocratic Jesuit named Francis Xavier, would not only produce an abundant harvest of souls but would also yield a serendipitous dividend in the form of art.

Along with two fellow Jesuits, Xavier landed on the island of Kyushu in southwestern Japan in 1549 and soon made the acquaintance of the daimio, the feudal overlord. The priest's unflagging energy, somber black robes and extensive learning made an immediate impression on the daimio, who gave him leave to carry his teachings throughout the fiefdom.

During two years of travel in southern Japan, Xavier formed an equally favorable impression of the people of this land. "It seems to me that we shall never find among heathens another race to equal the Japanese," he declared. "They have one quality that I cannot recall in any people of Christendom; this is that their gentry, howsoever rich they be, render as much honor to a poor gentleman as if he were passing rich." Xavier's original team soon expanded to more than a dozen missionaries, and within two decades they had built a church in the capital city of Kyoto, set up 40 Christian communities and baptized 30,000 souls.

Some of the Japanese converts embraced the new religion out of sincere spiritual conviction, and because the Jesuits made them welcome in the clergy. Others turned Christian out of worldly self-interest; the richly laden carracks sailed by the Jesuits' Portuguese countrymen promised them commercial benefits. And there was still another, subtler reason for the success of the Jesuits: They allowed the Japanese sufficient freedom of spirit to express the new religious beliefs in artistic forms already familiar to them. The result was an exotic fusion of European and Japanese themes and media, and an outpouring of *objets d'art* that served clergy and merchant alike.

Aboard a Portuguese carrack en route to Japan, Saint Francis splashes his feet in the waves. Legend holds that the priest miraculously turned the salt water to fresh so the ship's crew might refill their near-empty casks.

Kyoto's Jesuit church was in the form of a pagoda, as painted on this 17th Century fan. By applying Japanese esthetics even to mission architecture, the Jesuits did much to win the favor of their hosts.

56

A thriving exchange of goods and ideas

In 1570 the Jesuits established their headquarters at the town of Nagasaki on the west coast of Kyushu, in the territory of an already Christianized daimio. Nagasaki made an ideal site; it had a deep, sheltered harbor that could accommodate large cargo ships. Almost at once, carracks began arriving at Nagasaki from the Portuguese colony at Macao, bringing such merchandise as cordovan leather and Chinese silks to be exchanged for silver bullion and the distinctive lacquer ware turned out by Japanese craftsmen. The Jesuits, who had a fine sense of the practical, signed an agreement with the daimio empowering them to collect the harbor dues, to be split between the Jesuit missions and the region's feudal lords.

From their base at Nagasaki, the Portuguese priests ranged throughout the country in constant wonderment at the rarities of Japanese civilization. "It may be truly said that Japan is a world the reverse of Europe; everything is so different and opposite that they are like us in practically nothing," wrote one of the Jesuits. The Portuguese had high praise for the simple elegance of the nation's architecture, the intensity of its agriculture, the beauties of its green and misty landscape, and above all the gracious customs of its inhabitants. "You speak courteously even to the most menial laborers and peasants because they will not have it otherwise," remarked one visitor. Another, accustomed to

the general unkemptness of Europeans, exclaimed: "They wash twice a day!"

The Japanese were just as astonished by the odd ways of Europeans, whom they dubbed *nanbanjin*, or "barbarians from the South"—the direction from which the ships came. Japanese artists depicted the foreigners in fine and good-humored detail, exaggerating their height, emphasizing their strange, long noses, caricaturing their baggy pantaloons. The landing of the annual Macao argosy *(below)* made a favorite subject; so huge a vessel had never been seen before in Japan.

This rhapsody of mutual fascination lasted more than half a century. Then, under the pressure of a continuing European influx, it began to dissolve. Spanish Franciscan monks arrived and set up rival missions. Next came Dutch and English merchants, who opened a competing entrepôt at the city of Hirado. As the influence of the *nanbanjin* increased, so did conversion to Christianity; by the beginning of the 17th Century, Japanese Christians numbered some 300,000. The ruling shogun in Kyoto noted with alarm that elsewhere in the Orient Christianity had led to conquest. He had no intention of allowing that to happen in Japan. In 1614, pronouncing Christianity "a fanatical and pernicious sect, dangerous to the empire and ripe for any mischief," he decreed that all missionaries must leave.

Four lacquered boxes, richly inlaid in gilt and mother-of-pearl and neatly stacked one atop the other, reveal the superb artistry of 17th Century Japanese craftsmen. These—10¾ inches high when put together—depict two Portuguese merchants aboard a Chinese junk, a favorite mode of coastal transport.

Two painted paper screens, each about 5 feet by 12, display the unloading of a Portuguese carrack in Nagasaki harbor. Ashore, the ship's captain, shaded by a parasol, approaches a welcoming party of priests and (top) four Japanese Christians pray in a pavilion-like chapel. Japanese screens traditionally had depicted seasonal landscapes; after 1590 they began to reflect a fascination with the culture of the Portuguese.

A backlash that spared the Dutch

This porcelain bowl pictures an Indiaman of the type that would carry it to Europe. Such ware, with brightly colored figures on a blue underglaze, was developed for the export trade.

With the expulsion of the missionaries in 1614, the Japanese government began a 20-year campaign to curtail foreign influence and to stamp out Christianity. The Spanish and Portuguese trading posts were confined to Nagasaki, the Dutch and English to Hirado. Japanese citizens were forbidden to travel overseas. Those who had turned Christian were offered the alternative of recanting or facing an executioner's sword.

Some Christians simply went underground, and the government saw its worst fears of the alien religion confirmed in 1637. At Shimabara on Kyushu, 37,000 Christianized peasants rose in revolt against the local daimio and barricaded themselves in an abandoned castle. They held out for four months, until the shogun's warriors overran the castle and slaughtered them all. The government, now thoroughly terrified of Christian influence, banished most of the remaining *nanbanjin* from Japanese soil.

Having acquired a taste for trade, however, and recalling that the Dutch had shown no inclination to proselytize, the shogun allowed Dutch merchants to stay. But he confined them to an artificial island in Nagasaki harbor. Here they lived under onerous restrictions; they could have no religious books or services and no weapons, and their imports were heavily taxed. Even so, trade flourished for two more centuries, to the profit of both the Dutch and the Japanese.

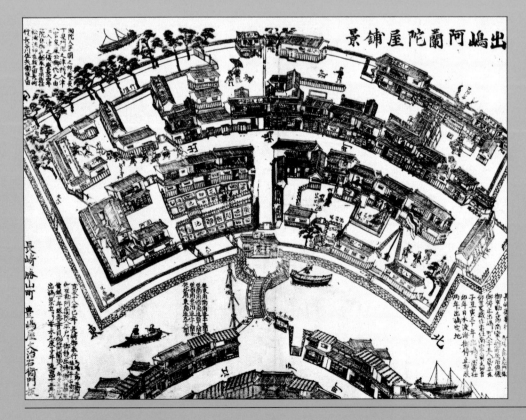

The Dutch compound of De-shima, built on landfill in Nagasaki harbor, links with the mainland by a single stone bridge, as detailed in this 18th Century woodcut. Japanese merchants needed permission from their own authorities to do business here with the Dutch.

The Netherlands tricolor at the
bowsprit and the name inscribed on the
stern identify the vessel in this 1782
woodcut as the East Indiaman Schellach,
which put in at Nagasaki in 1741 and
in 1744. In the 1700s four or five Dutch
vessels called at Nagasaki annually.

Chapter 3

A seaman's lot: misery, danger and empty pockets

At a romanticized coastal fishing port, three East Indiamen set off on the long and arduous passage to the Orient, as villagers gossip on the shore.

n a chosen morning in December every year during most of the 17th and 18th Centuries, Amsterdam was awakened by the insistent blare of trumpets, the shrill of pipes and a steady, compelling roll of drums. Children leaped from their warm feather beds and raced their parents to the windows. By the gray dawnlight they watched wretched little gangs of men shuffling through the narrow, brick streets and along the canal towpaths toward the source of the music.

Most of the men were pathetically thin, filthy, dressed in rags, pallid from weeks or months of confinement in stinking attics and cellars. They shivered and stumbled as they marched along, and impatient overseers prodded the laggards. Entering one of Amsterdam's main streets, the small groups converged in a flood of hundreds that quickened in pace as it neared the five-story headquarters building of the Dutch East India Company. Once they reached the imposing edifice, the men milled about, stamping their feet and blowing into their hands to keep out the cold, while the company's musicians inside the gates continued their martial siren song. The annual muster of recruits for the company's fleet was about to begin.

The hapless figures who were assembling before East India House were prospective seamen. They included drunks, derelicts, out-of-work slum dwellers and backward peasants from hundreds of miles around. The men who had marshaled the recruits and now herded them through Amsterdam's streets like so many cattle were crimps known by a chillingly appropriate name: *zielverkoopers*—"soul sellers." Although the East India Company's band provided a deceptively festive air for the occasion, the music amounted to a death march for many of the souls being sold by the crimps; the likelihood was that a third of the men who set sail on the long and arduous voyage to the East would not live to see Holland again.

Life was harsh on all ships in that era, and the East Indiamen were no exception. The work was "suitable for convicts," said a young Dutch soldier whose unit traveled east on an Indiaman. In consequence, stern disciplinary measures were needed to keep the men at their jobs. "At any show of reluctance," wrote Nicholaus de Graaff, who served as a surgeon aboard an East Indiaman, the sailor "is threatened and beaten with the rope's end." Rope was also the instrument of graver punishments, from keelhauling (pages 80-81) to hanging.

The ships themselves, while larger than most merchantmen of the day, were nonetheless cramped, miserably uncomfortable, smelly and verminous. But the worst aspect of serving on an Indiaman was the length of the voyages. The average journey to the Orient and back took about two years, and ill fortune could stretch it to three. The longer the voyage, of course, the greater the risks of disease, shipwreck, fire and attacks by pirates and privateers.

Most experienced Dutch seamen were well aware of the low survival rate in the trade to the Indies. They preferred to work on fishing boats or on ships plying European routes. Such vessels were smaller than the big East Indiamen, and living conditions on board were sometimes even more primitive; but the shorter voyages and the temperate climate gave the sailors a reasonable chance of coming back alive. The survival rate was slightly higher aboard English East Indiamen than it was on those of the Dutch (an English sailor who served on a Dutch ship attributed this difference to the poorer quality and quantity of rations provided by the economy-minded Dutch East India Company). Yet most English seamen, too, avoided the perilous voyages to the East when there was alternative work available, as did their counterparts in Portugal and France. In those countries, as in the Netherlands, crews for Indiamen were obtained largely by crimping.

No other seafaring nation had the practice down to such a finely honed system as the Dutch. Holland's *zielverkoopers* were part of an intricate network that involved all manner of citizens, from highly placed directors of the East India Company, who wanted their ships manned at whatever cost in chicanery, to the soul sellers' legmen, called "sharks," who hung about the city gates buttonholing likely prospects as they arrived in town. The Dutch kept 200 *zielverkoopers* busy in Amsterdam alone in 1778, and there were dozens more in the ports of Rotterdam, Hoorn and Enkhuizen.

Any waterfront down-and-out, anyone lost, homeless or penniless, any rustic come to town to escape the drudgery of digging dikes 16 hours a day, any poverty-stricken adventurer was prey to the *zielverkoopers* and their henchmen. Besides the chance of a berth on an East Indiaman, the crimps offered board and lodging until the next sailing of the fleet; all they asked in return was an I.O.U. for 150 guilders, to be collected from the man's pay. If a likely lad seemed hesitant, he was regaled with wonderful stories of life at sea and the riches of the East, of jewels and comely maidens for the taking. The more gullible were even offered a small hammer, the better to separate precious stones from the rocks in which they were embedded.

Once they agreed to the *zielverkooper*'s proposition, the men were hustled off to the lodgings that had been promised them, where they were kept under lock and key, very often in appalling conditions, to await the day of the muster. An eyewitness reported finding 300 men in a low attic "where they must stay day and night, where they perform their natural functions, and where they have no proper place to sleep, but must lie higgledy-piggledy with one another." In other instances large numbers of men were shut into cellars, sometimes for as long as five months, "during which time they had to breathe a very foul and sickly air. In some of these houses the death rate is so alarming that the owners, not daring to report the correct number of deaths, sometimes bury two bodies in one coffin."

When the men were marched to East India House on the morning of the muster, many of them were drunk, having been liberally supplied with brandy by their *zielverkoopers* as an encouragement to push and claw their way to the head of the line; every soul seller wanted to be sure his recruits got berths. Fighting was inevitable, and it became bloodier and more ferocious as the time drew near for the gates to be opened. Another scramble ensued after the rabble entered the courtyard, as the men pushed to get into the building where they would enlist. "It is almost incredible how they try to force their way in," wrote a Dutchman

Merchants gather in the courtyard of Amsterdam's East India House, headquarters of the great Dutch trading monopoly. During the last quarter of the 17th Century, the company paid salaries to 30,000 employees—half of them sailors, who assembled in this courtyard each December for assignment to ships that were bound for the East.

who witnessed the scene. He saw men "clamber up to the window of the second story, above the entrance door, and wait there, hanging onto the iron grating until the door was opened; they then immediately let go, fell on the heads of the men standing around the door, and in this way got carried into the house."

Many of Amsterdam's prosperous burghers, having hurried from their homes at the sound of the music, were on hand to observe this riotous procedure—and not just for the spectacle. Their money was at stake: They had bought the I.O.U.s of the would-be recruits from the *zielverkoopers* at a discount, and now they wanted to see whether the men whose notes they held managed to gain a place in the fleet.

Once inside and accepted, every recruit signed on for a minimum of five years' service at a monthly wage of 10 guilders, roughly the cost of a coarse suit of workingmen's clothes. Of the total 600-guilder sum, 150 guilders would be deducted to settle the I.O.U. extracted by the *zielverkooper*. This was not all clear profit for the soul seller, however. Besides paying for the recruit's lodging, the crimp had to provide 30 guilders' worth of gear for the new seaman: a chest, a hat, a pillow, a horse blanket and a knife. And he usually gave the recruit a few guilders for pocket money, enough to keep the man drunk at his boardinghouse until he joined his ship. In return, the *zielverkooper* (or the investor who bought the I.O.U. at a discount) received two months of the recruit's pay in advance from the company. He claimed the remainder of the 150 guilders as the man earned it; if the recruit died on the voyage before he had worked off this debt, the crimp or the investor was out of pocket. But the crimp had much more hope of financial reward than had the seaman, who would not receive his remaining 450 guilders until the end of his service five years hence—if he managed to survive that long. Thus, thoroughly skinned before ever setting foot aboard an Indiaman, the newly enlisted crews were marched back to their lodgings to await the sailing of the fleet.

Whether they signed on in Amsterdam, London or any other European port, it did not take new recruits long to discover that the reality of life on board an East Indiaman was dramatically different from the rosy pictures painted by crimps. With their great spreads of sail, elaborate figureheads, painted stern carvings, and flags and pennants streaming from their masts, East Indiamen of the era made a brave and glorious sight, but conditions on board were unremittingly grim. The crew lived in the gloomy and fetid space between decks. During the day, a little light filtered through the hatches and gunports—unless they had to be closed because of a storm. At such times, oxygen might be so depleted that a candle would not burn.

Many of the men, unaccustomed to the ocean, were seasick the first few days out and unable or unwilling to use the heads—the openings in the bows abovedecks; instead, they relieved themselves in the dark corners of the crew's quarters, adding to the noxious odors and disease-breeding filth. The drastic changes in climate during the voyage also could imperil the men's health. Unlike seamen on ships that navigated the trade routes close to home and encountered more or less the same

Dutch ships—models of perfection

The vessels that awaited the annual muster of Dutch seamen in the 17th Century were renowned for their quality—and rightly so. The technical skills and painstaking workmanship that produced them were unexcelled by any other seafaring nation in Europe.

Although no 17th Century Dutch ship survives, the superiority of the breed can still be glimpsed in some rare ships' models. These confections were made at the same time as were the ships themselves, to be given as mementos to the owners. Like the vessels they represented, they were masterpieces of craftsmanship, from the miniature capstans that weighed the anchors and hoisted the yards, to the tiny eyelets and laces that secured their sails.

Time has taken a toll on the models as well, but one of them—of the *Prins Willem*, which sailed between Amsterdam and Batavia from 1651 to 1662—has been given new life in a most appropriate way: Restorer Herman Ketting of the Amsterdam Rijksmuseum made a model of the model. The 40-inch replica, matching the original down to the last detail, appears at right and on the following pages.

By all accounts, Dutch shipbuilding technology was far in advance of that of the rest of Europe when the age of the East Indiaman dawned. While workers elsewhere labored at pit saws and turned out planks and spars that varied from ship to ship, Dutch shipyards used windmill-powered saws that had the advantage of sparing human muscle and also made it possible to cut the timbers to precise specifications.

In addition, the Dutch made sure every part and fitting was up to the function required of it. An anchor, for example, had to hold against the strain of a 1,400-ton vessel pulling on it in a churning sea. To test its strength, workers hoisted a newly forged anchor overhead by block and tackle and then dropped it on an iron cannon. Unless the anchor survived that exercise without a crack, it would not be sent to sea.

For all the pains they took, the Dutch still managed to build their ships swiftly: Because of their mechanized sawmills and extensive use of precut timbers, they needed only four months to complete an Indiaman—less than a quarter of the time the English shipyards spent on their ships in the same era.

This replica of the 17th Century model of the Prins Willem, done on a scale of 1 to 50, shows a Dutch Indiaman's full suit of sails. From the spritsail to the lateen mizzen, the Prins Willem carried a total of 13,000 square feet of canvas.

Backed by a row of gilded caryatids, a carved lion surmounts the Prins Willem's beakhead. This lattice-work structure served to provide purchase for the gammoning, the two heavy rope lashings that secure the bowsprit to the stem.

Blocks and coiled rope lie at the base of the mainmast, the belaying point for an Indiaman's main-topgallant sail and main-topsail rigging. The mast was a single fir timber three feet thick at the base and 92 feet tall, reinforced every five feet with a band of rope woolding.

Eight capstan bars crown a flawless timber that plummets 14 feet to the orlop deck. To weigh anchor, a gang of sailors heaved at the capstan bars topside while six men below hauled the anchor cable from the capstan barrel to its locker.

67

The maintop reinforces the mainmast by spreading the shrouds. In combat, the maintop served as a fighting post; soldiers fired muskets on the enemy from there and also doused fires in their own rigging by means of barrels of water.

Heavy wooden gratings cover the Indiaman's hatches, admitting a little light and air to the lower decks. In foul weather, tarpaulins were spread over the gratings and lashed to the hatch coamings to keep the lower decks dry.

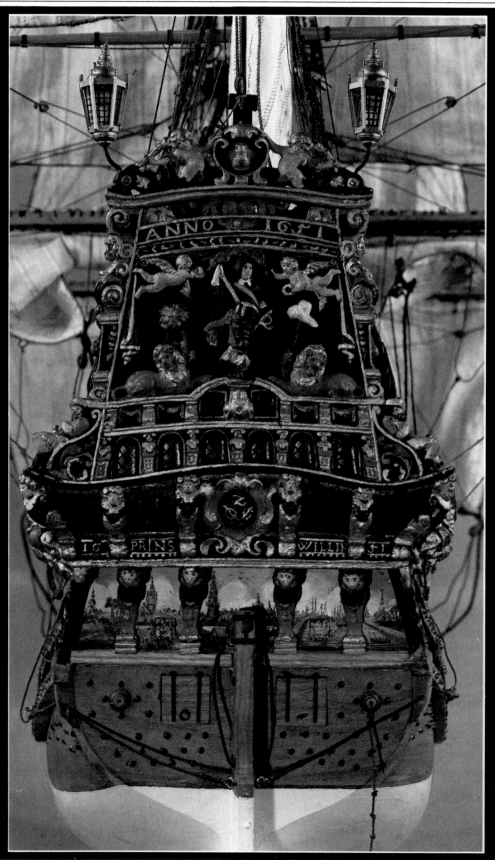

The Prins Willem's transom—
elaborately carved and ablaze with color
—displays (from top to bottom)
the date of the launching; a portrait of
Prince William II of Orange, the
vessel's namesake; and painted scenes of
Middelburg, where the ship was built.

weather at the end of a journey as at the start, those aboard East Indiamen went from the gales of a North Atlantic December to the oppressive heat of the Equator, where a ship might wallow in the doldrums for weeks on end. They then sailed through the tempestuous Southern latitudes of the Cape of Good Hope and voyaged back to the sultry tropics again as they reached the Indies.

The dozen or more skilled men aboard—boatswains, gunners, carpenters, cooks, coopers, calkers and joiners—occupied the forecastle, which was roomier and better ventilated than the crew's quarters. And those entitled to regard themselves as gentlemen—the captain, his mates, other officers, the surgeon and any merchants on board—lived in comparative comfort in compartments in the stern cabin, a large room, measuring some 25 by 30 feet, separated from the stench of the crew's quarters by a deck and from the forecastle by the ship's deep waist.

In addition to their greater allocation of space, the officers and merchants naturally enjoyed certain perquisites that were not granted the crew. The crewmen took their meals wherever they could find a perch, dipping their food from wooden bowls with wooden spoons. The officers and merchants sat down to a fine table that was covered with a white cloth and laid out with linen napkins, iron cutlery and pewter beakers. And there was no limit placed on the amount of wine and brandy the ship's gentlemen could drink—a fact that undoubtedly induced many an alcoholic haze that helped make the voyage more bearable. Crewmen were scarcely memorable for sobriety, but their grog—usually brandy or rum diluted with water—was rationed, and it sometimes ran out before the end of the passage. While it lasted, boatswains, cooks and carpenters were allowed two pints apiece per day, seamen one pint, and ship's boys half a pint. To prevent the men from hoarding and to take advantage of the beneficial effects alcohol was believed to have when imbibed on an empty stomach, all hands were obliged to drink their grog when it was doled out—at about 4 o'clock in the morning, three or four hours before breakfast.

For officers and crewmen alike, three hot meals were served every day, except on the occasions when rough seas made cooking impossible. Breakfast, at 7 or 8 o'clock, usually consisted of hot porridge cooked with prunes and covered with butter. Dinner, at noon, would be salt beef or pork three days a week and on other days stockfish (usually dried haddock or hake), served with peas or beans. Supper, served at 6, was a mixture of leftovers.

To provide this fare for a voyage of many months required lading the ships with enormous quantities of food. The provisions carried by a 600-ton East Indiaman that left London with 150 men in 1607 were typical: 37 tons of bread, 18 tons of pickled pork, 13 tons of marinated beef, six tons of dried salt beef, 210 bushels of peas, 105 bushels of beans, 141 bushels each of oatmeal and wheat, 600 gallons of cooking oil, 150 gallons of brandy, 28 tons of beer, 40 tons of cider, 41 pipes of ordinary wine for the crewmen and three pipes of fine wine for the captain, his officers and the merchants, and 80 tons of water. Also aboard were several tubs of cheese, butter, honey and delicacies such as sausage and coffee for the captain's table. Fresh provisions—meat on the hoof and baskets of fresh fruit and vegetables—were carried too, but they usually did not last longer than the first few weeks at sea.

If the quantity of food was impressive, its quality was dismal. The diaries and journals of those who sailed aboard East Indiamen tell the tale. "Beefe, beere and biskit all starke and stinking," reported the captain of one vessel after some weeks at sea in the early 1600s. Another seafarer recalled that the drinking water swarmed with organisms; the only way he was able to get it down was to hold his nose to keep out the smell and clench his teeth to strain the scum. Rats and cockroaches got into the supplies of foodstuffs easily, gnawed away at the contents and left their droppings behind.

Although little was known at the time about germs and disease, there could be no mistaking the connection between the state of the food and the high rate of sickness aboard. Christopher Fryke, a German who sailed as a surgeon on a Dutch Indiaman in the 1680s, asserted: "Many were not used to such a sea diet, namely bacon as salty as brine, half-boiled gray peas, rancid porridge and stinking water; our ship became a mere hospital, so many fell sick." Edward Barlow, an English seaman, in 1674 recalled that the crewmen were "very sickly through means of their bad provisions, having no bread but eating rice," and "the rice being of a waterish nature, bred a kind of dropsical disease, which swelled them up with water, and in a short time killed many." What Barlow observed were some of the symptoms of malnutrition.

The most dreaded form of shipboard malnutrition was scurvy, caused by a lack of vitamin C from fresh fruits and greens. In that respect, seamen who sailed with East Indiamen had better prospects than earlier long-distance voyagers, for by the mid-17th Century the Dutch had settled at Cape Town and planted vegetable gardens and orchards. So long as their governments were not at war with the Dutch, English and Portuguese vessels also were able to avail themselves of this oasis; breaking their voyage to the Indies at the halfway point, they could buy fresh Dutch produce that would cure the scurvy sufferers, provided the disease was not too far gone. Even so, the rest stops were a mixed blessing: While they cured some of the men of scurvy, they exposed others to the ravages of malaria, cholera and typhoid.

Lack of hygiene was yet another promoter of disease on board East Indiamen. The seamen cared little for personal cleanliness. Their clothing swarmed with lice, which carried typhus. And finally, virtually all these ailments were frequently accompanied by dysentery and its attendant dehydration.

To combat these ailments, almost all East Indiamen carried surgeons (pages 70-71). But their skills were limited, and so were their duties. Aboard Dutch vessels, the surgeons generally held sick calls twice daily, morning and evening, and all the ill sailors who could still walk were expected to report. Enemas, purging and bloodletting were standard treatments for almost all complaints, from smallpox to scurvy. The doctors aboard English Indiamen dispensed with the daily sick calls and went belowdecks for bedside visits, but few seamen respected either their abilities or their commitment. They "are very careless of a poor man in his sickness," wrote Edward Barlow, and did little more than

The father of seagoing surgery

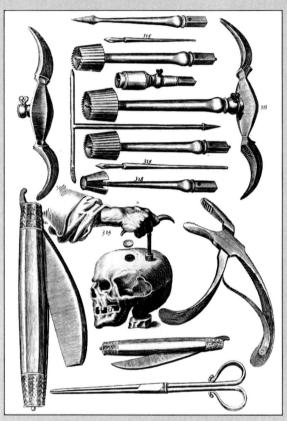

A page from John Woodall's manual shows the blades, forceps and auger-like trephine used in skull surgery.

Among the least popular members of a ship's company during the age of sail was the surgeon. Not only was his role associated with unpleasantness or worse, but his skills were often suspect: All too commonly, wrote a 17th Century seaman, the surgeon was "a drunken, careless and debauched fellow." One man, however, labored for some 30 years to change that sorry state of affairs. He was John Woodall, a dedi-

"take him by the hand when they hear that he hath been sick two or three days, thinking that is soon enough, and feeling his pulses when he is half dead, asking him when he was at stool, and how he feels himself, and how he has slept, and then giving him some of their medicines upon the point of a knife, which doeth as much good to him as a blow upon the pate with a stick."

Seventeenth Century mariners considered care of the soul to be as important as care of the body, and most vessels carried special personnel to look after the spiritual welfare of all aboard. On English East Indiamen the chaplains were usually ordained clergymen. Dutch ships frequently made do with lay readers, although religious devotions were accorded at least as much importance as on English vessels. The lay readers conducted prayers twice daily, before breakfast and supper, and attendance at the services was compulsory; anyone who was marked as missing forfeited his daily grog ration.

Like the English chaplains, Dutch lay readers were supposed to comfort the sick and dying—from which practice they came to be called *krank-bezoekers*, "sick visitors." Partly because their sick calls sometimes seemed insincere, and partly because they had a reputation for loose living, the *krank-bezoekers* were widely despised and commonly known as *drank-bezoekers*—"drink visitors." Jan Pieterszoon Coen, the East India Company governor who founded Batavia, described lay readers in terms that ranged from "clownish" to "idiots."

The sick visitors were often made the butt of practical jokes. In 1650 a Dutch official at Formosa asked for the services of a *krank-bezoeker* from a visiting East Indiaman and solemnly showed the fellow into a room containing an empty brandy cask. While local officials looked on and snickered, the *krank-bezoeker* was instructed to offer up a prayer for the restoration of the cask. The witness who recorded the incident did not comment on how the *krank-bezoeker* comported himself in the face of such ridicule.

Any deficiency of spiritual solace aboard East Indiamen was made all the more galling by the likelihood that sickness would end in death. Christopher Schweitzer, a German who served on Dutch East Indiamen in the 1680s, recorded that in one nine-day period on his first outward passage 63 persons died while the ship was in the doldrums. The toll was taken at all levels of the ship's company; among the dead were a chaplain and four of his children, the helmsman, four surgeons, three carpenters, two seamen and 31 soldiers. "We expected every soul should die out of the ship," he recalled grimly. When at last a favorable wind sprang up, "we had still a great many sick men, and not enough in health to be able to brace our mainsail."

Schweitzer himself was stricken and nearly succumbed—though not so much from his sickness as from a near-calamitous oversight on the part of his shipmates. "As I fell ill and was in a swoon, he that looked after the sick took me for dead, and fetched a new shirt out of my chest and was putting it on me," Schweitzer wrote. "The sailmaker too was going to sew me up, and he handling me a little roughly after all his pushing and tossing of me, I opened my eyes. Those that were gathered

cated and innovative London surgeon who was appointed the first surgeon general of the East India Company in 1612.

Woodall began at once to hire men who met his standards of medical skill (many of them, in fact, had been trained by him) and to oversee their fitting-out with proper medicines and instruments. Among the latter he included an invention of his own—the trephine *(left)*, a tool for removing splintered skull bone. The operation was an old one, but it had been performed with a cylindrical saw that wobbled and frequently cut too deep. Woodall's invention had a conical crown and center bit, which enabled the surgeon to steady the instrument as he bored and made it possible to cease drilling short of the brain tissue. The crowns and shanks, in different sizes, were interchangeable; a single handle suited them all.

Perhaps Woodall's furthest-reaching contribution was *The Surgeon's Mate*, a manual he wrote to instruct the surgeons in their work. Against prevailing practice, he urged caution in the use of that "great and terrible instrument," the saw. He pointed out that a surgeon's "over forwardnesse doth often as much hurt as good"—and added the pious but reasonable thought that "it is no small presumption to Dismember the Image of God." And, showing remarkable compassion for his day, he even advised the surgeon to spare mental anguish by hiding "his sharpe instruments from the sight of the Patient."

By the time of his death in 1643, Woodall's manual of instruction was in common use aboard East Indiamen, and it continued to be used for a good many years thereafter. His influence was so enduring that toward the close of the following century another English surgeon was to write that the recommendations made by Woodall "are in great part confirmed by modern practice."

about me were not a little startled, and said it was high time for me to open them, for if I had winked but a little longer, over I would have gone.'' Undoubtedly, many a feverish patient suffered the fate that Schweitzer so narrowly escaped.

Officers and merchants, at least, were accorded a ceremonious burial. The body of any important person was sewed up in a sheet and tied to a board with two cannon balls fastened at the feet to ensure that it sank quickly. After prayers had been said, a cannon was fired and the body was solemnly lowered into the water. No such trouble was taken over the corpses of ordinary seamen; sometimes they were not even wrapped in a sheet, but were simply thrown overboard and left to float away— a practice that generated a macabre curiosity among their surviving comrades. Surgeon Christopher Fryke, recalling his first encounter with shipboard burial, en route to the Indies on a Dutch ship, wrote that the incident ''gave occasion to a dispute among some of our seamen, concerning the dead bodies that were thus thrown overboard; some affirming that when they were loose, floating upon the water, you might turn them how you would, and they would still turn again, with the face or head toward the east.''

Fryke reported that there was one doubting Thomas among the crew who was unwilling to believe until he had tested the theory for himself.

A roistering welcome where two oceans meet

A crew of French seamen strolling on the beach at the Cape of Good Hope one day in 1619 were surprised to come upon a stone inscribed in Dutch. Rolling it over, they found two bundles enveloped in layers of lead and fabric; and inside all the wrappings, dry and intact after a lapse of several months, lay a number of letters that had been written by Dutch seamen and addressed to their comrades aboard other East Indiamen.

Despite the wild and untrammeled state of the Cape, this mail drop made perfect sense. Ever since 1488, when Portuguese explorer Bartolomeu Dias first reached the stormy tip of southern Africa, European seafarers had been stopping there to mend their ships and take on provisions, foraging off the land and bartering with the Hottentot village inhabitants.

The steady increase in ocean traffic inevitably resulted in a permanent Eu-ropean presence at the Cape. In 1652 the Dutch East India Company landed 80 colonists there and gave the little settlement the straightforward name of Cape Town. Unfortunately, more than half the members of this pioneering contingent found life in the wilderness not to their taste and returned to the Netherlands.

But the 1680s saw the arrival of another wave of settlers—many of whom were not able to go home again: They were Huguenots, refugees from the unsuccessful Protestant Reformation in France. Soon wheat, rye, barley and cultivated vegetables had replaced the wild grains and fruit on the meadows, and stone houses began to rise in the town, edging out the thatched huts of the Hottentots.

With their unerring instinct for commerce, the Dutch threw the port open to all comers. By the 1690s the Cape Towners were doing a thriving busi-ness supplying the requirements of some 200 ships that called there every year. To ships' provisions they added lodging—opening their houses to paying guests for the duration of the vessels' layovers.

Some visitors felt that there was a flaw in the Cape Town hospitality: An Englishman observed irritably in 1691 that he could find ''but 3 Houses in the Town that sell strong Liquor.'' But before the end of the decade, that deficiency was remedied—with so much success, in fact, that a Dutch governor reprimanded the Cape Town residents for their ''excessive cultivation of the vine'' and a clergyman from England was moved to complain that wayfarers ''Revel, bouze and break Glasses, what they please.'' For such roistering, this port of call between the Indian and the Atlantic Oceans earned a nickname that would endure for generations: the ''Tavern of Two Seas.''

He climbed down the side of the hull by the rope ladder "and with a pole turned the corpse about." The body "immediately turned again, by what cause I know not, but it convinced him that the others' assertion had somewhat of truth in it."

Some of the burials occasioned even more bizarre incidents. Schweitzer recalled that once, during the nine-day crisis that took so many of his shipmates, some of the surviving men caught a shark. "We designed to dress him and refresh ourselves," Schweitzer wrote, "but when we cut it open we found in the belly of it our sergeant that we had thrown overboard, not yet digested. The sight of this so turned our stomachs that none could find it in his heart to eat of the fish; so we threw man and fish into the sea again."

The accumulated pressure of such grimness, and the utter impossibility of escape from it, drove some men mad. Schweitzer told of two soldiers who jumped overboard in a raving fit. "Two of our best swimmers, perceiving, leaped in after them, and brought them into the ship again. But one of them after all this hanged himself that very night by his bedside." The other one died the following day, "having no regard to any good advice that was given him," by which Schweitzer seems to have meant that he was beyond reassuring.

If they were able to survive the food, sickness and madness, voyagers

As Dutch East Indiamen anchor off flat-topped Table Mountain, boats ferry sailors to the good cheer of Cape Town's taverns.

on East Indiamen still had to face a variety of threats to the ship as a whole. Perhaps the most terrifying of these was fire—an ever-present danger on wooden vessels that were loaded with gunpowder, illuminated by candles and manned by sailors with a fondness for smoking pipes. Captain Willem Bontekoe, a longtime servant of the Dutch East India Company, recalled that he was wakened from his sleep by cries of "Fire!" one night in November 1619 aboard his ship the New Hoorn in the Sunda Strait, the passage between the islands of Java and Sumatra. The steward's mate had accidentally dropped a lighted candle into a cask of brandy, and the resulting explosion of the alcohol fumes had caused the cask to burst. By the time Bontekoe had been alerted, burning brandy was spilling throughout the hold, carrying flames to the blacksmith's supply of coal.

Bontekoe lost no time in organizing the ship's company into a bucket brigade; one detail of sailors stood in a line along the rail and hauled up water from over the side in leather buckets; other seamen passed the buckets hand over hand to still more men in the hold, who dashed the water onto the flames. But before the fire could be brought under control, the acrid black smoke and sulfurous fumes from the burning coal drove the fire fighters out of the hold.

It was apparent that the bucket brigade was not enough; a more drastic remedy had to be tried. So Bontekoe ordered the carpenters to cut a number of openings in the hull at the water line to let in sea water. The fire spread faster than they could work, however, and Bontekoe, now fearing an explosion, next ordered men to start throwing the casks of gunpowder overboard.

But the fire had reached the barrels of cooking oil. "Then our courage was lost entirely," he recalled, "for the more water we threw, the worse the fire seemed to become, so high did it flame up through the oil. Then there arose such crying, groaning and shrieking in the ship as caused a man's hair to rise on his head, indeed the vehemence of fear and terror was so great that cold sweat poured from men's faces."

Some of the men now abandoned ship without orders, clambering over the side of the vessel and swimming to the safety of two boats that the New Hoorn had in tow. One of the sailors had the foresight to take along two barrels of bread. When both of the boats were filled, the men in them cut the painters that secured them to the New Hoorn and rowed away—leaving the 119 men who were still fighting the fire to fend for themselves.

Moments later the fire reached the 300 casks of gunpowder that had not yet been thrown overboard. The New Hoorn was blown to smithereens. When the explosion occurred, Captain Bontekoe was standing on the main gangway, far enough away from the powder casks to be spared instant incineration. The next thing he knew, he was in the water, surrounded by the debris of his vessel. Only one other man—an ordinary seaman—had been blown clear of the ship. The men in the boats, having watched the explosion from a safe distance, returned and picked up Bontekoe and the other survivor.

For the 72 men who were crammed into the two small boats, the nightmare was not yet over. They had no compass and only a vague idea

The true-life adventure of Captain Willem Bontekoe, skipper of the Dutch East Indiaman New Hoorn, unfolds in these sketches from his 1646 journal. After a fire in the magazine destroys the ship (top left), the vessel's yawl and longboat take on survivors (top right). The boats manage to stay together, propelled by sails made from shirts. Finally, the men crowd aboard the faster longboat (bottom), shown amid flying fish that helped keep them alive until they reached safety.

where they were. There was only enough bread for each man to get one tiny scrap a day, and they had no drinking water at all. But they stitched together some sails out of their shirts, and set their course in the presumed direction of land.

The elements were merciless. At night the temperature dropped so low that the men's teeth chattered; by day the sun scorched their skin raw. "Our distress became every day greater and heavier to bear," Bontekoe later recalled. The men grew so crazed with thirst that some drank their own urine, and others imprudently swallowed sea water, which, because of its salt content, only served to dehydrate their bodies more rapidly. After a few days the bread was gone, and "the men began to look with such despair, distrust and malevolence at each other as if they would devour each other; indeed they did speak of it among themselves, deeming to eat first the boys, and when these were finished, they should draw lots who should be the next one."

Bontekoe, "sorely troubled" at such a prospect, pleaded with the men to be patient, and they agreed that they would wait three days before resorting to cannibalism. On the third day, their 13th at sea, the men saw in the distance a small island covered with a green mantle of coconut trees. They were about 15 miles off the coast of Sumatra. When they landed on the island, they found food but were attacked by islanders. Sixteen of the Dutchmen were killed. The rest of the party managed to escape by boat to Java, a few miles across the Sunda Strait, where they found a Dutch fleet and safety.

Like most masters of Indiamen, Bontekoe was made of stern stuff; six years after the fire he showed similar courage in the face of another kind of disaster: a hurricane. He was captain of the *Hollandia* at the time, and was homeward-bound from Batavia in the company of two other ships, the *Gouda* and the *Middelburgh,* all of them carrying the season's yield of pepper. They had been at sea for six weeks and were about a thousand miles east of Madagascar when the great storm struck. At first the sea alternated between a calm as "smooth as a table" and waves that rose "so mightily that it seemed the ship would turn turtle." During the night, Bontekoe recalled, "the wind began to blow so terrifically hard that to him who has never heard or seen the like it would appear impossible for the wind to have such force." The gusts seemed to come from every direction, tossing the ship violently. "We stood together with our heads touching, yet could not shout or speak that we could hear one another." The wind snapped the mainmast and blew it overboard; then the hull sprang a plank below the water line, and the *Hollandia* shipped seven feet of water.

While the crew pumped without letup, Bontekoe recounted, "our blown-off mainmast lay clanking the whole night under the bottom and on the side of the ship," threatening to put a fatal gash in the hull. "The men in the hold called out: 'Cut away everything that holds it fast and let it drift!' We did what we could; we hacked the standing rigging through to windward, but on the lee side, as the ship rolled and swung so mightily, we could not get a foothold; we had to leave it so for the night." Not until the next morning were they able to free the ship from her damaged mast and tangled rigging.

Three Indiamen in a Dutch fleet battle a storm in the Indian Ocean in 1625; only Captain Willem Bontekoe's Hollandia (center) would manage to reach home. So filled with disasters was his published account of life at sea that "a Bontekoe's voyage" became a Dutch figure of speech for any star-crossed journey.

As the day wore on the weather cleared, and a dismal sight greeted the crew of the *Hollandia*. Lying to windward of them was the *Middelburgh*, with all her masts carried away. Where the *Gouda* should have been, there was nothing except an oily brown patch on the water. Later, one of the *Hollandia*'s seamen drew up a bucket of this brown water and found that it tasted strongly of pepper—the *Gouda*'s cargo.

The *Hollandia* and the *Middelburgh* limped to shelter in Madagascar, made repairs and then resumed their journey home. But only the *Hollandia* made it. The *Middelburgh* disappeared somewhere in the Atlantic. Bontekoe surmised she was the victim of an attack by pirates.

Pirates proliferated in most of the waters sailed by Indiamen, from the west coast of North Africa to the shores of China. Some were local inhabitants, who had begun preying on European merchant ships at the first intrusion of the Portuguese traders in the 1500s; others were European adventurers. In 1618 Sir Thomas Roe, the English Ambassador to the Mogul Emperor at Agra, sent word to London that the ships in his territory were beset by French, Danish and even English pirates in the Red Sea and the Persian Gulf, and warned that "iff measures bee nott tayken to prevent such expeditions, wee shall have the seas full of them and all trayde ruyned."

The only measures that governments and trading companies took against piracy were to arm their own ships and to send them out in convoy. Far from trying to eradicate the evil of predation, they gave underhanded support to a kind of legalized piracy by authorizing privateers to attack the Indiamen of other nations. In 1642 the government of France empowered French privateers to prey on English shipping off India, even while endorsing peaceable trade with England across the Channel. And in a single year, 1692, the English Crown authorized no fewer than 50 privateers, giving them carte blanche (and state-supplied armament) to prey on the merchant shipping of any trading rival. The crews of Indiamen had to be prepared to defend their vessels against such enemies on every voyage. But there was one peculiar case of maritime banditry—perhaps the strangest in the annals of East Indiamen—that involved neither pirates nor privateers, but an English captain who hijacked his own ship.

The ship was the *John*, an English Indiaman that sailed from London in February 1644 carrying £30,000 in gold and silver coins to the company's factory at Surat, on the west coast of India. At the time, England was in the throes of a savage civil war between Royalists loyal to King Charles I and Puritans led by Oliver Cromwell, who was trying to overthrow the monarchy. The East India Company tried to stay out of this conflict; but men of both loyalties were in company service, and passions sometimes ran high on company ships—as they did aboard the *John*. The vessel's captain, John Mucknell, was a Royalist; he was also a drunk. Edward Knipe, the senior merchant on board, was a Puritan with an inflated sense of his own importance and a bitingly sarcastic tongue. They would have found each other's company distasteful under any circumstances. And aboard an Indiaman, with its blurred division of authority between a captain who had control of nautical matters and a senior merchant who was in charge of all business affairs, the pair were irreversibly locked on a collision course.

In the initial stages of the voyage, Knipe reserved his criticism for lesser figures than the captain, such as a fellow merchant whose behavior was found wanting. "I butt acquainted him that his manner and carriage did rather become a fiddler than a merchant," Knipe recorded, "wherat he tooke soe much snuffe thatt hee hath not yet blowne itt oute. But I spake nothing in prejudice of his birth. I will say nothing in defence of itt because the partie thatt tolde mee he was borne in Venice of an Irish father and a Venetian mother, did not acquaint mee thatt they were lawfully married."

But it was the roistering behavior of the Royalist captain that particularly upset Knipe. Mucknell had a predilection for drinking at any hour of the day with the crew, inviting into his roundhouse what Knipe described as "the most debausht, and ungodlie people in the shipp." When the captain was in his cups, his voice could be heard throughout the vessel as he loudly proclaimed: "I am a prince at sea, I am the proudest man upon the face of the earth. I am an Englishman and were I to be born again, I would again be born an Englishman. I am a Cockney. That's my glory." The senior merchant shuddered at such undignified outbursts.

It was Knipe's intention to have the captain superseded when the ship

The British merchantman Experiment strikes her red ensign and surrenders to a Dutch fleet off Sumatra in 1672. Not until they were captured did the English learn that the two nations were at war.

arrived at Surat. But when the *John* reached Mozambique in August, a wonderful opportunity to humiliate the Cockney captain presented itself. The local Portuguese agent asked Knipe if he, his wife and his family, and a large number of African slaves could travel on the ship as far as Goa. As senior merchant, Knipe was responsible for arranging accommodations for fare-paying passengers and, without bothering to consult or even to inform Mucknell, he assigned the captain's quarters to the wife of the Portuguese agent.

On learning of the arrangements, Mucknell was enraged and was barely dissuaded from throwing Knipe and the Portuguese party off his ship. Knipe, now alarmed that he might have gone too far, sent the chaplain to placate the captain and promised to pay Mucknell 200 reals of eight in "good English gold." To the relief of the senior merchant, the chaplain returned to say that Mucknell had promised "reformacion of his liffe and conversacion."

Such was the change in the captain that at the *John's* next halt—the island of Johanna, in the Comoros north of Madagascar—he invited the merchants and the Portuguese to join him and his senior officers at a picnic on shore. During the course of this convivial gathering, a sailor arrived with the news that two members of the crew were preparing to fight a duel. Mucknell excused himself from the gathering and went off, vowing to put a stop to the fight. That was the last the picnic party ever saw of him.

It is not known whether the message about the duel was a ruse, but when the captain got back to the *John* he assembled the crew and announced he was seizing the ship in the name of the King. "You thatt are for the Kinge and will agree to this motion hold up youre hands," he said. On the promise of unlimited drink and a share of the treasure on board, all but 18 of the crew agreed to join Mucknell. The dissenters were thrown into irons, and the *John* sailed for home, leaving Knipe and his friends marooned on the island. After a few months there, living on handouts from the inhabitants, they were picked up by another ship and eventually taken to Surat.

The *John*, meanwhile, followed an erratic and drunken course back to England. It must have been a merry voyage, if Mucknell's account of a meeting with another English merchant ship off Madagascar is any indication. He jovially invited the captain and crew of the other vessel aboard and plied them with so much wine that, when the time came for the ships to be on their way, three of the visitors remained aboard the *John* because they were "too druncke toe bee put into the boate."

When the *John* reached England, Mucknell handed over the vessel—and the cargo of £30,000—to Royalist forces holding the port of Bristol. The King appears to have rewarded him with a knighthood, and the rest of the ship's company were gratefully given two years' pay in reals of eight, with the promise of more when the King should be restored and able to reward each "according to his deserte." The *John* was later commissioned a man-of-war and turned against the Cromwellian forces, with Mucknell in command. Needless to say, few hijackings of East Indiamen occasioned such merriment as did that of the *John*—or ended with so little harm done to the seamen.

Given the usual wretched conditions, the ubiquitous hazards and the high casualty rate, the wonder is that some men kept going out on East Indiamen again and again, year after year. Crimps usually put only the common seamen aboard; there were another 30 or more men on every ship, including the officers and most of the skilled specialists among the crew, who went of their own accord.

For some, like surgeon Christopher Fryke, the promise of adventure was lure enough. "Ever since I came to years that I could tell my own inclinations, I found the chiefest of my desires was to travel and to see strange countries," he wrote. "The more I read voyages, journals and other such books, which gave me an account of strange adventures, places, things, etc., the more my desires increased to see those things. Nor did the greatest of dangers that those accounts described so much frighten me from similar undertakings as the joyful deliverances out of them encouraged me."

Edward Barlow, a seaman who spent most of his lifetime aboard English East Indiamen, remembered similar yearnings. As a youngster living under the care of an uncle in London, Barlow recalled, "sometimes I would stand where I could see the ships and boats sail along, taking great pleasure therein." When he first announced that he longed to go to sea, his uncle tried to dissuade him, warning him against the crimps who prowled the waterfront and telling him that a seaman "earns his living with more pain and sorrow than he that endures a hard imprisonment." But "I would not hearken to his counsel," Barlow said; he voluntarily signed up for an apprenticeship of seven years, and found that his boyhood dreams of adventure were sufficiently fulfilled for him to decide to make a career of seafaring.

In the minds of most men, vague ideas of adventure combined with grandiose dreams of wealth. Christopher Fryke told of a lucky drummer boy who, in a military campaign on Java, stumbled upon the jeweled crown of an Oriental potentate; his commanding officer paid him the handsome sum of 30,000 guilders for it, and gave him his freedom and a pass to return to Holland.

But such finds were rare indeed. The real wealth for which the East Indiamen were famed went only to a lucky few, mainly the powerful men who—without ever suffering the torments of the sea—directed the companies' activities from London and Amsterdam. The crews who actually endured the dangers and discomforts aboard East Indiamen received pitifully low wages: The English company paid an ordinary seaman no more than one pound a month (about the equivalent of the Dutch seaman's 10 guilders) and mates got between three and five pounds a month. But everyone on an Indiaman expected to make a good deal more from what he called his "privilege."

On East Indiamen of all nations, privilege was the right granted to officers and men to trade on their own account on both outward and homeward voyages. Every member of the ship's company was allotted an amount of space, graded according to rank, to stow his personal ventures—goods he hoped to sell at a considerable profit at the end of the voyage. Customs duty had to be paid on these shipments, and the companies specifically forbade private trade in the products on which

Grim penalties for shipboard offenses

Ships' companies and townsmen gather to witness a ducking at the yardarm. The unfortunate culprit hangs just to the left of center, about to plummet into the sea.

Of all the terrors besetting the men who sailed East Indiamen, none was worse than the prospect of shipboard punishment. A Dutch saying had it that sailors were treated "like men ashore and like donkeys on board." But because sailors were presumed to be an unruly lot, both law and seafaring tradition sanctioned a Draconian discipline.

On Dutch East Indiamen, simply throwing food overboard—surely a desperate temptation at times—earned a flogging, on the ground that, no matter how unappetizing, the food had to be made to last. Using a ship's boat without permission also drew a flogging; the company feared desertion by the men. And because the welfare of the ship was devoutly believed to be in the hands of a wrathful Providence, swearing was considered a transgression that was worthy of both a flogging and a fine.

For the most part, punishments were graded ac-

they had monopolies, such as spices, pearls, gold and tea. But privilege was a system that invited abuse, and everyone—from the cabin boy to the captain—abused it.

As early as 1609 the directors of the Dutch East India Company recorded sourly that the "senior merchants, junior merchants, skippers, officers, assistants and all other persons in the service of the company" were buying up and bringing or sending back to Holland "the best and finest porcelain, lacquer ware, and other Indian rarities, contrary to their oath of engagement." Thirty years later, the illicit private trade had grown to such an extent that the Dutch company was having a difficult time selling its imports because the shops in Holland were so well stocked with contraband.

In England, so much private trade merchandise was smuggled on and off East Indiamen that King Charles I was prompted to issue a royal proclamation in 1627 reiterating the restrictions vainly imposed by the company. "Many abuses are laytely crept intoe the East India trayde," the proclamation began, "by reason of the practice of officers and others ymployed by the sayde Companie and their confederates in gayning att theyre own profitt by driving a secret and underhand trayde wherebye his Maiestie is defrauded of his Customs and Subsidies and the sayde Companie of its Freyte and Goodes." There followed a list of the permitted imports and exports, and strictures limiting each man's private trade to "Suche Onelie as may be packed in a chest of Fower Foote long, one foote and hauf a fotte broade, and one foote and one hauf deepe. Duble this quantities being permitted to Commaunders, Factors, pursers, Captains, and Master's Maytes." But since captains and merchants wanted to smuggle aboard more than their personal allowances, they looked the other way when the rest of the ship's complement did the same, and private trade continued to expand.

The Portuguese, too, tried to limit the privilege to liberty chests of standard measurement—with similar lack of success. On Portuguese Indiamen, all the deck and cabin space except the hold was usually filled with personal goods, and sometimes the crates and bales were piled so high that sailors were forced to clamber over them when going from one end of the ship to the other. In addition, boxes, barrels and baskets were slung over the side of the ship or lashed to planks projecting over the gunwales; overloading was frequently cited as the reason for the loss of homeward-bound Portuguese East Indiamen during the first half of the 17th Century.

Regulations designed to control the abuse of privilege on East Indiamen failed because graft and corruption riddled the entire structure of European trade in the East. Most of the clerks and merchants sent to man factories in lonely and fever-ridden ports had only one aim: to get rich as quickly as possible. They were paid barely a living wage by their employers, but the opportunities for fraud, embezzlement and illicit dealings were endless—particularly in the so-called country trade, the commerce between ports in the East (pages 112-119). A quantity of opium, for example, could be bought in Bengal for 70 rupees and sold in Batavia for 220, yielding a nice profit even after pay-offs for the captain, senior merchant and port officials were deducted.

cording to the severity of the crimes. A seaman who started a fistfight was clapped into irons and given only bread and water to eat. One who pulled a knife was ducked three times from the yardarm. If he pulled it again, he was keelhauled—ducked from one yardarm, dragged under the ship's bottom and hoisted up to the opposite yardarm.

If a fight drew blood, the culprit had one hand tied behind his back and the other affixed to the mast with the knife; in that position he was left until he was able to free himself. If a fight resulted in murder, the guilty party was tied back to back with his bleeding victim and pitched overboard like so much shark bait.

There were some captains for whom even these measures were not enough. A naval journal reported that one British captain used to triple the number of lashes "when any one *squeaked*, as he called it," while undergoing a flogging. The only restraint on such a man was his knowledge that, once the ship reached shore, sailors whom he had mistreated might lie in wait for him and exact a revenge as brutal as the punishment.

Trafficking in contraband had its risks, of course. Christopher Fryke, for instance, made only one attempt at dabbling in forbidden goods—and barely missed a dire fate. In Amboina he exchanged some cheese and tobacco for seven two-quart bottles of oil of cloves—second only to pepper as the Dutch East India Company's most important commodity. Fryke managed to get his illegal purchase as far as the roadstead of Batavia, and carried it with him as he joined a party going ashore in a boat. Luckily, he confided in a congenial seaman before customs officers approached the boat; the sailor craftily tied the ill-gotten bottles to a cord and suspended them over the side. As the customs men drew perilously close, the seaman unobtrusively cut the cord, sending the precious oil of cloves to the bottom of the sea. The customs officers found the part of the cord that was still attached to the boat, "which made

In this frontispiece to a treatise called The Light of Navigation, *published in Amsterdam in 1620, scholars and seamen pore over nautical paraphernalia under the glow of a ship's lantern. The gods of wind and sea loom over them, and in the background a Dutch fleet of Indiamen sails in search of trade.*

them give us an ugly look, but it was not sufficient to give us any further trouble,'' Fryke recalled.

He soon found out just how fortunate he had been. Aboard another East Indiaman, the customs officials caught a lieutenant who was trying to smuggle "a piece of gold of some pounds weight." The lieutenant was hanged. "This poor man's hard lot made me not regret my loss so much; I rather hugged myself that I had let my oil of cloves go. But it cured me from ever again attempting anything of that nature. This may serve to let you see how dangerous such undertakings are; and that such contraband goods are not so easily brought off. So that if men have no other end in going to the Indies, I advise them as a friend to stay at home while they are well."

Craftier entrepreneurs made plenty of money on ostensibly legal commerce between ports in the East. It was said that Dutch Indiamen loading at Batavia for Japan were so "pestered" with private goods that there was sometimes no space for the company's own cargo. Some well-placed servants of the companies were able to amass vast fortunes in a comparatively short time.

One of these servants was Elihu Yale, who joined the English East India Company in 1672 as a writer—a bookkeeping clerk—at a wage of £10 a year. He quickly rose through the lower echelons of the company and was appointed Governor of Madras in 1687. Taking advantage of that lofty position, he found many opportunities to enrich himself through private trade in diamonds, rubies, seed pearls and timber. In 1690 a group of company officials alleged that he had evaded freight charges and customs duties, but the accusation was never proved. Yale retired and returned to England in 1699 with a private fortune of £175,000—more than half the sum of the English East India Company's working capital for the same year—and used a portion of it to endow the American university that bears his name.

Meanwhile, the English East India Company had been making repeated efforts to curb private trade. In the fiscal year 1674-1675, when such dealings accounted for £135,000 of the £565,000 worth of exports that went east on the English company's ships, the company set a limit on privilege goods: five tons on outward-bound voyages and five per cent of the chartered tonnage homeward—a very large allowance in ships of 500 to 700 tons. The company employed "waiters" to intercept returning Indiamen off the coast of England and search for prohibited goods or excess over the allowance. They were most effective against the small-time private trader.

Edward Barlow was caught when the *Kent* arrived off Plymouth in 1684, as he described bitterly in his diary: "We met a ketch, which had our East India Company's waiters, which are sent by them on board of all ships coming from India to oversee and look whether they can see or find any person that brings any mulctable goods home with them, and if they hear of any, to inform the Company of it, although a man may have but a piece or two for his own use or for his wife and family; I having two pieces of calico which cost in India both together five shillings and ninepence, they put to me four shillings open charges before I could have them in my own possession, the Company showing such kindness to poor seamen, their waiters being then as welcome to us as water in a ship which is ready to sink."

Poor Barlow continued to be singularly unsuccessful with his attempts at private trade. In 1701 he returned to England from China on the *Wentworth* with a considerable venture of silk, tea and lacquer ware, only to discover that in his absence the government had slapped an extra duty of 15 per cent on most goods imported from the East. Worse, he found that all imports had to be warehoused until their value had been ascertained by public auction.

By the time Barlow had paid all the duties and charges involved—he described them sarcastically as "wateragge, wharfrige, portrige and cartrige"—he had incurred a loss of 30 per cent on the tea and lacquer ware. The silk he brought home fetched £908 at auction, although "when I came to receive what the Company allotted for me, it was no more than £454." He did not say whether this represented a profit or loss, but added ruefully that had he bought gold he "could have made near 50 pounds profit."

Captains of East Indiamen, who were notorious for the single-minded pursuit of personal wealth, tended to enjoy the greatest success in circumventing company restrictions. Indeed, private trade helped make command of an English Indiaman a much sought-after position. Unlike the Dutch company, which held title to its ships, the British company hired its vessels from private owners, and these owners also supplied the captains—at a handsome profit to themselves. They sold commands for prices that reached as high as £10,000 by the end of the 18th Century. But the man who bought the command of an East Indiaman was almost certain to recoup his investment: Some English captains made as much as £12,000 from private trade on a single two-year voyage. And they rarely missed other opportunities to make a little extra on the side, at the expense either of the company or of their crew. For instance, gains could be wrung from the sale of liquor, tobacco and clothes to the seamen. In 1677, after complaints of overcharging became so numerous they could not be ignored, the English company ruled that captains should not sell necessities to the crew at a profit of more than 50 per cent. The rule was, of course, largely disregarded.

Careful choice of dunnage—the material used to pack the cargo to prevent its rolling about or being damaged—also provided useful income for the captain. Bamboo or rattan, supplied free by Eastern merchants for dunnage, fetched a good price in Europe, where it was used to make furniture. Many East Indiamen carried excessive amounts of dunnage on homeward voyages.

Some skippers put personal gain before the welfare of their crews by cutting back on the men's rations in order to sell the surplus on their arrival in the East. The luckless Barlow had the misfortune to fall in with a thoroughly dishonest captain on his last voyage to the Orient, in 1702. This young man, Barlow noted with undisguised contempt, had been a "milliner of small wares" before he married a wealthy baker's daughter, and got together sufficient money to buy command of an East Indiaman, the *Fleet Frigate*. The captain profited, Barlow said, by "selling the beer out of the ship at Batavia and buying rack"—a cheap local brew—"and

85

Returned from the East Indies and flush with back pay, a Dutch sailor (top) struts on the wharf in Amsterdam with souvenirs of his journey—an exotic cockatoo, a jug of liquor and a sea chest that overflows with the rest of his worldly possessions. Below, another seaman carouses in a waterfront dance hall.

disposing of it as he pleased, and making us drink water all the time we were in China, and several times afterward, although it is a custom for men to be allowed rack to drink when the beer is done, a pint every day. But he was much like all other commanders, to gain what they can, either by hook or crook."

When the time came for Barlow to be paid his fee for piloting the ship from Batavia to Canton, the captain counted out the money by the light of a single flickering candle. Next day, Barlow found 12 of his 100 Spanish dollars were "cross dollars"—coins similar in size but worth much less. "That was no great matter," Barlow sighed, compared "to what he pinched otherwise."

East of the Cape of Good Hope, few seamen dared complain about such treatment for fear of being left behind in some remote Oriental port. But when the ship was approaching home, it was not unusual for resentment to boil over and for the members of the crew to settle old scores. An eyewitness on a Dutch East Indiaman in 1701 reported how seamen dragged from hiding a cook who had been shorting their rations for his own private gain, and beat him with his own kitchen implements so severely that "he was maimed for a long time and could not even go to the East India House to get his sea chest and wages." The skipper of the same vessel managed to keep out of the way of his mutinous and angry sailors until they reached harbor in Holland, where the crew "told him to his face, in the presence of the directors who were paying us off, that he was a scoundrel, a ration thief and a bully, and they threatened to pay him his due ashore. As indeed they did at Middelburg, where they beat him almost to a jelly."

In Amsterdam the Dutch sailors who were returning from the East were known as "lords of six weeks," since this was approximately the length of time it took these men to flaunt and squander their sudden wealth. One seaman, in possession of literally more money than he knew what to do with, hired three coaches—one for his hat, one for his pipe and tobacco box and a third for himself—and then drove through the streets of Amsterdam in regal procession until his money ran out. But no sailor had to go to such extremes. He could get rid of all his money without ever having to leave the waterfront, where the grogshops and brothels abounded.

The prosperous citizens of Amsterdam were openly contemptuous of the returning seamen; one observer noted that the mariners quickly reduced themselves from affluence to being "as naked as Adam." But the city's burghers made no efforts to improve the lot of the seaman, for they found his habits convenient. "Where does the money that they have squandered remain?" the same man asked—and answered his own question: "In Amsterdam. And who has derived the profit from it? The inhabitants of that town."

When the seamen had nothing left but a few blurred memories, they found they were no longer welcomed by the tavern keepers. Those who did not find other employment hung around the waterfront, penniless and hopeless. Soon enough the *zielverkoopers* would send them back to sea again; but this time, at least, they would have no illusions about what awaited them there.

Chapter 4

An empire brewed from tea leaves

British warships bombard the French fort of Chandernagore in 1757. In London, news of its fall boosted the British company's stock by 12 per cent.

f all the wondrous commodities of the Orient transported back to Europe in the creaking holds of East Indiamen, none had more impact on the fortunes of Great Britain than the faintly aromatic, shriveled, dark brown leaf called *tcha* or *tay* in the East and "tea" in the West. From its beginnings in Britain as a luxury item prized by an elite handful of Londoners, China tea became a national staple in less than one generation. In the process, it catapulted the Honourable East India Company—familiarly known as John Company—into a position of wealth and power undreamed of by its founders. The company's merchants became the first Europeans to secure a foothold in one of the great seaports of China, the city of Canton. Then, as the China trade began to reap dividends, tea supported the company as it battled a host of jealous competitors at home and outfought the French and Dutch for the riches of India. The struggle between aspirants to supremacy in Eastern trade had many venues—palaces and parliamentary halls in Europe, obscure waterfronts in the Orient, and inland strongpoints on the Indian subcontinent. But at heart, it was a story of the great ships that linked two worlds.

The first packets of tea, purchased by the crews of East Indiamen from Chinese junks trading in India or Batavia, arrived in London in the 1650s. By 1658 sufficient quantity was available for it to be put on public sale. An advertisement in the September issue of the newspaper *Mercurius Politicus* notified Londoners that the "excellent and by all Physitians approved China drink, Tee, is sold at the Sultaness Head, a copheehouse in Sweetings Rents, by the Royal Exchange, London."

On September 25, 1660, the ever-inquisitive diarist Samuel Pepys recorded his first sampling of the new beverage in Garraway's Coffee House, a popular watering hole near the Royal Exchange: "I did send for a cup of tea (a China drink) of which I never had drunk before." Pepys next mentioned tea in his diary on June 28, 1667—this time in a domestic context: "Home, and there find my wife making of tea, a drink which Mr. Pelling the apothecary tells her is good for her cold and defluxions."

The English East India Company did not make its first official purchase of tea until 1664, when it paid four pounds five shillings for a tin of "good thea" weighing two pounds two ounces, and presented it to King Charles II. The company's gift evidently found royal favor: Two years later, another 22 pounds 12 ounces was purchased for the King at a price of 56 pounds 17 shillings 6 pence. Soon the rage for tea spread beyond fashionable London—although not without certain confusions as to its proper mode of preparation. When the Duke of Monmouth's widow sent a pound of tea to relatives in Scotland in 1685, they boiled it, threw the liquid away, served the leaves as vegetables, then wondered what their southern cousins were so ecstatic about.

In Holland, samples of tea had been brought back by East Indiamen as early as 1610, yet England's arch rivals in trade did not take to the drink with enthusiasm, preferring the stronger-tasting beverage brewed from Arabian coffee beans. Ruddy-cheeked Dutchmen derisively labeled the pallid tea-leaf infusion "hay water." Those who partook of the drink did so mostly for medical reasons. In 1641 the celebrated Amsterdam physician, Dr. Nicholas Tulp, declared tea to be a remedy for virtually all ills.

SUPERCARGO JOACHIM BONSACH

SUPERCARGO PETER MULE

Foot-high figurines—ceramic except for hair wigs, cloth caps and the wooden chairs that seat them—represent the captain and three merchants who initiated Danish trade with China in 1731. The Canton artists' quarter had a number of "face makers" who specialized in this realistic form of portraiture.

His assessment was supported by the court physician, Dr. Cornelius Bontekoe, who recommended that his royal patients drink from 50 to 200 cups of tea every day.

Tea was also accorded medicinal value in England. As the beverage became more generally available, wild claims of tea's "particular Vertues" were circulated on printed broadsides throughout London. "It maketh the body active and lusty; it vanquisheth heavy dreams, easeth the Brain, and Strengtheneth the Memory," proclaimed one circular. More to the point, piping hot tea simply suited the taste of most Englishmen. By the late 1670s, when annual tea sales in London alone reached £94,000, the East India Company resolved to redouble its efforts to open direct trade for such a profitable cargo from its source in China.

Since its inception in 1600, the company had striven without success for trading privileges at a major Chinese port. Under the Ming Dynasty, which ruled the Celestial Empire in the early 17th Century, Chinese merchants were enjoined from trading with foreigners, especially Europeans, who were dubbed *fan kwai*—barbarians. The Ming emperors declared trade with the fan kwai unnecessary, distasteful and dangerously subversive, and the Manchu Dynasty, which succeeded to power in 1644, fully shared these sentiments. Among all the European powers, only the Portuguese, at Macao, had managed to push the door ajar—at the price of huge annual contributions and presents to the Emperor.

Without legal access to a Chinese port, the English and Dutch East India Companies engaged in a stealthy commerce at the coastal city of Amoy—controlled by a Ming loyalist warlord named Coxinga, who was holding out against the conquering Manchus—and in the semiautonomous buffer state of Tonkin, where Chinese exports were readily available. In these commercial backwaters the company merchants got a foretaste of the frustrating—and often infuriating—business practices that prevailed throughout the Celestial Empire.

Merchants aboard the English East Indiaman *Zant* received a typically rude introduction to the tea trade in 1672. Laden with cloth, lead, sulfur, pepper, sandalwood, drugs and silver bullion, the *Zant* dropped anchor in the muddy waters of the Red River at Tonkin on June 25. Without delay, the vessel's captain dispatched a letter to the King of Tonkin requesting permission to trade. Six days passed before a small party of silk-clad officials, dubbed mandarins by Europeans (from the Portuguese word *mandar*, to order), was rowed out to greet the fan kwai ship.

The Chinese were welcomed aboard the *Zant* by the ship's officers and the company's supercargoes—the agents who would actually conduct any business to be done. When the formalities were over, the mandarins politely asked for a complete list of the ship's cargo and a statement of what presents were intended for the King and his oldest son. They also wanted to know what presents they could expect to receive themselves. Trade would not even be considered, they said, until these important preliminaries had been settled.

Stunned, the English gave up hope for any trade. William Gyfford, the chief supercargo, explained to the Chinese that his "Honourable Employers" would not do business on such terms, and he applied for permission to leave. The request was brusquely refused. Before they an-

A clash of cultures in a Chinese court

All during their tenure as traders in China, the English never ceased to wonder at the peculiarities of their hosts—and vice versa. In February 1807, when 52 sailors from the Indiaman *Neptune* got into a drunken row with a crowd of Cantonese and left a customs officer wounded, commerce halted for two months while officials on both sides sought to accommodate each other's idea of justice without sacrificing principle.

A Chinese security agent initiated the proceedings, telling the *Neptune's* Captain Thomas Buchanan that, for a consideration, news of the incident would be withheld from the higher authorities. But when the customs officer died, officials learned about it and demanded that the English surrender the murderer for punishment under Chinese law—which called for strangulation. When the English refused, saying no evidence pointed to an individual culprit, the Chinese forbade the English fleet to leave the harbor.

Matters stood at an impasse until March 28, when a provincial judge ordered Buchanan to bring his crew to the English hong for questioning. When he did, all the men denied having committed the deed. At last, the Chinese singled out one Edward Sheen, on the flimsy ground that he had been wounded in the fray. The English were ordered to detain him to await the verdict. The other men returned to the ship, and the fleet was given permission to sail.

The Chinese were astonished when the fleet refused to budge until Sheen's fate was determined. After two weeks the judge delivered an unexpected decree that made no mention of murder: Edward Sheen merely had to pay a fine—later set at four pounds. Satisfied with the outcome, the English departed.

They never received an explanation. Presumably when the Chinese found them willing to detain the entire fleet for a single seaman, they feared a permanent stoppage of trade. In any event, the Chinese would endure a far more humiliating setback to their legal authority four decades later, when Britain defeated China in the Opium War and won the right to exempt British nationals from Chinese law.

During interrogation of the Neptune's crew, a seaman goes before a Chinese magistrate in the great hall of the English hong at Canton.

chored in the river, the English were informed that they were free to come and go as they chose; now they were told that their presence in the King's realm rendered them subject to his power. What the mandarins did not state was that they intended to milk the fan kwai merchants of the *Zant* for all they were worth.

While the English fumed, another worthy emissary arrived with a long list of goods requisitioned by the King ("without price, manner or time of payment," one of the *Zant's* supercargoes noted bitterly). Among the desired items were 17 bales of cloth, more than a ton of sulfur, almost that much lead, seven great guns and several hundred pounds of drugs. After these goods were handed over, the emissary personally demanded half the silver bullion on board—some 10,000 reals, worth about £2,300. If his demand was not met, he warned, the sum might be extracted by force. The English managed to pacify him with an offering of 100 reals, but a veritable parade of covetous officials came aboard the *Zant* in the days that followed, all of them demanding "satisfaction."

At last the supercargoes were summoned ashore to hear from the King how much he would pay for the goods he had taken. It was a third of what they had cost. In return, the English were generously offered the opportunity to buy silk at 40 per cent above the going rate, a proposition the hapless supercargoes could not afford to accept. At that point, discussions came to an end, and the *Zant* was finally allowed to leave.

Despite repeated indignities of this kind, more East Indiamen were sent to the Chinese coast, and by 1676 the company had managed to establish tenuous trading links on the island of Taiwan and at Amoy. Unfortunately, Manchu armies captured Amoy in 1680, forcing suspension of operations there. As for Taiwan, the main business seemed to consist of paying bribes to an apparently endless queue of local officials.

Obviously, a new port of entry had to be found, and in October 1682 the company dispatched the East Indiaman *Carolina* from London with orders to try to establish a factory at the port of Canton, 70 miles northeast of Macao, at the mouth of the Pearl River. The *Carolina's* supercargoes were advised to be "very wise and circumspect" when dealing with the Chinese, "they being a very cunning, deceitful people." The agents had scant opportunity to follow this advice, for no sooner did the *Carolina* reach Canton's bay than she was warned off by Manchu war junks. The English were told that no European would ever be allowed to trade there. After five months of shuttling from port to port, the *Carolina* headed for home. "We might stay here untill the bottom of our Ship did drop out," one of the supercargoes wearily noted, "before we should have trade from any persons of their countrey."

Meanwhile, in December 1682, the *Delight*, another English East Indiaman, was sent out from London with orders to join the *Carolina* if possible. After calling at Achin on Sumatra, the *Delight* pressed on toward Macao. But when she was only about 150 miles southwest of her destination, the September monsoon struck with full force, causing her to retreat to Bangkok. There the *Delight's* supercargoes learned from a Portuguese ship that the *Carolina* was already on her way back to England, her mission to Canton a failure. With the supreme optimism characteristic of 17th Century traders, the men of the *Delight* decided to see if the Manchu conquerors of Amoy had reconsidered their ban on trade with Europeans. They arrived in the Chinese port on May 26, 1684.

The first step, as always, was the distribution of presents to local mandarins, civil magistrates and their secretaries. By June 5 the English believed everyone had been satisfied and that trade would be permitted. But at a meeting on shore between Chinese officials and the supercargoes, an unforeseen problem arose. The *Delight* was carrying a large number of brass guns, muskets and barrels of gunpowder, and this collection of armaments seemed to trouble the Chinese. Perhaps, the mandarins slyly suggested, they were meant as a present for the Emperor.

With sinking hearts the Englishmen pointed out that the weapons were for sale and that the Emperor was welcome to buy them, but as humble merchants they could not afford to give such expensive presents. Their reply sent the Chinese into a fury: They accused the English of attempting to supply arms to Coxinga's rebels, still holding out on Taiwan, and issued dark threats that failure to present the guns to the Emperor would "hazard" their ship. The *Delight*'s supercargoes argued as best they could, but in the end they glumly handed over 24 of their 30 brass guns, 220 of their 250 muskets and 100 of their 150 barrels of gunpowder. This produced smiling assurances from the Chinese that trade would shortly be forthcoming.

For the whole of June and July the crew of the *Delight* waited patiently. Nothing happened. By the beginning of August the ship was leaking badly and permission was sought to careen her ashore to make repairs. The mandarins immediately raised objections, saying they could not approve the work without the Emperor's authorization—which was, of course, impossible to obtain at short notice. The inevitable corollary followed: For a suitable consideration, the officials might authorize repairs on their own. Their price was 1,100 taels of silver (about £340). No sooner was the extortion paid out than a second magistrate, claiming that he had the power to block the authorization, demanded a sum equal to that already handed out. When he was satisfied, the three officials who were to supervise the unloading of the *Delight*'s cargo stepped forward and demanded their dues. They were each bought off with a gift of cloth, which immediately prompted their already bribed superiors to stake new claims. The superiors each received 12 pieces of fine cloth. Only then could the ship be careened.

But the *Delight*'s fortunes quickly turned sour again. While the ship was being repaired, a richly laden Dutch Indiaman, the *Chylida*, arrived in Amoy harbor, providing the Chinese with an excuse to peremptorily instruct the English merchants to reload their cargo so that the Dutch goods could be stored in the local warehouse. By means of a new spate of presents, the English managed to have their competitors shunted off to Foochow, a port about 150 miles to the north.

On October 18, nearly five months after the *Delight* reached Amoy, a Manchu official performed a ceremony that seemed to indicate an end to the visitors' troubles: He removed an official storage permit called a *chop*—a strip of paper affixed across the doors of the building that housed the ship's cargo—and read an imperial proclamation declaring that the English were free to trade. Naturally, a steady diet of presents

Chinese Emperor K'ang-hsi, who ruled the Celestial Empire from 1661 to 1722, wears a silk robe adorned with dragons symbolizing his absolute power. During his long reign, he broke with China's isolationist tradition, seeking information on Western technology and opening his ports to European trade.

was required to keep the trading wheels oiled. The final insult came from a newly appointed governor of the port, who demanded a duplicate set of the gifts and considerations that his predecessor had received. The *Delight* escaped the clutches of Amoy on December 19, with some of the goods she had brought from Europe still on board and with only half a return cargo. Bribes, presents, fees and duties paid out totaled £2,000, not counting the value of the guns and gunpowder.

But the news she carried was not all bad. In 1684 the Manchu Emperor, K'ang-hsi, loosened the restrictions on foreign trade and declared that Europeans could enter the China Sea and call at South China ports on a limited basis. Even more encouraging, the *Delight* conveyed a message from the Manchus inviting East India Company agents to establish a factory at Amoy or, as the *Delight's* captain reported, "any other place in ye great Emperour's Dominions." The company directors wasted no time. In May 1685 the hopefully named *China Merchant* was sent to Amoy to set up and operate a factory. Her supercargoes received a cordial welcome, and a building was offered at a reasonable rent. Though trade procedures continued to be vexatious and the mandarins retained their polished rapacity, the *China Merchant* was the forerunner of a great fleet of Indiamen plying between China and England.

The commercial success of the early English voyages to China depended almost entirely on the skill, shrewdness, diplomacy and courage of John Company supercargoes. Despite the thinly veiled contempt that the Chinese felt for all Europeans, the supercargoes had to avoid any actions that might cause offense. They had to grease appropriate palms, yet resist extortionate demands. They had to know whom to trust and not to trust. They had to haggle to get the best price they could for English woolens and lead, and haggle again to buy return cargoes at a price that would yield a suitable profit in Europe. Instantly, they had to calculate whether the tea being offered was of a quality worth one shilling a pound or double that amount. Moreover, they had to judge the value of a bewildering variety of commodities, many of which had scarcely been seen in Europe, let alone sold—woven silks, for example, or China root, a species of sarsaparilla.

On top of all their business dealings, the supercargoes had to straighten out any number of problems stemming from the behavior of British seamen. In 1685, when sailors from the *Loyal Adventure* shot and wounded "a Tartar from a Siam Junk" who had stolen two hats from their tent on shore at Amoy, the company's supercargoes smoothed over the affair by bribing a militia officer, all of the witnesses and a grasping old peasant who swore he was the father of the wounded man. The payoffs kept the incident from being reported to the Manchu Viceroy at Foochow. Had he learned of the contretemps, he would certainly have ordered the *Loyal Adventure* to leave immediately. Shortly after the *Loyal Adventure* incident, a drunken English sailor broke into the Amoy customhouse, a crime punishable by death. A supercargo pleaded the sailor's case before the commissioner for foreign trade and won a comparatively mild sentence for the offender: 100 lashes in public.

The first truly serious clash between English seamen and the Chinese occurred in 1689 at Macao. Local regulations required British ships to unstep their mainmasts while at Macao and stow them ashore. As the day of departure approached for the vessel *Defence,* Captain William Heath took a party of 20 to 30 armed sailors ashore to collect the spar. He presented the wrong permit to the wrong official, who simply threw it away. Exasperated, Heath ordered his men to start rolling the mast into the water. This was an unpardonable breach of procedures, and the Chinese tried to stop Heath's men. Blows were exchanged. Then, as the English sailors attempted to lash a towline from their longboat to the mast, the Chinese began throwing stones. At this point, Heath made a last, disastrous miscalculation: He ordered his men to use their guns. Several Chinese fell, and in the ensuing confusion a number of English sailors were stranded on shore as the longboat hurriedly pulled for the *Defence.* One of those left behind was the ship's doctor, who was cut down by the mob on the beach in full view of the men in the longboat.

The next day Portuguese officials rowed out to the *Defence* and urged the English supercargoes to settle the affair in the time-honored fashion of the Orient—with a hefty bribe. The ship's fourth-ranking supercargo, a Mr. Watts, volunteered to go ashore and speak with the mandarins. It was an act of considerable courage, but a futile one, for Watts's superiors

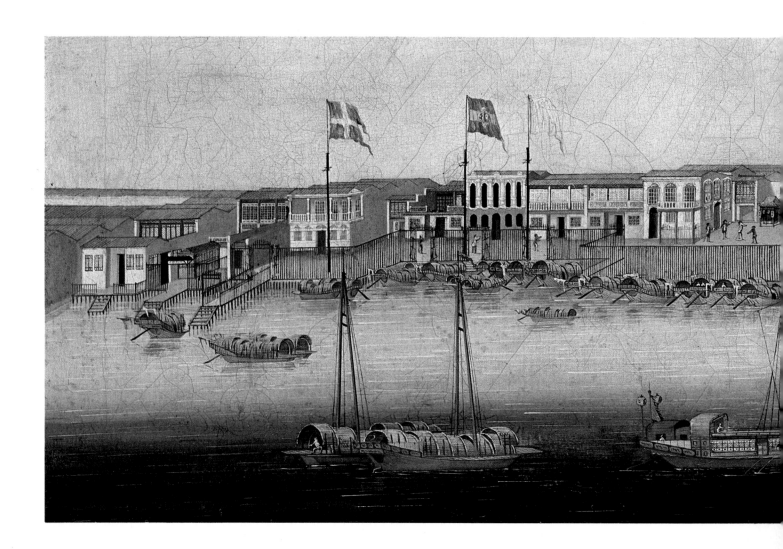

authorized him to offer only 2,000 taels recompense—3,000 less than the outraged mandarins demanded. When the news was relayed that the offer had been rejected—and that Watts was being held—the remaining supercargoes decided there was "no prospect of the mandarins lowering their demand" and persuaded Captain Heath to sail out of Amoy harbor—after giving 198 taels of silver to a Chinese merchant who promised to seek the release of the unfortunate Watts.

Although Watts was never heard from again, the *Defence* melee did not seriously hamper John Company's relations with China—and the incident was soon overshadowed by a dramatic shift in Manchu policy toward foreign trade. In August 1699, when the Indiaman *Macclesfield* dropped anchor at Macao, a high Manchu official came down from Canton to issue the necessary permits. It was the first indication that the Manchus had decided to actively encourage trade with the Europeans.

That same year the English were allowed to establish a factory at Canton, a walled South China seaport of more than a million citizens—four times the population of 17th Century London. Canton offered the best trading facilities in China. Situated at the mouth of the Pearl River and sheltered from the open sea by a funnel-shaped bay 30 miles long,

The flags of Denmark, Spain, France, Austria, Sweden, England and the Netherlands fly in front of hongs—leased trading stations—lining the Pearl River just outside Canton. The hongs served both as warehouses and as living quarters for the European merchants.

The china that was taken home to Europe

The emblem of Portugal's King Manuel adorns this 10-inch dragon-spouted ewer —one of the first porcelains known to have been commissioned for a Westerner.

In 1604 the Dutch captured the Portuguese carrack *Catharina* on her way from the East and auctioned off the cargo in Amsterdam. Among the contents of the ship were tons of Chinese porcelain, used by the Portuguese as ballast—but a treasure-trove in its captors' eyes. Made of a fine white clay unknown in Europe and fired at temperatures as high as 1,500°, it had a translucent hardness that made local pottery seem crude by comparison.

Before then, porcelain had had little circulation outside Lisbon. Now it became a craze throughout northern Europe—the only Chinese import to rival tea in popularity. Over the next 50 years the Dutch alone imported three million pieces of porcelain, from diminutive saltcellars and mustard pots to immense vases and basins. By 1712 China's main porcelain-making center, Ching-te-chen, 500 miles north of Canton, had to keep 3,000 kilns fired day and night to satisfy the demand.

The wealthy collected porcelain on a grand scale. Augustus the Strong, Elector of Saxony, had no fewer than 10,000 pieces. But middle-class folk were swept up in the craze too; satirist Daniel Defoe twitted his countrymen for piling china on "every chymney-piece, to the tops of ceilings, till it became a grievance."

The earliest porcelain imports were glazed in blue-and-white designs that were traditional among the Chinese—landscapes in combination with abstract patterns. But Chinese artisans soon introduced Western elements—a Dutch house or a winged angel, for instance—into their decorations. Eventually whole scenes were copied from drawings, prints and medals.

Toward the end of the 18th Century the effects of mass production diminished the quality of the products. And, too, the West was learning to make porcelain for itself. Decades of experiment—and, eventually, the discovery of good porcelain clay—produced a European china that was competitive in all but price. Soon protective tariffs ranging as high as 150 per cent took care of the price, and the trade ceased as abruptly as it had begun.

This 18th Century bowl depicts the Canton trading stations of Sweden, England and the Netherlands, with their flags.

An early-17th Century blue-and-white
plate features a traditional water scene at
center and, on the rim, alternating
panels of wild flowers and abstractions.

Two Royal Highlanders, of the
regiment later famed as the Black Watch,
crowd the Chinese landscape onto the
rim of a mid-18th Century plate.

Superimposed on a monochrome
landscape, the coat of arms of English East
India Company director John Elwick
personalizes this standard 1720s pattern.

In this scene, Western merchants
inspect the porcelain in a Cantonese shop.
More than 100 such firms also took
special orders for personalized china.

the metropolis was one of the commercial hubs of the Celestial Empire, serving as the terminus of a number of overland trade routes. Supplies of tea, silk and porcelain were abundant and prices reasonable.

In the early 1700s, as the English East Indiamen began to call regularly at Canton, the Manchus created a unique trading system, designed to produce maximum profits for the Chinese and also to guarantee a minimum of intercourse between the mainland population and the fan kwai merchants. At the pinnacle of this system stood the Emperor's personal merchant, or *hai kwan pu*—pronounced "hoppo" by the English—the sole broker for the purchase and sale of all European cargoes. The position of hoppo was a Manchu sinecure, and the noble who held it was not himself a merchant. To share his monopoly, the hoppo licensed a dozen or so trading firms, or *hongs* (Chinese for "warehouse"), which conducted the day-to-day business with the European supercargoes.

When an East Indiaman approached Canton's anchorage of Whampoa—a large island just outside the city's walls—it was customary for her supercargoes to go ahead in a pinnace to obtain a chop and hire a hong for storage of their European cargo. Once these formalities were

In the counting room of a Cantonese warehouse equipped with a huge tripod support for a scale, laborers pack tea into chests with their feet, while clerks (right) keep track and a Western merchant (left) negotiates for a cargo. By 1750 Chinese tea accounted for more than half the English company's trade.

Two doll-sized ceramic figurines represent a tea bearer (above) and a tea packer. Cantonese artisans did a brisk export business in such curios during the 19th Century; this pair reached Salem, Massachusetts, in 1803, almost 20 years after America entered the China trade.

concluded and the harbor dues had been paid, word was sent to the ship to move upriver to Whampoa and start unloading.

In the hongs that lined the riverbank at Whampoa, business was conducted mostly in broken Portuguese, the lingua franca of the China trade—largely due to the presence of Portuguese missionaries on the China coast for more than 150 years. Hong merchants would buy limited quantities of iron, lead, English broadcloths and worsted woolens. Opium, smuggled from the Indian province of Bengal, could always be sold; eventually it would be imported in staggering quantities, despite numerous attempts by Chinese authorities to stop the trade. But in the 17th Century the bulk of the return cargoes of tea and silks had to be purchased with silver bullion, more valuable in China than gold.

Predictably, the Chinese established a strict set of procedures for the selling of tea. Freshly harvested crops of tea were packed and sealed in wooden chests, affixed with a government chop and shipped to Canton, where they were consigned to one of the hong merchants. Before bidding on a shipment, European supercargoes were permitted to sample the tea at the Consoo House, or Tea Hall, located near the Whampoa anchorage and owned jointly by the hong merchants. A knowledgeable supercargo could tell from the taste when the tea had been picked. The most popular tea in Europe was bohea, named after a mountain in the neighboring province of Fukien and made from leaves gathered in early summer. Leaves harvested later in the season lost their freshness quickly and produced a coarser-tasting tea that could be bought more cheaply.

Because European sailors were not allowed ashore at Whampoa, all return cargoes were rowed out to the waiting East Indiamen in sampans by Chinese stevedores. First to go in a great ship's hold was ballast — usually tutenag (an alloy of copper and zinc) or tightly stacked wooden chests of porcelain cups, saucers, plates and bowls, all packed in palm-leaf confetti. Porcelain was heavy for its bulk and appealed to the captains of Indiamen because they could make a tidy profit on the sale of the chinaware at the end of the voyage. Next on board was the tea, packed in zinc-lined wooden chests weighing about 170 pounds each and hammered into place to prevent shifting at sea. Then came the bales of silk and finally, to fill the remaining space, an infinite variety of small goods—drugs, quicksilver, camphor, crystallized ginger and sugar candy, lacquer ware, scented wood and precious stones. When the cargo was aboard and the hatches sealed, the supercargo secured a second chop, granting the vessel permission to leave Whampoa harbor.

Although John Company agents had been the first Europeans to take advantage of the opening of Canton's port, the tea trade did not remain an English monopoly. By the 1750s the flags of many different nations could be seen fluttering over the warehouses on Thirteen Factory Street at the Whampoa anchorage. But the English East India Company continued to dominate the trade, if for no other reason than that the English took to tea with an enthusiasm unmatched in any other European country. Annual totals of imported tea rose from 79 pounds in 1670 to 90,000 pounds in 1700, 121,000 pounds in 1715 and 238,000 pounds in 1720. By the second half of the 18th Century, East Indiamen were shipping about five million pounds of tea into England every year.

Tea was not the only import that sold well. Daniel Defoe, one of England's leading men of letters, reported that even Queen Anne "was pleased to appear in China and Japan, I mean China silks and calico. Nor was this all, but it crept into our houses, our closets and bed chambers: curtains, cushions, chairs, and at last beds themselves, were nothing but calicoes and Indian stuffs, and, in short, almost everything that used to be made of wool or silk, relating either to the dress of the women, or the furniture of our houses, was supplied by the Indian trade."

The spectacular successes of John Company in the last decades of the 17th Century stimulated a host of domestic competitors, all eager to cash in on England's market for tea and Oriental imports. In legal terms, the company's position was unassailable: Its royal charter gave it the sole right to import goods from China and India, and specifically prohibited other merchants from engaging in the East Indies trade. But the protection of law turned out to be less than total. In 1680 Parliament slapped an excise duty of five shillings per pound on all imported tea—instantly creating a black market for the untaxed commodity. Whole fleets of seafaring smugglers, who called themselves "free traders," began to cross the English Channel to France and the Low Countries, where plentiful supplies of tea imported by other East India Companies were available for two shillings a pound. Brought back to England, the clandestine shiploads of tea were sold for less than one third of John Company's lowest price. Parliament finally had to lower the tea duty to one shilling per pound to make tea smuggling unprofitable.

In the 1690s a more direct challenge to the trading monopoly was mounted by an influential assemblage of independent London merchants who had been excluded from owning shares of East India Company stock. The group, called the Committee of the New East India Company, lobbied vigorously for permission to dispatch a fleet of merchant ships to China, and on January 16, 1690, a Parliamentary committee recommended to King William III that a new joint-stock company be established for East Indian trade. The King remained silent on the issue, but the independent merchants began to hold regular meetings in London's Skinner's Hall to publicize their campaign against the trading monopoly. For the next eight years John Company's directors fought desperately to maintain their privileges.

In its defense, the company published a series of essays on the value of its service to the nation. Not the least of its contributions, claimed the articles, was the build-up of England's maritime strength. There were between 30 and 40 ships in the company's fleet, each employing up to 100 seamen and bringing into the country vast quantities of tea and porcelain, as well as smaller amounts of drugs, saltpeter, indigo and pepper for home consumption and reexport. The value of the goods imported was six times greater than the specie exported and generated some £150,000 annually in customs duty.

When the issue of the East Indies trade monopoly was debated in the House of Commons, Sir Josiah Child, governor of the Honourable East India Company, distributed thousands of pounds in bribes to win favor in Parliament and at court. In 1698 the company attempted to gain the

The mixed blessings of Batavia

The Portuguese "mean to settle for the rest of their lives," observed a Dutch soldier stationed in the Indies, "but a Hollander thinks: 'When my six years of service are up, then I will go home again.'"

To the hundreds of Dutchmen who left home annually to staff the East India Company factory in Batavia, life in far-off Java seemed like exile. The climate was oppressive and enervating after the brisk, cool air of the Netherlands. The tall, gabled houses and tree-lined canals with which city planners had endowed Batavia served only to sharpen nostalgia for Amsterdam—yet word from home came just three times a year, when the fleet arrived. Heat, boredom and homesickness led to heavy drinking: By one reckoning, alcohol killed more Dutch settlers in Batavia than did dysentery and fever combined.

Nevertheless, Batavia had some powerful attractions. Household slaves were omnipresent; one bride wrote home that she had 59 at her command. Officials shamelessly borrowed the pomp and circumstance of

Oriental potentates—some even going about in public attended by suites of standard bearers, trumpeters, musicians and armed guards.

When they did go home, Dutchmen who had acquired a taste for these perquisites found the plain ways of the Netherlands a bitter comedown. For one thing, no Dutch servant would perform such tasks as holding a parasol in the midday sun (below). For another, the silks and jewels they sported on even the simplest social occasion cost considerably more at home than in Batavia. The diminishment of their style of life put many a returning Hollander perversely out of sorts. "No sooner have most of them stepped ashore," wrote the company directors in 1656, "than they wish they were back in the Indies again."

Jacob Mathieusen, senior Dutch East Indies merchant in the 1640s, points proudly to the company fleet, while a slave holds a silken parasol over him and his wife.

King's support by offering to lend the government £700,000 to help meet debts incurred during the recent war with France. It was not enough. The same day, a group of the rival merchants offered two million pounds in return for a charter for East India trade. In July 1698 the King assented to a Parliamentary bill allowing the formation of a new East India joint-stock company.

Most of the investors in the new company were well-known merchants who had long been agitating for a share in China trade, but the largest single shareholder, with a stake of £315,000, turned out to be a financier named John DuBois—an officer of the old company. The Honourable East India Company was simply hedging its bets. This precaution eventually proved to be unnecessary. The result of having two competing English East India Companies was chaos, as darkly predicted in a letter from the directors of the original company to its servants in the Orient: "Two East India Companies in England can no more subsist without destroying one the other, than two kings, at the same time regnant in the same kingdom."

At Canton, Calcutta, Madras and Bombay, English merchants representing the rival companies undersold goods unloaded from their respective East Indiamen and outbid each other for return cargoes.

At home, the increase in imports undermined the English textile industry. Cheap silk and cotton from India flooded the domestic market, and thousands of unemployed English weavers were forced to move to Ireland, where their skills were less endangered by the bustling activity at the East India docks along the Thames.

Rivalry between the two companies soon turned to intense hatred, and profits slumped. By 1700 the directors of both companies realized that to survive they would have to join forces, and in 1702 their directors agreed upon merger terms, to become finally effective in 1708. The list of properties that passed into the control of the newly amalgamated company—formally titled the United Company of Merchants of England Trading to the East Indies, but still known to most people as John Company—included dozens of forts and factories throughout the Orient, and "other forts, etc., between the Cape of Good Hope and the Straits of Magellan, and lastly, their warehouses and premises in Great St. Helen's London."

Shortly before the English companies finally settled their differences, India entered a period of turmoil that was to have far-reaching effects on the nature of European trade with the subcontinent. The Mogul Empire, after two centuries of expansion and conquest in India, began five decades of stagnation and decline. On February 20, 1707, Emperor Aurangzeb, the last great Mogul conqueror, died at his camp in the Deccan in southern India. He was followed by a series of weak and short-lived rulers, and the great Empire began to disintegrate. With the collapse of imperial India, all of the European trading companies in India swiftly took measures to protect their varied interests: forts, settlements and agricultural lands acquired by treaties with the Mogul authorities and geared for the production of cotton piece goods, saltpeter and indigo. At Bombay, Madras and Calcutta, John Company officials recruited mercenary armies from the local population to defend English property—a step that soon led to political control of whole provinces.

In spite of the political troubles in India, the United English East India Company enjoyed a period of peace, stability and increasing prosperity during the first half of the 18th Century. Annual tea revenues alone reached £6,288,588. The company's directors ambitiously invested most of these funds to expand their operations on the Indian subcontinent. Between 1711 and 1722, John Company still managed to pay yearly dividends of eight to 10 per cent. East Indiamen established such a regular and reliable link between Europe and the Far East that in Madras English agents placed bets on the exact day in June when the incoming fleet would be sighted.

By the 1720s the boom in East India trade had swamped the legions of John Company clerks in London: Bookkeeping fell months, then years, behind as more and more ships were loaded and unloaded at the company's docks. At East India House on Leadenhall Street, at least half of the company's eight regular operating committees were always in session, and its 24 directors met at least once every week. September was the busiest time of the year, for the biannual sale of imports from the East coincided with the assembling of outward-bound cargoes for the first fleets due to leave in November. Between 1717 and 1727 the number of ships freighted for the Orient increased from 100 to 150 and their total tonnage from 41,000 to 62,000. Proceeds from trade spiraled even higher, until by 1727 profits reached one million pounds a year.

In every way, John Company's future looked bright. The company could depend on political support from Parliament and on the Bank of England to supply working capital for day-to-day operations. Public confidence in its operations was at an all-time high, and the price of shares of its stock was second only to that of the Bank of England.

The company's counterpart in Holland also seemed to be in robust health. The Dutch East India Company warehouses in Amsterdam were filled with rich and costly goods. Each year 30 to 40 ships sailed to the Orient, and the Dutch enterprise paid handsome dividends like clockwork. But appearances were deceptive: Only its directors knew that the Dutch company was in trouble and that the dividends came from cash reserves or from borrowed funds.

The Dutch company's expenditures had begun to exceed its income some time toward the end of the 17th Century, although the losses were not immediately evident because of deficiencies in its system of accounting. Since spices sold in Europe for two and a half to three times what they cost in the East, the public never dreamed that the Dutch company, which monopolized the spice trade, could do anything but make a profit. Yet even before 1700 the Dutch East India Company's policy of acquiring territories and guarding against any incursion on its spice trade was beginning to cripple its resources of money and manpower. Capital expenditures on ships, forts and factories, not to mention a force of some 12,000 men permanently stationed in the East Indies, had obliterated practically all of the company's profits—yet none of these expenditures appeared on the spice-trade balance sheets.

And overspending was only part of the problem. After a century of trade supremacy in the Far East, the Dutch company's overseas ranks were riddled with corruption. Merchants and administrators alike

Flanked by the skeletons of sister ships being built in other berths, an East Indiaman is fitted out in a Thames River shipyard. In the mid-18th Century, the British trading company maintained about 100 Indiamen, replacing elderly vessels with a dozen new ones annually.

availed themselves of every opportunity to make profits on their own account, whether by smuggling, extortion or speculation with company funds. Moreover, the Dutch failed to anticipate the potential of the tea market. In the early 18th Century, while John Company consolidated its commercial gains in Canton, the Dutch had contented themselves with buying tea from Chinese junks calling at Bantam. Direct voyages between Holland and China were not started until 1729—too late to challenge the English grip on the traffic in tea. Dutch operations in India were similarly overshadowed by the English, who had been forced many years before to concentrate their trading ambitions on the subcontinent because of Dutch determination to exclude all comers from the East Indies' island spice trade.

The English company's biggest rival in India was not the Dutch but the French. A French East India Company had been formed in 1664 and had established a factory at Pondicherry, 75 miles south of Madras on India's east coast. But for decades the French company devoted most of its resources and energies to establishing a colony on the island of Madagascar in the Indian Ocean. The effort was unsuccessful and brought the company to the verge of bankruptcy. The French enterprise did not begin to flourish until the early part of the 18th Century, when an infusion of government capital breathed new life into its trading fleets and factories, and it began to concentrate on the more profitable East Indies business. Between 1720 and 1740 the French company's revenue increased tenfold, to a total of about £880,000 a year, nearly half the annual revenues of John Company in India. After 1724, the French maintained a fleet of about 35 East Indiamen and annually dispatched as many as 20 ships to the East.

For nearly a century the English, Dutch and French East India Companies managed to coexist more or less peacefully in India. But tensions began to rise in June 1745, when news reached India that England and France had declared war the previous year. Joseph Dupleix, the governor of the French headquarters at Pondicherry, proposed to his English counterparts at Madras, Calcutta and Bombay that there should be a truce east of the Cape of Good Hope during the course of conflict in Europe. The English cautiously replied that, although they nurtured no hostile intentions, they could not speak for the Royal Navy. In fact, a squadron of three English ships of the line and one frigate had already sailed for India under Commodore Curtis Barnett. Arriving in Indian seas, Barnett tracked down and captured four French East Indiamen. When Dupleix heard the news, he sent an urgent appeal for aid to the tough and able Admiral Mahé de La Bourdonnais at the French colony on the island of Mauritius in the Indian Ocean.

La Bourdonnais had personally organized the French naval base at Mauritius and was spoiling for action. After Dupleix called for help, La Bourdonnais began to convert eight French East Indiamen lying at Mauritius into warships. By February of 1746 the alterations were complete and the French were ready to act. By May, La Bourdonnais was sailing in search of Barnett's squadron.

He found the English ships late that spring and proceeded to devastate them. After a two-hour battle, Barnett's fleet was so battered that it was forced to break off and flee toward Calcutta. But La Bourdonnais and Dupleix were not satisfied with this resounding victory. They next decided to attack John Company's Fort St. George at Madras. In July 1746 French forces, allied with the troops of a local Indian prince who was promised possession of Madras if the English were defeated, laid siege to the fort. In defense, the English could recruit only about 200 mercenary soldiers. The contest was settled, with a comic-opera denouement, when La Bourdonnais maneuvered his ships into position to bombard the English strongpoint. While their gunnery was not particularly effective—only six persons were killed—a stray shell broke open the doors to the fort's liquor supplies, and in a few hours the garrison was drunk and mutinous. The English commander had no choice but to surrender.

That was the only Indian land battle of the war. With the return of peace in Europe in 1748, Madras was handed back to the English. But the ease with which La Bourdonnais and Dupleix had conquered the seaport demonstrated—both to the European companies and to a host of Indian princes—that all of southern India was open to conquest. As rival Indian rulers fought for territory along the Coromandel Coast of the Carnatic provinces, the English and French East India Companies unashamedly lent support to opposing sides. In 1749 French-backed princes won control of most of the Carnatic, and the French company gained jurisdiction of a tiny fiefdom, including 80 villages in the region of Pondicherry. Meanwhile, the English strengthened their position at Madras. The in-

The French trade: Orient to Lorient

In the early 1660s the biggest European consumer of spices and Eastern textiles was France—the one power of any pretensions without even a toe hold in the Orient. Instead of buying directly from the producers, France made its purchases from England and Holland, taking more than a third of their total imports. But a pamphlet that appeared anonymously in 1664 signaled a change in this situation. Pointing out that England and Holland were growing rich and powerful at France's expense, it proposed that Frenchmen form an East India company of their own, and touted the proposition as "a design that one of the greatest princes of the world has a mind to support."

The great prince to whom the pamphlet referred was the 26-year-old King Louis XIV. But the real instigator of the proposal—as indeed of much else in the young King's reign—was his Finance Minister, Jean-Baptiste Colbert, a gouty man who worked toward his country's betterment with a cold, fixed determination that earned him the sobriquet "North Star." Colbert had no trouble enlisting the interest of his King, who readily subscribed three million livres from the royal purse toward the proposed company. But when it was chartered in 1664 the Finance Minister had to strain his considerable coercive powers to find the rest of the money to fund it; in effect, he forced loans from merchants reluctant to have the state meddling in commercial affairs.

Funding was only one of the problems Colbert faced. He needed experienced personnel to run a trading company; he solved that by raiding the competition, hiring factors and ships' pilots away from the Dutch. He also needed vessels; on an estuary of the Bay of Biscay he created a shipyard and a port that became known as Lorient (a corruption of "the East").

For all the resistance it met at the outset, Colbert's idea eventually paid off handsomely. By the second quarter of the 18th Century, the French were sending out an average of 19 Indiamen a year, and ranked second only to the English among traders in India. As an added dividend, Lorient grew into a major seaport, with a population of more than 14,000 and an annual traffic worth more than 18 million livres—twice Colbert's initial capital.

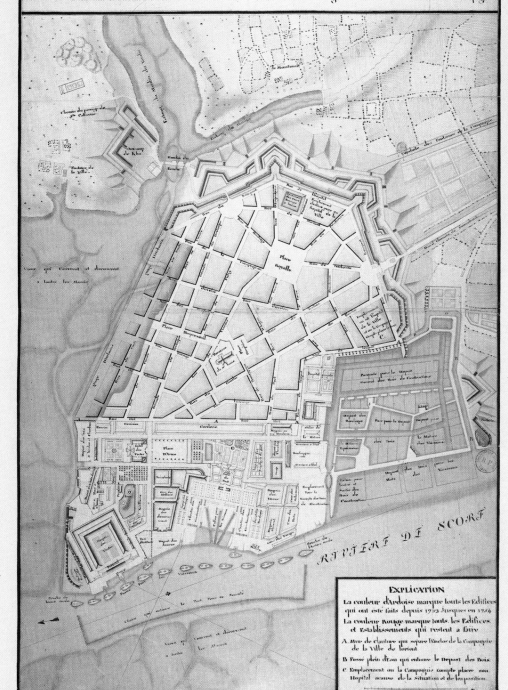

French Finance Minister Jean-Baptiste Colbert ponders state papers in his office in Paris. The map at left, drawn in 1754, shows the port of Lorient, which was founded at his urging in 1665.

evitable clash between the English and French factions in southern India came in 1751, when Indian princes allied to Governor Dupleix besieged the Carnatic capital of Trichinopoly, whose ruler had supported the English. A French victory seemed just a matter of time. But now a new and extraordinary figure appeared on the scene—a young man named Robert Clive, whose boldness would shape India's future.

In 1744, at the age of 18, Clive had come to Madras to serve as a clerk in the English company's offices. Two years later he had been taken prisoner by La Bourdonnais and Dupleix in the battle for Fort St. George, but escaped by blackening his face, donning Indian clothes and making his way on foot to the English outpost of Fort St. David, 100 miles to the south. There, Clive volunteered for military duties. He spent the next five years urging his superiors to take direct action against the French, rather than fight them with proxy forces. In December 1751, when news of the French attack on Trichinopoly reached Fort St. David, Clive convinced his commander that the siege of the Carnatic capital could be broken in a lightning stroke.

Ignoring the winter monsoons, Clive led a party of 210 English troops on a 70-mile forced march to the city of Arcot. He surprised and captured the city, in the process routing an Indian army of 3,000 and cutting the French supply lines to Trichinopoly. The little English force then held Arcot against repeated assaults by French-Indian forces until an English

Robert Clive wears the star-shaped insignia of the Order of the Bath in this 1764 portrait by an unknown painter. Proclaimed a "heaven-born general" by statesman William Pitt, Clive won for the English East India Company its empire. But he was hounded by political enemies on his return to England, and committed suicide at the age of 49.

Arriving at Fort St. George in Madras, British seamen debark from two Indiamen in small boats, while a friendly man-of-war fires a welcoming salute. The English East India Company established its Eastern headquarters here in 1652.

relief column arrived almost two months later. On June 18, 1752, the French abandoned their siege of Trichinopoly. Six months later, Governor Dupleix fell afoul of his directors in France. Just a year after receiving the company's praise for "the glorious action of your troops" in the Carnatic, Dupleix was recalled in disgrace; his superiors had discovered that he had amassed colossal debts in pursuit of his military victories.

No sooner did the political strife in southern India begin to abate than a new power struggle erupted in the populous, fertile province of Bengal, where the Ganges River flows into the Indian Ocean. In the days of Mogul dominance, Bengal had funneled its exports inland, toward the imperial city of Delhi. But in the 18th Century, with the decline of the Moguls, the province began to look seaward to the increasing numbers of English, French and Dutch traders who came to compete for Bengal's lucrative exports of opium, saltpeter, silks and sugar. For decades the European companies had gained trading concessions by paying nominal tribute to a Bengali Prince, or Nawab, who had seized power from the Moguls. But in April 1756 the old Nawab died, leaving all of Bengal to his impulsive and headstrong 27-year-old grandson, Siraj-ud-Daula.

Within eight weeks of coming to power, Siraj-ud-Daula ordered Roger Drake, the English East India Company's governor in Calcutta, to cease constructing a moat around Fort William, an old English trading post that was located near the town's harbor and guarded the Hooghly River, one of the Ganges' main tributaries. When Drake was summoned by the young Nawab to account for the suspicious strengthening of the fort's defenses, he replied that he was worried about a French attack, and he refused to stop work on the moat. The irate Siraj-ud-Daula immediately raised the ante: He told Drake that he would not only have to desist digging but must fill in the moat. Drake replied that the Nawab could fill in the moat with the heads of his own subjects.

The dialogue ended there—but not the quarrel. The Nawab amassed an army of some 30,000 foot soldiers and 150 elephants—supplemented by a party of French, Portuguese and Dutch artillerymen who were promised the ownership of Calcutta as a reward for fighting the English—and led them to the gates of the settlement on June 16. Despite the imposing forces confronting his 520 men, Drake was unimpressed. He did not credit Siraj-ud-Daula's army with any real fighting ability. In any case, two heavily armed English East Indiamen were moored in the broad Hooghly.

To the surprise of the English, the Nawab mounted a ferocious assault. Although hundreds of Indians fell before the British muskets, the steady pounding of the French artillery set part of Calcutta ablaze. In the early hours of June 19, the English retreated behind the walls of Fort William, and Governor Drake gave the order for the European dependents to be evacuated by ship. Thirty children and women were rowed out to the *Dodaldy*, the Indiaman nearest to the fort. Despite angry protests from some of the women, the 16-year-old wife of a British sailor was not allowed on board because she was Indian. She was taken back to the fort.

Later that morning, with the Nawab's troops advancing through the burning town, a rumor swept the English garrison that the supply of gunpowder had run out. Panicked soldiers and civilians stampeded for the riverbank, hoping to get a boat out to the *Dodaldy*. One of them was Captain George Minchin, the garrison commander. Those men who had stayed at their posts watched from the parapets as Governor Drake ran after Minchin, ostensibly to stop him. To their astonishment, Drake waded into the water, clambered into one of the boats and was rowed out to the *Dodaldy*. Not once did he turn to look back at the fort.

As soon as Drake was on board, the *Dodaldy* weighed anchor and began to move slowly down the Hooghly, leaving 170 English soldiers behind. Their only hope of rescue was the other East Indiaman, the *Prince George*, lying farther downriver. In the afternoon she was sighted rounding a bend in the broad Hooghly and heading for the fort. A ragged cheer died on the lips of the watching soldiers as the *Prince George* ran aground on the maze of sandbanks in the river channel. Soon fire arrows soared through the air from Indian soldiers on the riverbank, and the helpless *Prince George* was set ablaze, forcing her crew to abandon ship.

Nothing could now save the doomed garrison, and within 24 hours Fort William was in the hands of the Nawab. What followed was a ghastly act that would sear the pages of history. The survivors—63 men and the girl who had been turned away from the *Dodaldy*—were locked for the night in a room only 18 feet long and 14 feet wide. The next morning only 23 of them, including the girl, were still alive. Their prison became known as the Black Hole of Calcutta, and the horror of that night became infamous. The following day the Nawab sent the surviving prisoners to another European settlement downriver.

When news of the fall of Calcutta reached Madras in August 1756, John Company officials in Madras organized a powerful expedition to retake the Bengali city. The expedition, 3,000 men strong, left for Bengal in a fleet of 10 ships. In command was Robert Clive, recently promoted to lieutenant colonel. On January 7, 1757, Clive retook Fort William and Calcutta, without opposition.

Then, in a ruthless assault, he turned on the main French station in Bengal—a fort at Chandernagore, 75 miles upstream on the Hooghly. With the fleet blockading the river, the French fort was bombarded for a week. The defenders surrendered shortly before Clive was due to attack from the land side. Now the English were in a position of clear superiority in Bengal. The humiliated Siraj-ud-Daula fled his throne and was replaced by an elderly Indian general of Clive's choosing.

The year 1757 marked the beginning of the end for French territorial ambitions in India. They fought stubbornly and not without some successes, but the strength of John Company's power base in Bengal proved decisive. By April 1761 there was not a single French military post left in India. The French East India Company continued to trade on the subcontinent, but only on English sufferance.

With the defeat of the French, only the Dutch East India Company remained to challenge John Company's grip on the rich Bengal trade. For nearly a century the Dutch had monopolized the region's opium exports. The British now threatened to take over the opium trade for themselves, but the Dutch did not intend to stand idly by. In August 1759 John Company's council at Calcutta received word that a large fleet

Crazed by thirst and airless heat, Englishmen trample their dead and dying comrades in a mad rush for a drop of water in the Black Hole of Calcutta, a 14-by-18-foot cell at Fort William. When Indian rebels seized the garrison in 1756, they crammed its 64 occupants into the minute cell; one lone rebel guard, taking pity on his captives, dispensed occasional water by the hatful (above).

As shown in a plan view, a new Fort William—built near the old one after Robert Clive's British forces retook Calcutta from Indian rebels—bristles with spiked salients that made it virtually impregnable. The fortress cost an unprecedented two million pounds, but it more than justified that sum by securing Britain's hold on the rich Ganges plain.

was being armed at Batavia and that its likely destination was Bengal.

Clive, by then Governor of Bengal, unhesitatingly ordered all Dutch ships moving up the Hooghly River to be stopped and searched, a directive that resulted in indignant protests from the Dutch. The Dutch fleet—seven Indiamen carrying 700 European soldiers and 800 Malays—arrived at the mouth of the Hooghly in October. Only three English East Indiamen were then in the river: the *Calcutta*, the *Duke of Dorset* and the *Hardwicke*. Clive ordered them to follow the Dutch ships.

When the Dutch delivered a formal protest at their ships' being searched, Clive delayed his answer, taking time to reinforce the English batteries and forts along the river. Finally he sent a cool and calculated message. It was by order of the Nawab, he said, that Dutch ships were being stopped, and therefore the Nawab was the proper person to apply to. Aware that the Dutch knew that the Nawab was a mere figurehead, Clive mischievously said that the British stood ready to "interpose our friendly offices" if required, to "mitigate his resentment." Even Clive later recalled that his offer "savoured a little of audacity."

Certainly the Dutch thought so, for they seized seven small English ships lying at the mouth of the river, took the officers prisoner and

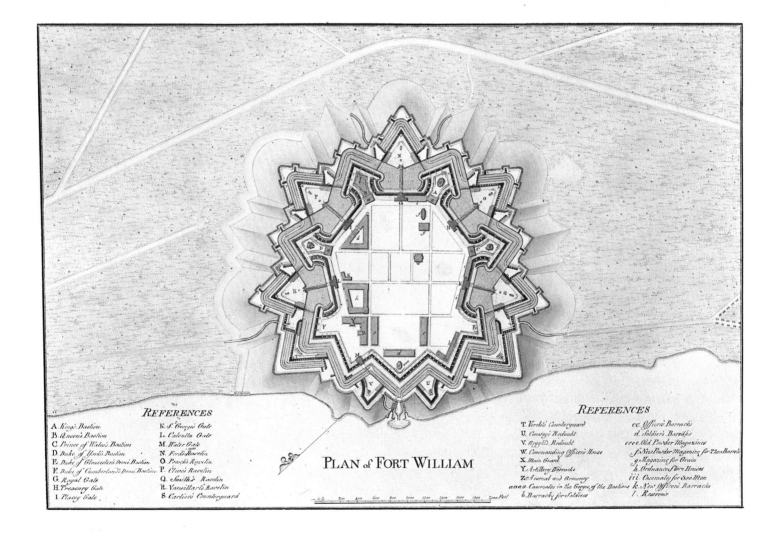

REFERENCES

A. King's Bastion
B. Queen's Bastion
C. Prince of Wales's Bastion
D. Duke of York's Bastion
E. Duke of Gloucester's Demi Bastion
F. Duke of Cumberland's Demi Bastion
G. Royal Gate
H. Treasury Gate
I. Plassey Gate

K. St George's Gate
L. Calcutta Gate
M. Water Gate
N. Ford's Ravelin
O. Peacock's Ravelin
P. Clive's Ravelin
Q. Smith's Ravelin
R. Vansittart's Ravelin
S. Carlier's Counterguard

PLAN of FORT WILLIAM

REFERENCES

T. Verelst's Counterguard
U. Coustay's Redoubt
V. Appyl's Redoubt
W. Commanding Officer's House
X. Main Guard
Y. Artillery Barracks
Z. Arsenal and Armoury
aaaa. Casemates in the Gorges of the Bastions
b. Barracks for Soldiers

cc. Officers Barracks
d. Soldiers Barracks
eeee. Old Powder Magazines
f. New Powder Magazine for 22000 Barrels
g. Magazine for Grain
h. Ordnance Store Houses
iii. Casemates for 800 Men
k. New Officers Barracks
l. Reservoir

transferred guns and ammunition to their own fleet. Until this attack, Clive had hesitated to use force against the Dutch, since England and Holland were not at war. "In this situation," he had noted, "we anxiously wished the next hour would bring us news of a declaration of war with Holland; which we had some reason to expect by our last advises from England." Now, with the Dutch seizure of British ships, he considered himself free to deal with the situation by force, war or no war.

Shadowed by the three English East Indiamen, the Dutch fleet moved on to the port of Sankrail, where it disembarked its troops not far from the English batteries protecting Fort William. The ships then dropped back to a place called Point Melancholy. On November 22, Captain George Wilson of the Calcutta wrote to the Dutch that he was "surprised to hear their troops had debarked on the territory of the English company, without permission obtained from the governor and council at Fort William." He added that if one more man was landed, he would "construe it as an act of hostility, and exert himself to the utmost to sink and disperse their ships."

The Dutch were given little time to reply. As soon as Clive heard that the Dutch fleet and its troops had separated, he boldly decided to bring them to battle both on land and on the river. On November 23 he ordered Wilson to demand immediate restitution of the captured English ships, their crews and arms. If the Dutch refused, Wilson was to attack immediately. On November 24 the demand was made and refused. The three English Indiamen cleared for action, their gun decks lined with bags of saltpeter to screen the crews from shot.

Anchored in a line of battle, the Dutch had every reason to be confident. Four of their seven Indiamen were 36-gun ships of the line. Their margin over the three English East Indiamen seemed overwhelming.

In a fitful wind, the Duke of Dorset was first to engage, drifting into the heart of the Dutch fleet toward the commodore's ship, the Vlissingen. To the dismay of the English, no sooner was the Duke of Dorset committed to fight than the wind died, compelling the Calcutta and the Hardwicke to stand by helplessly while the Dutch fleet poured fire into the beleaguered Indiaman. The Duke of Dorset was almost torn to pieces before a light breeze stirred the sails of the Calcutta and the Hardwicke, enabling them to join the battle. With all three English Indiamen now involved, two of the smaller Dutch ships cut their cables and ran, and a third ship was driven ashore. As the fighting continued, the Dutch suffered very heavy casualties, while the English, sheltered behind their barricade of saltpeter bags, were hardly scathed.

After two hours of battle, the Vlissingen's decks were bloodied with dead and dying, and the Dutch commodore struck his colors. The other Dutch ships, with one exception, followed suit. Only the Bleiswyk, second-in-command of the Dutch fleet, refused to surrender; with guns still blazing, she made a run for it downriver, only to be intercepted and captured by two English men-of-war, the Oxford and the Royal George, which were moving up belatedly to support the Indiamen. During the action, more than 100 Dutch sailors were killed. The English Indiamen did not lose a single sailor, even though the Duke of Dorset had taken 90 pieces of shot in her hull.

The 100-gun man-of-war Royal George sails along the south coast of England in this 1778 oil painting. Two decades earlier, on the Hooghly River downstream from Calcutta, she had played a vital role in driving the Dutch from India.

The following day, on the plain of Bedarah, the English and Dutch troops clashed. In a bloody engagement lasting less than half an hour, the Dutch were put to flight, destroying any Dutch hope that their company might supersede the British in India.

The power and influence of the English East India Company would never again be seriously challenged east of the Cape of Good Hope. In 1769 the French company was so obviously bankrupt that King Louis XV ordered its liquidation and turned over the Eastern trade to private merchants; the Dutch company continued to sink deeper into debt, until it too was forced to declare bankruptcy in 1792.

Events following Clive's victory over the Dutch were to change John Company's role in India. It was indisputably the dominant power in Bengal, and in 1765, with the agreement of the powerless local rulers, it took over the administration of the province—the richest in all of India. Clive, appointed governor general of the province in March 1764, recommended to the company directors in London that they halt all shipments of silver bullion to Bengal to purchase Indian exports. Henceforth, he asserted, the Bengal treasury—controlled by the English—would finance the procurement of these goods out of its own tax revenues, and would still produce a surplus of about two million pounds annually. By its conquest of Bengal, John Company had acquired the foundation of an empire.

Extraordinary ships in an exotic commerce

Concerned with amassing its own huge profits on trade between Europe and the Orient, the British East India Company from its beginning tolerated private business deals by its employees, some of whom made small personal fortunes in private commerce between ports in the East. At first this country trade, as it was called, was carried mostly in small brigs that were bought or hired by syndicates of company employees. But by the middle of the 18th Century the country trade had become so voluminous that British investors commissioned a special vessel for the business—larger than a brig, but kettle-bottomed so that it could maneuver in the shallow coves and inlets that led to many local ports.

The spur to this development was a surging traffic in illicit opium. Until 1729 the British East India Company itself legally shipped large quantities of Bengal opium into China; the drug was the commodity the Chinese most wanted in exchange for tea. But that year the Emperor of China outlawed all trading in opium, and the company was warned to desist or lose its commercial privileges there. The country traders were not so hampered. Through a network of bribed port officials in Batavia and Macao, they made clandestine contacts with Chinese smugglers and kept the opium moving. The company, which sold the opium to the private traders in the first place and thus got the currency it needed to buy China's tea, gave its protection to these ambitious entrepreneurs.

Country ships were custom-built in Indian shipyards to resemble the mighty English Indiamen that Eastern pirates had learned to fear, but they were in many ways superior to their European look-alikes. Their hull planking was cut from Malabar teak, a strong, oily, almost knotless wood that often lasted a century without rotting. Each plank was rabbeted into its neighbor so tightly that calking was unnecessary. Instead, an iron-hard resinous glue was laid between the planks, giving the finished hull the appearance of having been cut from one solid piece of wood. Below the water line, the hull was smeared with a remarkable compound of fish oil and lime that both repelled wood-devouring teredo worms and prevented the accumulation of layers of mossy sea flora that clung to the copper plating used on British vessels.

The country ships were rigged with rot-resistant rope turned from the fibers of coconut shells, and they carried sails cut from Bombay canvas—a coarse, golden-hued material akin to dungaree. Many of the lighter booms and spars were made of bamboo. These colorful touches blended with banks of hand-carved gilded molding to make the country traders as beautiful as they were seaworthy. One Englishman, witnessing a flotilla of country ships setting off on a voyage similar to the one that is reconstructed on these pages, was moved to exclaim,"Behold the finest fleet of merchant shipping in the world."

An Indian prince, a rich English widow and three East India Company employees (left) agree to pool their capital to buy opium and other commodities, and outfit a small fleet of ships for a country-trade venture. Amid Calcutta's quayside hubbub (right) one of their vessels takes on its cargo while two smaller ships in the fleet wait in the Hooghly River at right. The opium—stacked to the left of the country ship's galleried stern—was stored on a specially ventilated deck to keep it from spoiling. At left, a British man-of-war lies at anchor amid smaller craft.

Intercepted by pirates in the Malay Archipelago, the country trader's crew—mostly Indian seamen—flock to the rails with cutlasses and pikes to beat back attackers trying to scale the merchantman's smooth hull. The pirate vessels, called proas, each carried about 30 men and were reinforced against shot with double planking and layers of bamboo two feet thick along their sides. The plaited coils of rattan cable at their gunwales gave added protection. The proas were fitted with tripod masts of bamboo, which, because it splits lengthwise instead of breaking when it is struck, could stand up well to gunfire.

From the sterns of the proas, pirates fire swivel guns and muskets over the heads of their comrades. In the background, smoke billows from one of the smaller country ships as her sails lie slack in the calm air. The pirates have followed their usual practice of waiting until the English ships are becalmed and then moving in under oar power toward their victim's bow or stern, where they would be clear of broadside cannon fire. The oarsmen, chained to their seats (inset), were usually New Guinea slaves. In the foreground, one lies dead, slain by langrage, a miscellany of broken bolts, nails and glass fired into the proa.

Saluted by the whir and rattle of fife and drums, two Dutch customs officials board the country ship at Batavia. For a substantial bribe, officials not only overlooked the illegal opium when they inspected the cargo beneath the hatch covers, but would set up meetings for the traders and Chinese opium smugglers.

At a moonlit rendezvous in a cove near Batavia, a Chinese smuggler warily tastes the bitter opium to test its purity. Cakes of the perishable drug—wrapped in poppy leaves and cotton cloth—lie before him in a wooden chest, and two Indian guards from the country ships stand by to assure his honesty. For their opium, the Englishmen would receive tea and gold coins—money the Chinese took in the year before from the East India Company in exchange for tea, and which the country traders could use to buy more opium from the company.

Main-topsails backed to hold to a steady crawl in deep waters, a country trader (right) and a British Indiaman meet in the Bangka Strait, east of Sumatra. Hatches have been opened on both ships, and a crane on the trader's port side off-loads the tea received at Batavia in exchange for opium. For a freight fee, the East Indiaman would transport this cargo back to England; the country trader, having already turned a handsome profit, could continue her voyage, picking up new cargoes before sailing home.

Enjoying one of the few luxuries that life at sea afforded, company and country seamen barter belowdecks, swapping goods that they carried with them in their individual privilege chests. Ivory, liquor, tobacco and even books changed hands as each sailor tried to improve the value of his private holdings, which he would later sell when he got into port.

Chapter 5

A passage to India

or sheer majesty, few nautical sights of the late 18th and early 19th Centuries could compare with that of the outward-bound British East India fleet parading down the English Channel: 20 or more great three-masters in double line, escorted by frigates of the Royal Navy. Under billowing clouds of canvas, the Indiamen surged through the ruffled sea with flags streaming proudly from their mastheads.

A closer view would have revealed a somewhat motley but no less moving aspect of the scene. Lining the rails on every ship was an unlikely collection of shipmates: soldiers on their way to join the company's army in India, impoverished younger sons of the gentry hoping to make their fortunes, spinsters seeking husbands, fugitives escaping scandal or worse, company officials and their families headed for some remote outpost. At this moment of leave-taking, each of them strained for a last glimpse of England. If many were silenced by lumps in their throats or had tears streaming down their cheeks, that was understandable, for they knew that they might never set foot on their home soil again. And if, when the English coastline was no more than a smudge on the horizon, the passengers began eying one another in critical assessment, suspicion or hope, that too was understandable, for they would spend the next five or six months together on a voyage that was sure to be tedious and uncomfortable—and perhaps perilous as well.

Passenger traffic on outward-bound English East Indiamen increased rapidly as the nature of the company's business underwent a fundamental change after the long and bitter power struggles with the Dutch and the French. Governing large areas of the subcontinent by means of its standing army, the company got more income from taxes and rents than from trade, and what it most needed in India was not merchandise but men. So company ships carried less broadcloth and iron for the Indian market and more people to operate and protect its nascent empire. Because most of these people died prematurely from the various dangers facing Europeans in the East—notably disease and overindulgence in drink—the outward-bound traffic of replacement personnel was constant. East Indiamen heading for India became the precursors of passenger liners; only the China-bound ships continued to trade as before, bringing home the tea that the British consumed so avidly.

The increased passenger traffic was welcomed by the captains; the fares were part of their income, one of the perquisites that made commanding an Indiaman such a profitable and desirable occupation. Company servants had to pay their own fares, but these were set at relatively low rates that varied according to rank, ranging from £50 for cadets to

All dressed up in their redingotes and bonnets, travelers join officers in the stern gallery of the Indiaman Halsewell for a musical farewell to the coast of England in 1786. By the last quarter of the 18th Century Indiamen were carrying nearly 1,000 passengers annually to tend to company business in the East.

£200 for general officers. Passengers not in the company's service had to drive the best bargain they could with the captain or his agent, the ship's purser. Depending on the accommodation being offered, individual fares ranged from £200 to £1,000.

For the more affluent travelers, booking a passage to India usually began with discreet inquiries about the relative merits of the available ships and then a social call on the captain at his London home. The worldly-wise followed up by inviting the captain to dinner and entertaining him royally. After these civilities, the prospective passengers often visited the ship at her mooring in the Thames and decided with the purser the position and size of their accommodation for the voyage. Cabins on East Indiamen were infinitely flexible, since the bulkheads dividing them were only light wooden panels or stretched canvas screens, either of which could be struck in a few minutes if the decks had to be cleared for action.

The most expensive space was in the roundhouse, the large compartment beneath the sternmost portion of the poop deck (*pages 126-127*). Most of the cabins created by partitioning the roundhouse had ports, providing the occupants with light and air. Ladies traveling alone were usually berthed in the roundhouse, partly for privacy and partly so that they would have the captain's protection. Immediately forward of the roundhouse cabins was another large enclosure called the cuddy, which was often divided into two spaces—the captain's stateroom on one side of the ship and the dining room on the other. Glass doors connected the cuddy with the quarter-deck. Underneath the roundhouse was the great cabin, usually divided into spaces for bachelor army officers and other gentlemen passengers who could not afford the roundhouse. Forward of the great cabin was the steerage, an unpartitioned area normally occupied by cadets, subalterns and clerks traveling on the cheapest fares. On either side of the steerage were cabins for the ship's officers.

Although East Indiamen provided the most luxurious passenger accommodations afloat during their era, the choice of cabins, even for wealthy passengers, was a matter of selecting the least uncomfortable space rather than the most comfortable. Residents of the roundhouse had to endure the incessant noise of feet on the poop deck above, but the great cabin beneath had more serious drawbacks.

Emma Roberts, a British woman who published a journal of her voyage on an Indiaman, drew the comparison. "To ladies, whether married or single, the upper, or poop-cabins are certainly the most desirable, the disadvantages of the noise overhead being more than counterbalanced by the enjoyment of many favourable circumstances unattainable below." The roundhouse cabins, she continued, "are much more light and airy: it is seldom, even in the very roughest weather, that the ports are compelled to be shut; and it is almost inconceivable to those who have never been at sea, how great a difference it makes in the comforts or discomforts of a voyage, whether a delicate person can have the enjoyment of light and air in bad weather, or be deprived of both, condemned in illness to a dark, close cabin, without the possibility of diverting the mind by reading, or any other employment.

"There is also another advantage above stairs, which is the comparative degree of seclusion attainable in these cabins. A few steps lead from them all to the cuddy, or general apartment: there is no necessity to go out upon deck, or to go up or down stairs to meals; thus avoiding much of the annoyance of a rolling vessel, and all the disagreeables attendant upon encountering persons engaged in the duties of the ship. It may seem fastidious to object to meeting sailors employed in getting up different stores from the hold, or to pass and repass other cabins, or the neighbourhood of the steward's pantry; nevertheless, if ladies have the opportunity of avoiding these things, they will do well to embrace it; for, however trivial they may be in a well-regulated ship, very offensive circumstances may arise from them."

After the roundhouse, the quality of accommodations fell off sharply. William Hickey, a veteran English traveler and bon vivant, could find little positive to say about the second-best choice, the great cabin. Its most objectionable feature, he noted, was "that of being completely debarred of all daylight in tempestuous weather by what is very expressively termed 'the dead lights' being then fixed in to all the windows in order to prevent the sea breaking in." Furthermore, the dead lights were not always effective. "I was often set afloat in my cabin by heavy seas breaking against those dead lights, and entering at the seams, especially so at the quarter gallery door and window, where it poured in in torrents, beating even over my bed. You have also at times the horrid screeches and crying of children or what is full as bad, their vociferous mirth when playing their gambols, added to which grievances is frequently being half poisoned by a variety of stinks."

Steerage, of course, was worse—particularly in the matter of ventilation. This section of the ship was, as one voyager explained, "an open passage, totally devoid of privacy, exposed to violent currents of air, not always of the sweetest, and subject to many obvious inconveniences." The cabins on either side offered portholes, but that was their only amenity. One passenger scathingly described the quarters there as "worse than a dog-kennel."

Having booked a cabin, a passenger next had to furnish it; nothing was provided by the company but the space. The simplest way to solve the problem was to visit one of the tradesmen around the East India docks who bought furniture from passengers on incoming ships and sold it to outgoing passengers. The generally accepted minimum requirement was a table, sofa, washstand, cot and bedding. If there was enough room, a couple of chairs and bookshelves were recommended. Wise travelers also took with them a water-filtering machine, candlesticks, some means of making tea and coffee, and usually a private stock of wine. In addition, tobacco, soap and brandy were useful as inducements for sailors to do small chores.

Not all passengers were content with a spartan minimum of cabin furniture. Mr. Peter Cherry, writing home from Madras to his three daughters, who were to sail out on the *General Harris* to join him, suggested for their cabin a piano and harp, two or three small bureaus with bookshelves, a washstand with two pewter basins, a small bathtub, three chairs and "two or three sea couches with drawers to convert into sofas in the day time." He was as concerned about his daughters' decorum as he was about their comfort, warning the young ladies against hanging out their washing: "Nothing is so indelicate, indeed so indecent, as from the windows of the ladies' cabins to see anything towing overboard or being hung out to dry."

Most passengers joined their ship at Gravesend, 20 miles down the Thames from London, several days before she sailed. Arriving at the anchorage there, they found a scene of barely controlled chaos. Stores and baggage were being loaded from boats clustered round the hull; the decks were cluttered with barrels and crates of all kinds; terrified cows and pigs penned in the hold and chickens and geese on the poop deck added a farmyard cacophony to the bleep of the bosun's pipe and orders shouted by the mates. The noise and general confusion were compounded by crowds of friends, relatives and well-wishers who had come aboard to bid farewell to loved ones and enjoy the spectacle of an East Indiaman preparing for sea. An open house was maintained in the cuddy for these guests, who ate and drank with enthusiasm; indeed, the party atmosphere was so agreeable that visitors often stayed on board overnight, sleeping on tables and chairs.

Before the ship got under way, passengers were advised to secure their possessions in their cabins in order to prevent them from sliding about when the vessel heeled with the wind. Wealthy travelers sent their servants ahead to make such arrangements; the less fortunate spent a couple of hours on their knees hammering cleats and staples into the deck and lashing down their furniture, trunks and boxes. The decks of older ships often were full of holes from previous passengers' efforts to secure their belongings.

At last the bosun piped "topmen aloft," and a pilot took the ship out of the Thames. The outward-bound East India fleet usually mustered off Deal, Kent, to await a favorable wind. There, more passengers joined the vessel, most of them having traveled from London by post coach in order to delay boarding the ship for a day or so. The Deal boatmen, who rowed passengers out to their ships, were notorious for their avarice, and demanded extortionate sums for their services. Passengers had no choice but to pay, since other boatmen would refuse to take them.

Seventeen-year-old Thomas Twining was one of the passengers rowed out to the *Ponsbourne* off Deal in April 1792, and his first few minutes on board an East Indiaman were never to be forgotten:

"Having made a bow to the Captain and officers, whom I found upon the quarterdeck, or part between the main and mizzen masts, and glanced my eye, for a moment, upon the ship from head to stern, I inquired where my cabin was. I was conducted down a ladder to it, on the lower or gundeck, not far from the stern, on the larboard side. Here, the port being shut, there was scarcely light enough for me to survey my new apartment. I soon found, also, that the ship had considerably more motion than was apparent from the boat, and that the relief which I felt in coming on board was of very short duration. For I was scarcely able to stand without laying hold of some fixed object. I also became exceedingly oppressed by a close suffocating air, and by a sickening offensive smell, to which I know nothing comparable, and can only designate it by its usual appellation on board—the smell of the ship. My head and

A beauty with less than met the eye

To a casual waterfront stroller in the 1770s, a British East Indiaman must have seemed a floating palace, the very apotheosis of classical grandeur. The heraldic shield and floral ornaments on her carved taffrail gleamed with gold leaf, and the oriel windows of the stern and quarter galleries jutted over the water like a castle's balconies. The massive, rounded lines of the oak hull accentuated the ship's majestic proportions—140 feet long and 35 feet at the beam, twice the size of an ordinary 18th Century merchantman.

The discerning eye of a sailing man, however, would have construed these dimensions quite differently, seeing an ungainly hull much too long for its breadth. The ratio between keel length and beam—a reliable gauge of a ship's sailing qualities until the sleek hulls of the clipper era rendered the formula obsolete—was 3½ to 1 in an Indiaman, as opposed to the 3-to-1 ratio of other merchant vessels. The difference came about through a quirk in the English ton-

nage laws, which after 1773 computed tax assessments and harbor fees chiefly on the basis of a ship's beam, but took little account of her length and none at all of her depth. In order to stow the maximum quantity of cargo for the lowest possible fees, the British East India Company built its ships long, narrow and very deep.

An 800-ton Indiaman like the one below could stow nearly 1,000 tons of tea—but she was a notoriously poor sailer. With her bluff bow and rounded bottom, she plowed through the water at only three or four knots in the best of circumstances, half the speed of a contemporary warship. Sailing close to the wind, she made almost as much leeway as headway because the wind pushed her high superstructure sideways like a sail. And worst of all, even in calm waters and with heavy ballast, an Indiaman was dreadfully cranky, subject to wallowing with an interminable, lurching roll that made all but seasoned mariners seasick.

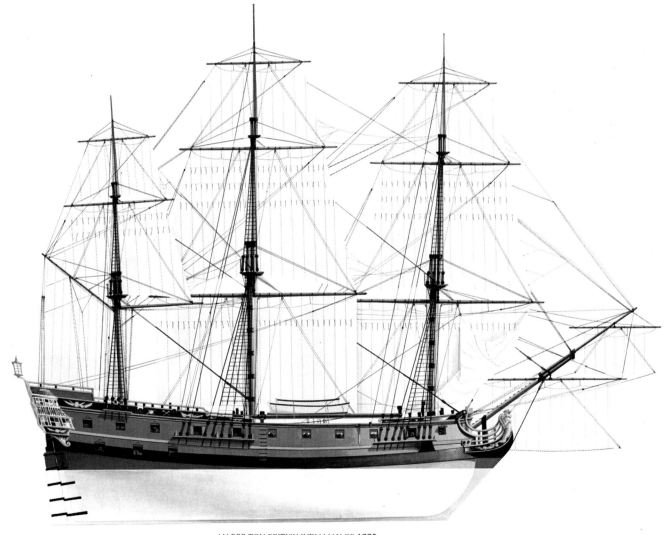

AN 800-TON BRITISH INDIAMAN OF 1775

The East Indiaman was a hybrid among ships. She came into being as a cargo carrier, but because she might have to defend her freight, she was armed like a warship. And because the British East India Company needed so many servants to manage its affairs abroad, she took passengers too.

For all these reasons, cargo, arms and people were crowded together as on no other vessel. The 100-odd tons of provisions necessary for the ship's company went in the hold. Trading goods owned by the captain and crew were generally lashed to the lower deck, where they were safest from spray and leakage. The armament for an 800-ton Indiaman consisted of thirty-two 18-pound cannon; but to make room for the passengers and their stores, many of the guns had to be stowed in the hold, where they were useless. In any event, the stores and passenger cabins so encumbered the decks that clearing for action could take two hours—much too long to save the ship if an attack took her by surprise.

The passengers' accommodations varied in quality from barely livable to comparatively luxurious. Worst off were the seamen and army recruits, who had to find catch-as-catch-can arrangements in the claustrophobic lower-deck steerage, so called because ships once were steered from this space. Officers and company officials got cubicles in the great cabin with one- or two-tiered bunks. Families traveling on company business might have a measure of privacy in five-by-seven-foot cabins rented from the ship's officers; but to sleep, a passenger might have to sling a hammock over a cannon. Only a handful of persons aboard had accommodations consistent with the aura of the outer ship: The wealthy passengers who lodged in the roundhouse cabins (the number varied from two to six) might crowd in some of the comforts of a Georgian home (right).

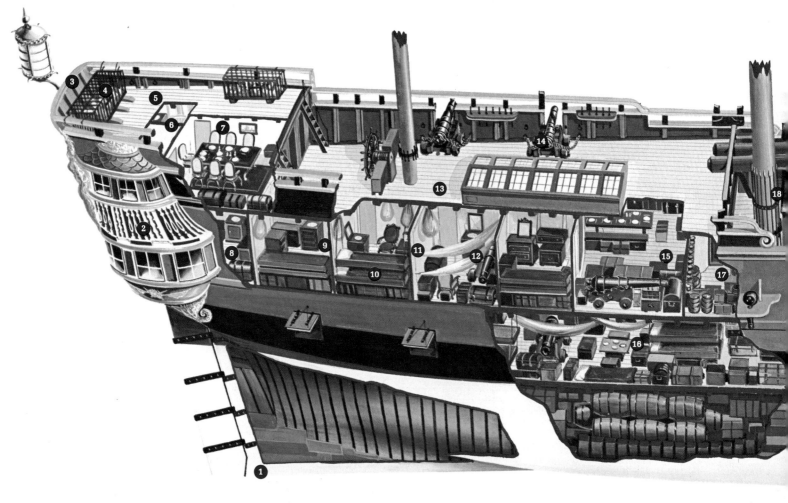

1. KEEL	5. POOP DECK	9. CABINS	13. QUARTER-DECK
2. QUARTER GALLERY	6. ROUNDHOUSE CABINS	10. HANGING COTS	14. 18-POUND CANNON
3. TAFFRAIL	7. CUDDY DINING SALOON	11. CABIN PARTITION	15. MAIN-DECK STEERAGE
4. POULTRY COOP	8. GREAT CABIN	12. HAMMOCKS	16. LOWER-DECK STEERAGE

A typical roundhouse cabin had a couch, a table and chairs, a bureau and a washstand. To these a passenger might add personal possessions such as a harp (foreground) and a decanter (on the table). Heavy furniture was permanently lashed down; the decanter was easily packed away if the weather worsened.

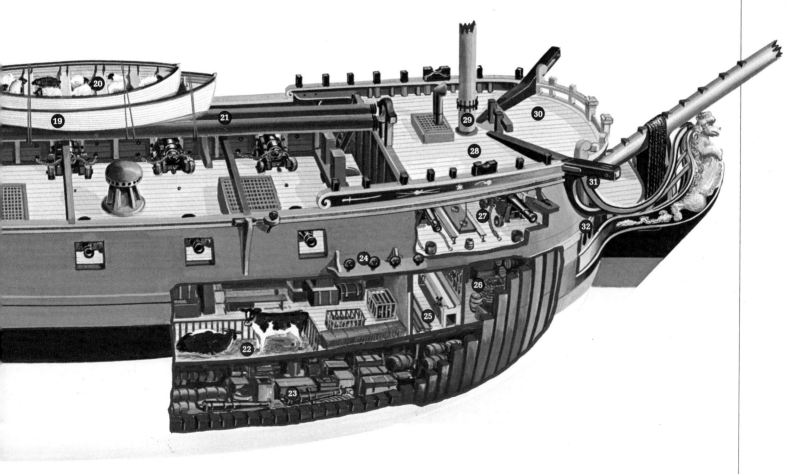

17. PANTRY	21. SPARE SPARS	25. CARPENTER'S WORKSHOP	29. BELAYING PINS
18. BOARDING PIKES	22. CATTLE	26. BOATSWAIN'S STORES	30. BITTS
19. SHIP'S BOATS	23. DISMANTLED CANNON	27. CREW'S MESS	31. CATHEAD
20. SHEEP	24. CHAINS	28. FORECASTLE DECK	32. HAWSEHOLES

stomach soon began to yield to this irresistible combination. I could hardly help returning to the deck to breathe a little pure air."

All passengers were given copies of regulations issued by East India House "for the promotion of orderly behaviour in the Company's ships," and many spent their first hours at sea studying these rules and generally acquainting themselves with shipboard customs and etiquette. They learned that male passengers had to touch their hats in salute before coming onto the quarter-deck, that whistling was forbidden on deck (it was considered disrespectful and unlucky), and that at meals "no debauching or late seats are ever countenanced." They were required to familiarize themselves immediately with the quarter bill. This was a list the captain made out and posted as soon as the fleet was at sea, assigning every man on board—passengers included—to an action station. Danger from enemy men-of-war, pirates or privateers was ever-present, and the quarter bill was essential to prevent confusion in the event that a strange and possibly malevolent sail appeared on the horizon.

In the first days at sea, most passengers had more immediate difficulties to worry about than hijackers, as James Wallace, a surgeon on his way to India in 1821 on the *Lonach*, noted in his diary. "At the call for breakfast, I went in, although I had little inclination for the meal, to take my seat at table along with the rest; but I found few others there; and even these few, as soon as the eating articles were produced, and caterer had commenced sending them round, got up and made their exit rather hurriedly. I followed very soon, for I found things far from being right, and, like the others, took the way to my cot, into which I tumbled in a most pitiable condition." Along with the other landlubbers aboard, Wallace was being introduced to seasickness.

"All Friday it continued to blow, and all that day, I and many others, were, as we supposed, in a state of greater misery than ever mortal was in before. The moment we raised our head from the pillow, such horrible sensations ensued, that we were glad instantly to get it down again. Some who fought against their feelings, and got out of bed, had scarcely reached the floor, when a tumble of the vessel sent them tumbling to the other side of their cabin; and before they had time to recover themselves another roll would send them as quickly and roughly back again. Others who got the length of beginning to dress, in the attempt to draw on a stocking, or in any other act which occupied both hands, and put the body on rather a ticklish balance, were thrown down with such violence, that for some days afterwards they had cause to remember it. And to increase the misfortune, the same lurch that upset the man, generally upset along with him, some of the cabin furniture."

William Hickey, on the first morning of his first voyage to India on the *Plassey*, took to his cot in a "lamentable condition" and stayed there for 10 days. "So ill was I that it was actually indifferent to me what became of the ship, and I should verily, I believe, have heard with composure that she was sinking." Days later, a friend tipped him out of his cot and insisted he get some fresh air. On deck Hickey found the ship close to the island of Tenerife and the sea serene and smooth. By evening he felt well enough to eat half a boiled fowl and drink a pint of wine, which left him "quite renovated."

As an East Indiaman heels sharply to starboard, diners, meals and chairs pitch from the captain's table in undignified disarray. Such mishaps were common on the stormy passage to the East. "The chairs were very fond of skating," recalled a traveler who sailed to India in 1826.

The captain's table in the cuddy was rarely fully occupied until after the ship had crossed the Bay of Biscay and the last passenger had found his sea legs. Only the high-ranking passengers, those occupying the expensive accommodations in the roundhouse and great cabin, dined in the cuddy with the captain and his leading officers. If there were too many to fit around the table at one time, some were relegated to a second sitting—without the company of the captain. Lower-ranking passengers ate in the steerage mess, with the third mate at the head of the table.

Fresh food was available for a time. In addition to the livestock and poultry carried by all East Indiamen, salad greens and other vegetables were sometimes grown in boxes of earth. While these lasted, the fare on board was generally good. The quality deteriorated as the weeks passed, but there were rarely complaints about the quantity of food. In 1797 Lady Anne Barnard, a passenger on board the *Sir Edward Hughes,* noted that the menu for dinner included pea soup, roast leg of mutton, hogs' puddings, two fowls, two hams, two ducks, corned round of beef, mutton pies, pork pies, mutton chops, stewed cabbage and potatoes, followed by "an enormous plum pudding and washed down with porter, spruce beer, port wine, sherry, gin, rum etc." This was for just 16 people.

The bell signaling the change of watch at 8 o'clock in the morning also called the passengers for breakfast—usually tea, biscuit, rancid butter, corned beef and tongue, or curry for old India hands. It was not a popular meal, and the ladies often passed it up, preferring to stay in their cabins and nibble some delicacy from their own provisions.

One of the problems with breakfast was that the biscuits offered on board an East Indiaman were usually extremely hard. Hickey recalled that one passenger on the *Plassey* bet another man five guineas that he could not dispose of a biscuit by his teeth alone within four minutes. "A watch being laid upon the table, at it he went with a set of remarkably strong teeth, but strong as they were, we all thought he must lose his bet, and he was twice in extreme danger of choking, by which he lost several seconds. Notwithstanding this however, he, to our great surprise, accomplished his object, and won the wager, being six seconds within the given time."

Dinner was served at 2 o'clock in the afternoon and was announced by a sailor tapping out a drum roll titled "Roast Beef of Old England." The meal consisted of at least three courses, and both ladies and gentlemen dressed for the occasion with the same formality that would have been expected on shore. The mealtime ritual lost some of its polish in rough weather, however. For one thing, the galley was near the water line, and an especially high sea gushing through the port might extinguish the cooking fire, causing a delay in the delivery of courses. If the ship started to roll excessively, the tables and chairs in the dining room were lashed to staples in the deck, and the plates and dishes were held in place by long rolls of cloth tied across the table between the place settings.

When no such precautions were taken, the results could be disastrous, as a passenger on an Indiaman in 1810 recorded: "The dishes would forsake their place on the table, and mutton, gravy and all deposit itself in the lap of him who sat nearest it: whilst, on rising from the desolate meal, it was an even choice whether to retire to the dark, close, uneasy cabin, or to parade the deck in the midst of the spray."

After dinner the ladies retired, leaving the gentlemen to enjoy a glass or two of port from a decanter that was circulated around the table a number of times, depending on the generosity of the commander. When the captain got to his feet and bade his guests good afternoon, everyone withdrew. Tea was served at 6 o'clock, followed at 9 p.m. by a supper that usually consisted of soup, cheese and cold meats. The decanter was circulated only once after supper, and then all the passengers turned in for the night.

According to regulations drawn up in 1799 "for the Preservation of good Order on board the Company's Ships," candles in the cabins had to be extinguished by 10 o'clock at the latest. Even before that hour, the utmost precautions had to be taken to prevent any lights from being visible to other ships passing in the night; it was the hallowed custom of East India captains to shorten sail at dusk, and while dawdling through the darkness under easy canvas, the ships were sitting targets for a privateer or pirate.

East Indiamen usually made their first stop at the island of Madeira, where they took on water, fruit, vegetables and, most important of all, the local wine, which was very fashionable and popular in India. There

Aboard an Indiaman with brush and sketchbook

Toward the end of the 18th Century a new kind of passenger set sail for India: the artist, who went out to satisfy the demands of a public eager to have views of the Orient. At least 58 painters traveled aboard East Indiamen between 1770 and 1825.

Few of them struck it as rich as did the uncle-and-nephew team of Thomas and William Daniell, energetic Londoners who, with sketchbooks always at hand, voyaged to China in 1785, then doubled back and spent the next eight years touring India.

They returned home with a portfolio that for the rest of their lives was to yield dividends in the form of aquatints, water colors and oils—all rendered from the same initial sketches. Their outbound trip alone resulted in 50 aquatints; some of them appear here and on the following pages.

Off the quays at Gravesend, ships ride at anchor in a scene sketched by Thomas Daniell before he and his nephew embarked on what they called their "adventurous track in the deep."

As the Indiaman Atlas heels in a blow, crewmen and a pair of tethered goats balance precariously on the spray-swept quarter-deck.

In a traditional shipboard hazing ceremony, a passenger who is crossing the Equator for the first time pays homage to a sailor dressed as Neptune. "The appearance of Neptune and his retinue is highly grotesque," reported William Daniell; their "oozy locks are composed of long, half-wet swabs bespattered with oatmeal, and the faces are painted with red ochre."

Barrels, crates and a line are flung from the poop deck of the Atlas in an effort to save the life of a sailor swept overboard during a storm. Moments later, a boat was lowered, but the man had disappeared.

"This part of the ocean abounds in sharks," remarked William upon reaching the island of Java. After sailors speared one, he reported, they cut up the carcass, "reserving the fins and tails for the Chinese market, a rich nutritious soup being extracted from those materials."

Lying at anchor off Macao, a Chinese trading junk dwarfs the diminutive coastal craft. The Daniells thought that the city, a Portuguese settlement, looked quite European in style—except for the windows, which were made of translucent oyster shells instead of panes of glass.

was time for sightseeing excursions ashore, and captains sometimes entertained their passengers and local dignitaries at a ball on board. After Madeira the ships picked up the northeast trade winds for the long haul across the Atlantic toward Brazil, where they would turn and head southeast across the Atlantic once again to the Cape of Good Hope. This roundabout route enabled them to avoid the worst of the doldrums.

After a few days on the westward transatlantic leg, boredom set in. Passengers sought diversion in shooting at sharks for sport, visiting other ships when the fleet was becalmed, playing endless games of cards and producing amateur theatricals. Mary Sherwood, who traveled to India on the *Devonshire* in 1805, described how a seagoing version of ordinary society gradually evolved. "By the middle of May, when we passed St. Lucia and St. Vincent Islands, we on board had begun to understand each other, and to fall into little parties and societies. We had our little plots and under-plots, our likings and dislikings, our jealousies and small spites and real kindnesses, and I had formed my plans for spending my days. I arose early and got out of my horrid cabin, and came upon deck, and sat under the awning, by the wheel, at the door of the dining-room. With sewing, reading, or being read to, passed the time till it was necessary to dress for dinner. After dinner I was generally invited into Mrs. Carr's cabin, or all the ladies went and took their tea on deck, and the gentlemen talked to them, and not unseldom there was a dance on deck."

Studious and ambitious young men going out to enter the company's service sometimes found the voyage an opportunity to learn a useful foreign language—usually Persian, Hindustani or Portuguese. But concentration was not always easy, as Sir James Mackintosh discovered when he tried to study philosophy on board the *Caroline* in 1811. There were 10 children on the ship, creating as "many noises and distractions as ever tried the presence of mind of Julius Caesar," he noted in a letter. "It is the severest test to which the power of attention of a student of philosophy was ever subjected."

Few passengers, however, had such self-improving instincts. They much preferred to yawn and gossip and grumble and intrigue and quarrel. Even the festivities on crossing the Equator—during which a sailor dressed as King Neptune presided over the ceremonial shaving and dunking of travelers who had never crossed the Line before—were often a cause for squabbling. The ceremony could easily degenerate into brutality, and there were reports that on some ships passengers had to protect themselves with pistols. In 1802 a passenger who had traveled aboard the *Scaleby Castle* actually sued the captain because of the rough treatment he received crossing the Line, and the court at Bombay awarded him damages of 400 rupees.

It was not, in fact, unusual for the passengers and the captain to fall out during the voyage. The captain of an East Indiaman was an autocrat; his authority on board was absolute and his privileges extensive. Walking on the windward side of the quarter-deck, for example, was reserved for the captain alone, and it was considered an insult, said one company servant who made the voyage east, for anyone to "pass between the wind and his nobility." While captains were required by company regulations to pay due attention to the contentment of their passengers, some did nothing of the kind. Captain Charles Chisholme of the *Gatton*, outward-bound for Bengal in 1778, behaved so disagreeably to his passengers that not one of them would exchange a single word with him during the last two months of the voyage. The fact that he had on board a large and noisy pack of foxhounds that he was planning to sell in India for his own profit cannot have contributed much to the comfort of the voyagers. A couple of years earlier, Captain Jonathan Court of the *Prince of Wales* put his passengers on short water rations, despite their protests, so that there would be sufficient water for the foxhounds that he, too, was transporting to Bengal.

Lady Maria Nugent, a passenger on the *Baring* in 1811, kept a journal in which she diligently logged the "violent and distressing outrages" committed by the captain, Henry Templer. The trouble started soon after a stop at Cape Town. Its initial cause was a dispute over seating protocol, which was always a potentially inflammatory subject among status-conscious passengers and officers on Indiamen. Seating at the captain's table was arranged strictly in order of social precedence, beginning with the two most important female passengers, who were given the chairs on either side of the captain. Lady Nugent, the ranking woman on the *Baring*, required a change of seating position because of the delicate state of her vision.

"Some new arrangements at the dinner table, made on my account—the medical man at the Cape saying it was injurious to my eyes to sit opposite the glare of the sun on the sails," she recorded. This meant the rest of the diners had to be shifted accordingly, but "a Captain Midwinter, of the Company's service, insisted upon keeping his seat, which would place him and his wife next to me and Sir George." Sir George was Lady Nugent's husband and the ranking male passenger on the *Baring*. "As this was Captain Templer's place, and Colonel and Lady Charlotte Murray next, Captain Templer would not submit to it. There was, in consequence, much confusion, and it ended in Captain Midwinter retiring to his cabin, and ordering his and his wife's dinner to be sent to them there. This was all very uncomfortable to us. I would have given much to be allowed to dine in my cabin, or to have resumed my former situation, but this was not permitted."

Lady Nugent judged Midwinter to be in the wrong, but her opinion of Captain Templer's character was none too high—and it sank further when the obstinate commander made matters worse by banishing the army officer from the table altogether; Midwinter was required to take the rest of his meals in his cabin. Several weeks later the choleric skipper hit a soldier, knocked him down and then heaped scornful insults on a young army officer who tried to intervene. After this "painful occurrence," said Lady Nugent, a number of the gentlemen passengers declared they would no longer dine at the captain's table. "In short, all was unhappiness," she wrote, "and I have never left my cabin since." In the end, the young officer whom Templer had insulted demanded satisfaction from the captain, and a duel was fought on shore near Calcutta. They fired at the same time and both missed, but honor was preserved.

Young Captain Thomas Taylor, of the *Glory*, was less fortunate. Only

28 years old, he was killed by a passenger in a duel at Madras in March 1804, at the end of his first voyage as commander of an East Indiaman. His opponent was a man with whom he had quarreled over the affections of a young lady on board. Indeed, the presence of women on Indiamen almost always caused friction among the men, many of whom seemed incapable of completing the voyage without falling in love. "Notwithstanding the utmost vigilance on the part of the captain," one lady passenger noted disapprovingly, "attachments will spring up amongst the young people on board, and fortunate may it be considered when these are confined to the single of both sexes."

Worried parents issued to their daughters clear instructions on how to avoid romantic entanglements. No more than two glasses of wine were to be taken at dinner, for example, and any invitation to play cards or backgammon was to be firmly refused. It was permitted, "from the motion of the ship," to avail oneself of the supporting arm of a gentleman during a walk on the deck, but particular care should be taken to keep the conversation general. Chaperons were sometimes engaged to ward off lovesick fellow passengers. One such overseer, a Mrs. Eliza Fay, escorted three young ladies to Calcutta in 1784 and later triumphantly wrote home: "We were only five times on deck during the passage, owing to a previous arrangement between the captain and me, to guard against imprudent attachments which are more easily formed than broken; and I am happy to say the plan succeeded according to our wish."

The concern of parents was no doubt intensified by popular stories of shipboard romances on East Indiamen. One told how three passengers fell in love with the same girl and resolved to fight for her affections the moment their ship arrived at Cape Town. Hearing what was afoot, the young lady intervened and settled the matter by lightheartedly promising to marry each of her suitors in turn. It was a promise she was in due course able to fulfill, because the Indian climate obligingly carried away her first two husbands.

As Indiamen approached the Cape of Good Hope they were often buffeted by violent northerly and northwesterly gales that lashed the seas in the area for months at a time. William Hickey, typically, managed to find amusement in the region's rough weather. He had gone into the roundhouse to comfort one of his fellow passengers, a Mrs. Smith, when "a sea broke over the ship that for a time quite overwhelmed her. Down she went upon her beam ends. The shock was so violent and sudden everything yielded to it. Mrs. Smith, who was sitting on her bed with a child on each side, came, cot and all, bodily over to leeward, as did chests, trunks and every article in the cabin. Although for some moments I actually thought the ship had upset, I could not help smiling at the scene that presented itself, the female servants floundering about in all positions, Mrs. Smith screeching to them to cover their nakedness, whilst she herself was employed in gathering up curls, toupees, and various articles of her toilette she would not upon any consideration have exhibited to profane eyes."

During this phase of the journey, conversation among the passengers often turned to the unhappy fate of the *Grosvenor*, an Indiaman wrecked

John Coxon is dressed in the uniform he wore as captain of the Grosvenor in this contemporary miniature. When the ill-fated Indiaman came to grief under his command in 1782, one survivor recalled that the captain's conduct was "well-collected, patient and brave."

on the coast of South Africa more than 500 miles east of the Cape. Her loss caused a sensation in England. It was not just that she was carrying a small but valuable quantity of diamonds—which, in the telling and retelling, became a fortune in diamonds, rubies, sapphires, emeralds, and gold and silver bars. It was not just that her passenger list included a large number of names from socially prominent families. What made the *Grosvenor* the subject of endless speculation was the fact that the 105 people aboard her simply disappeared into the hinterland of Africa.

Disaster befell the *Grosvenor* in stormy weather during the early hours of Sunday, August 4, 1782. Captain John Coxon was in his cabin for the night, having calculated his ship to be some 300 miles from the nearest land. But a sailor, ordered aloft to strike the fore-topgallant yard, twice descended to say he thought he saw land directly ahead through the squally darkness. He was not believed at first, but on his second report several men on deck said they, too, could discern land. The third mate, who was officer of the watch, was so sure they were wrong that he refused to walk across the deck to look for himself. Defying the watch officer, one man ran to rouse the captain from his cabin. Coxon hurried onto the quarter-deck and ordered the ship to be put about. The maneuver was almost completed when the *Grosvenor's* port bow struck a submerged rock with a force that sent a sickening shudder through the ship and brought everyone up onto the deck. Coxon, shouting above the screams and wails of the passengers, appealed for calm.

In the gray light of dawn, they could see the shore 120 yards away, separated from them by a daunting barrier of boiling surf. The *Grosvenor* was shipping so little water that the captain underestimated the damage and at first tried to refloat the vessel. The fore-topsail, jib and staysails were hoisted; as the sails caught the wind, which was blowing from landward, the bow heaved off the rocks with a grinding shiver. But as soon as the *Grosvenor* floated free, she began to sink rapidly and was saved from going down only because her stern rammed hard on the rocks seconds later. When Coxon ordered the gunner to fire distress signals, the powder room was found full of water. The ship's biggest boat, a yawl, was lowered, but it was immediately smashed to pieces on the rocks.

At this point, two Italian crewmen volunteered to try to swim ashore. Clenching in their teeth the ends of light lines that would be payed out from the ship while they swam, they plunged into the thundering surf. One of the Italians, Joseph Barkini, was drowned in the attempt, but the other, a man named Roque Pandolpho, finally made it to shore. He scrambled up the steep rocks at the water's edge, watched by a group of curious Africans who had gathered nearby. Emboldened by the success of Pandolpho, three lascars—Indian sailors—jumped into the water and followed him to land.

The four men then used Pandolpho's line to pull a seven-inch hawser ashore, and secured it to the rocks. A large metal eye was slipped onto the hawser, and a metal grating was slung from it by ropes to serve as a makeshift breeches buoy. But after one passenger had made it ashore by means of this rig, the line that was used to pull the grating got hung up on rocks and could not be disentangled.

Meanwhile, some of the sailors had fashioned a raft from spars and

As storm surf smashes the Grosvenor on an African coastal reef, her passengers await their turns at a life line slung ashore. The vessel was one of four Indiamen shipwrecked in 1782.

other timbers. After the breeches-buoy rig broke down, they launched the crude craft, but it was destroyed by pounding waves almost as soon as five men set out on it. Four of them drowned and one swam to shore. Next, some of the crewmen tried swinging hand over hand along the hawser; a few made it, but 15 dropped into the surf and disappeared.

The frantic attempts to reach safety continued all day as the ship disintegrated. At about 12:30 p.m. the *Grosvenor* suddenly broke in two, and the bow section swung round alongside the stern. Sometime between 3 and 4 p.m. the stern half began to fall apart. Most of the people were on the starboard quarter, to which the hawser was fixed, and this section of the stern began to inch toward the shore, driven by waves and a wind that had shifted and now blew from seaward. At 5 p.m. the crowded hulk was beached in shallow water. After all the desperate efforts and loss of life, those who had stayed aboard simply waded ashore. The only man left in the starboard quarter of the wreck was the cook's mate, who was so drunk he could not be persuaded to leave the comfort of his berth. It is not known what became of him.

The captain mustered the group and found that 123 people had made their way to safety. These survivors salvaged casks of salted beef and flour that had washed up on the beach. They also found two sails, from which a rough tent was constructed for the women and children. The Africans who had watched the whole drama from the shore disappeared at dusk, leaving the embers of a fire, which the seamen were able to use to get three more fires going with driftwood. The next morning the Africans reappeared to plunder what they could. They were interested primarily in metal, and spent most of the day burning pieces of the wreckage to free the iron fittings from the wood. But when they saw some of the sailors carrying salvaged cooking pans, the Africans indicated by signs that they wanted those prizes and, when refused, boldly wrested the pans from the sailors' hands. At one point they invaded the tent to see if it held anything to their liking. Their demeanor caused considerable alarm, and Captain Coxon heard no disagreement when he suggested that the survivors strike out at once for the nearest Dutch settlement. By his calculations, he said, the trek would take 15 or 16 days.

One hundred seventeen days later, six seamen stumbled into a Dutch settlement some 300 miles east of the Cape. They were starving, half deranged and dressed in rags—and they had a terrible story to tell. Constantly harassed by Africans and followed by wild beasts, the 123 survivors had stayed together only a few days. When the stronger people began complaining about the slow pace set by the injured and those with children, the group had split up, and later divided again into smaller and smaller parties. The six seamen had crossed trackless stretches of desert, forded fast-flowing rivers and fought their way through dense forest. Africans had stripped them of everything but the tatters hanging from their emaciated frames. They had survived—just—on land crabs, snails, shellfish, wild sorrel and a whale they had found stranded on the shore. They did not know what had become of the others. A search expedition mounted from the Cape turned up 10 more sailors and two passengers. None of the others were ever seen again.

For years it was rumored that many of the *Grosvenor's* survivors were

French privateer Robert Surcouf made a fortune hijacking English shipping off the coast of India between 1795 and 1809. A fearless warrior who believed in leading by example, he charged into every fray brandishing a pair of custom-made pistols (below). At 36, he retired to a life of respectability as a financier.

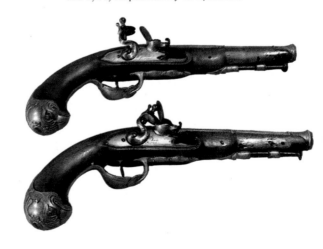

still alive, enslaved by African tribesmen. An English explorer in 1788 visited the spot where the ship had been wrecked and was told by an African that a white woman was living in the vicinity with his countrymen; she had a child, whom she "frequently embraced, and wept bitterly." Later, visitors received reports of fair-skinned children being seen in the same area—presumably the offspring of the female passengers from the ship.

Additional details were presented in an account of the tragedy published in 1812. "It is said by officers at the Cape that some of those unfortunate females who survived the shipwreck had it in their power to return; but, apprehending that their place in society was lost, and that they should be degraded in the eyes of their equals, after spending so great a portion of their lives with savages, who had compelled them to a temporary union, they resolved not to forsake the fruits of that union, and abide with the chiefs who protected them."

No doubt many such theories circulated in Cape Town, where the adventures of East Indiamen were the common currency of conversation. Cape Town was the halfway house between Europe and Asia, the place where outward-bound Indiamen met homeward-bound ships and swapped news (pages 72-73); Dutchmen called it the "Tavern of the Two Seas." It was the custom at the Cape for passengers to live on shore at their own expense while their ships were taking on provisions and supplies in Table Bay. Lodgings were provided by respectable Dutch families and were for the most part excellent. "The tables are plentiful, the houses are clean, and the people obliging," an English lady traveler noted. "What makes it extremely comfortable," she added, "is that most of them speak English."

Entertainment consisted largely of expeditions upcountry to the Constantia winery and scenic Table Mountain and, of course, dinner parties and dances. Eleven young ladies who arrived on board the *Thetis* in early 1793 caused a tremendous stir when they stepped out in the latest fashion from England—very high-waisted dresses. No one in Cape Town had ever seen the style before, and at a dance a shocked Dutch gentleman was heard to observe: "Ah, God help their poor parents, how miserable must they be upon perceiving the situation their daughters are in!" When Captain Bullock of the *Thetis,* who was within earshot, asked him what he meant, the Dutchman replied testily, "Is it not apparent they are all with child!"

After the Cape, India-bound ships often made a further call at Johanna in the Comoro Islands, where people in outrigger canoes paddled out to meet the incoming fleet and sell poultry, eggs, fish, pineapples, oranges and bananas. Passengers on preceding ships had given many of these local entrepreneurs mischievous names, usually of prominent European statesmen. Thus some near-naked islander was liable to proclaim himself to be the Prince of Wales, or Robespierre, or William Pitt.

From Johanna the fleet struck out on the last, and sometimes the most dangerous, leg of the journey. The risk of a sea battle increased considerably east of the Cape, where British Naval strength was inadequate to protect East Indiamen from the great numbers of pirates, privateers and

enemy men-of-war that prowled the Indian Ocean. Mary Sherwood, traveling aboard the *Devonshire* in a fleet of Indiamen in 1805, faithfully recorded an encounter with three French men-of-war:

"In a very short time after the enemy had been seen, one of the strangers lay to, whilst the other two came down, and, passing close to our rear, hoisted French colors almost before we had time to form our conjectures of what they were. The colors were no sooner up than they began to fire, and at the same crisis all hands were engaged on board our ship to clear for action. Every cabin which had been erected between the last gun and the forepart of the ship was torn down, ours of course among the rest, and everything we possessed thrown in heaps into the hold or trampled underfoot. All the women were tumbled after the furniture of the cabins into the same dismal hole at the very bottom of the ship, and the guns prepared in the shortest possible time to return the compliment which the enemy had already paid us."

Privateers from Robert Surcouf's Confiance swarm aboard the giant East Indiaman Kent in this painting by a Frenchman who took part in the raid. The moment the ships locked together, men high in the rigging of the Confiance dealt a savage blow by dropping grenades on the Kent's crowded decks.

In the hold Mrs. Sherwood and her companions were below the water line. "We were quite certain that if anything happened to the ship nothing could save us, for they had taken away the ladders, probably to keep us in our places. Our husbands and all our late companions were above, and we heard the roar of the guns, but had no means of learning what was going on. We were warned not to approach the opening lest a ball might roll in on us, and there we were for some hours, not in the least knowing what was going on. There was, however, no fainting, screaming or folly amongst us; it is not on occasions of real trial that women in general behave weakly.

"It was quite dark, though I know not the hour, when notice was given that all was over, and no mischief done in the *Devonshire*." The outnumbered French warships had withdrawn. "And then ensued a strange ceremony, for the men began to hoist up the women instead of providing steps for us. They took the ladies up first, lifting them from one to another as if they had been so many bales of goods. There were larger and taller women amongst us than myself, but the men made no difficulty with any of us. We all repaired to Colonel Carr's cabin, where we congratulated each other on the happy termination of the affair, and much enjoyed some negus"—a hot wine punch—"and biscuit."

One privateer particularly feared in the Indian Ocean was a Frenchman named Robert Surcouf. He had first won fame—or, from the English point of view, notoriety—in a six-month voyage that began in late 1795, during which he captured five British merchant ships in Indian waters. At the time, Surcouf's command was the *Emilie*, a small vessel with only four guns, and yet his prizes on the cruise included the *Triton*, a big 26-gun Indiaman. Surcouf surprised the *Triton* by approaching under an English ensign and holding fire until he was within pistol range. The British got off only three shots—all of which missed the *Emilie*—before Surcouf boarded with a mere 18 men and routed the 150-man crew of the *Triton* in hand-to-hand fighting.

In 1800 Surcouf was given command of the 18-gun corsair *Confiance* by an owner eager for a share of privateering loot. The *Confiance*, said an East India captain named Robert Eastwick, was a "remarkably beautiful" ship. "She sat very low upon the water, and had black sides with yellow molding posts, and a French stern, all black. She carried a red vane at her maintop-gallant masthead, very square yards and masts without the smallest rake either forward or aft. Her sails were all cut French fashion, and remarkable, having a great roach and steering sail, very square. There was not a ship in those seas that she could not overtake or sail away from. It was the custom of her commander to ply his crew with liquor, and they always fought with the madness of drink in them."

Surcouf's exploits were, of course, a frequent conversational topic among passengers on British Indiamen. Probably the most memorable—and certainly the best recorded—encounter between English travelers and the French privateer occurred on October 7, 1800, when the East Indiaman *Kent*, outward-bound with 100 crewmen and 42 passengers aboard, fell in with the *Confiance* in the Bay of Bengal. The *Confiance* was not flying an identifying ensign, but Captain Robert Rivington of the *Kent* had little doubt about the intentions of the strange sail bearing down on his ship: He ordered all hands to quarters, the guns run out and matches lighted before the *Confiance* came to within hailing distance. When Rivington received no answer to his shouts asking the ship to identify herself, he ordered a shot fired across her bows. The *Confiance* hoisted her French colors and replied with booming cannon.

Before the battle, the three women on board had been hustled down to the comparative safety of the ship's bread room. While they were there, they were joined by a man. In the gloom they could not see who he was and were even unaware of his presence until one of the women stepped on him. The women huddled as far away from the intruder as they could get, and the man remained silent.

For about an hour, the two ships maneuvered for advantage, each blasting the other with cannon and musket fire. Then the *Confiance*, her rigging damaged from cannon fire, took in her main topsail and dropped back, apparently not anxious to continue the fight. The men on the *Kent* were jubilant, but the battle was not yet won. The Indiaman's third officer, anxiously watching the activity on the privateer, became convinced she was going to attempt a boarding. Captain Rivington treated his observations with indignant contempt. "A likely thing indeed," he snorted, "that such a vessel as that, which is a dozen feet below the level of our upper deck should have the presumption to attempt boarding, it is utterly impossible."

No sooner had he spoken than the ship's carpenter, an old and experienced seaman, shouted, "By God, they are coming up to board us!" The *Confiance* had crowded on every inch of sail and was heading directly for the *Kent*. Before the big Indiaman could take any evasive action, the privateer's forerigging was entangled with the *Kent's* mizzen shrouds, and hatchet-waving Frenchmen began jumping from the upper rigging of their ship onto the Indiaman's poop and mizzen decks. All the male passengers had been armed with cutlasses, and they fought bravely alongside the *Kent's* crew, but they were no match for the savage fury of the attackers. Within a few minutes the Frenchmen were in control. One of their officers hauled down the *Kent's* colors and triumphantly hoisted the *Confiance's* ensign. Robert Surcouf, dressed as an ordinary seaman so that he could not be identified, had led the boarding party; he now assumed command of the *Kent*.

The women were brought up from below and saw a bloody shambles. Among those killed during the fighting were Captain Rivington, 16 of his crew and five passengers. Thirty-four men were wounded. While they were being treated, a senior passenger who had been reported missing, Major General Henry St. John, suddenly reappeared, totally unscathed. The other passengers had assumed he had been thrown overboard in the fighting, and they were puzzled by his presence—until they deduced that he was the mysterious man in the bread room.

At this point, the *Kent's* fifth mate recalled that just before the battle he had overheard an angry exchange between General St. John, who wanted to go below, and his aide-de-camp, who protested that it was the general's duty to stay on deck and help defend the ship. "Upon my word I shall not stay here," said General St. John, "as I do not conceive we are in any way bound to risk our lives in attempting to defend a merchant

After arriving at Madras on an East Indiaman, passengers ride cockleshell boats through breakers to shore. Travelers to Bombay ended their journey more sedately: East Indiamen tied up at company docks in the deepwater port.

ship, the property of the East India Company." With that, he disappeared belowdecks. His aide-de-camp, a Captain Pilkington, stayed on to fight and received a vicious ax wound that laid open one side of his face from his temple to his throat. He survived, but bore the ugly memento of his passage on an Indiaman for the rest of his life.

Captain Surcouf behaved with great civility to his prisoners, ensuring that the wounded men received the best possible care and that the women were treated with respect. The *Confiance* and her prize set a course for the French base at Mauritius, but 14 days later Surcouf captured a small merchantman and allowed all the passengers and the wounded to continue their journey to Calcutta in that ship.

News of the battle had already arrived in India. Details of the conduct of General St. John were also widely known, and most of his fellow passengers assumed that he would be socially ostracized in the colony. To their astonishment, he was met by a coach and six horses sent by the Governor General, Lord Wellesley, and conveyed directly to Government House, where a suite of apartments had been prepared. "This unexpected reaction," said William Hickey, who was in Calcutta when the *Kent's* company arrived, "prevented the General meeting that contempt he merited, for the whole settlement were mean enough to follow the example of their Governor-General, all courting the infamous poltroon." Nonetheless, for the remainder of his career, General St. John was known in India as the "Bread Room General."

Chapter 6
The splendid façade of a crumbling company

he drama and pageantry of an East Indiaman's launching always attracted thousands of Londoners, but the scene near William Cleverly's Gravesend shipyard on the cold, wind-whipped morning of March 7, 1787, was extraordinary even by the standards of the age. The Thames teemed with yachts, launches and wherries, all wearing a colorful panoply of pennants and flags. In the lane outside the locked shipyard gates, weather-beaten East India captains, rigged out in blue coats and black velvet capes, gathered in clusters to discuss the company's affairs with merchants and shipowners. Vendors hawked hot chestnuts and meat pies, an organ-grinder played, and fashionable ladies—bundled in ruffled cloaks, fur hats, muffs and wooden clogs that protected their delicate satin shoes—gathered in the lee of the shipyard's stone wall to shield their complexions from the wind off the river.

From within the gates came the dull tattoo of sledge hammers striking wood as carpenters smashed two-foot-square oak keel blocks to splinters, gently easing the new ship down onto its launching cradle. Above them the varnished yellow hull of the Indiaman *Nottingham* gleamed within a shadowy latticework of timber scaffolding. Even though she was not yet crowned with her intricate, soaring web of topmasts, yards and rigging, the ship possessed a palpable aura of majesty. She was, marveled the London *Morning Chronicle*, "the largest ship ever built for the service of the Honourable East India Company," 1,152 tons, 160 feet long and 40 feet at the beam—20 feet longer and five broader than the standard 800-ton Indiaman of the day.

At about 11 o'clock the shipyard's gates were thrown open and the crowd poured through, overflowing onto the banks of the Thames. While a band played popular airs, William Cleverly carefully eyed the height of the incoming tide, which would determine the moment to launch this, his first East Indiaman. Just after noon the choppy water submerged the lower end of the ways, and he strode to the knot of dignitaries at the ship's bow. At his signal, workmen checked the maze of timbers beneath the ship one last time and began shooing rambunctious children behind the wooden barricades that restrained the crowd. While the spectators craned to see, Cleverly shouted for the workmen to knock out the dogshores, braces that held the cradle in place.

As the huge timbers clattered to the ground, the ship began to inch toward the water. At that moment some honored lady standing on a platform at the bow (her name has been lost to history) smashed a crystal flask of wine against the ship's cutwater and intoned the traditional phrase, "I name this ship *Nottingham*. May God bless her and all who

At a London shipyard, hundreds of spectators gather to watch the launching of the 1,315-ton Edinburgh on November 9, 1825. She was built half again as large as Indiamen of the previous century, making it possible to carry more and bigger guns to defend against the depredations of rival ships.

sail in her." As the crowd cheered and the band struck up "God Save the King," the *Nottingham* gathered speed, rumbling stern first down the ways and into the Thames with the force of an avalanche.

While the ship was warped alongside a dock to receive her masts and rigging, more than a hundred guests—including, said the *Morning Chronicle*, "several persons of distinction"—adjourned to Cleverly's mold loft for the customary banquet, which was followed by an elegant ball. The merchants and shipowners who enjoyed the festivities that evening presumably toasted the *Nottingham* as the precursor of a great new epoch of prosperity for John Company, just as the newspapers did.

All of the signs seemed propitious: Company armies led by Robert Clive and his successors had conquered much of India, installing a company-run civil government that was expected to remit stupendous sums of surplus tax and rent revenue to Britain. And the China trade, stimulated by lower English customs duties on tea, was importing 15 million pounds of the leaf each year.

But even amid the euphoria of the launch, a few farsighted men must have harbored private doubts about the future of the East India Company and its 120-ship fleet. The company was two years in arrears on payment of customs duties and freight bills and had total debts of more than five million pounds. It remained solvent only by raising money with new issues of stocks and bonds, and even then it was so impoverished that it could not pay tradesmen in cash. This scandalous situation, while unknown to the general public, had prompted Parliament in 1784 to install a government Board of Control to supervise the company—a step that some insiders considered a prelude to a complete Crown takeover.

A large part of the problem lay overseas. Ever since Clive's victories in the 1750s, the directors—learning, perhaps, from the example of the failing Dutch East India Company—had been chary of territorial conquests, admonishing their governors general in India not "to involve us in the endless and turbulent distractions" of military campaigns. But such directives from London, 12,000 miles and five months of arduous travel away, took no account of the quicksand of Indian political intrigues, in which military force often seemed to be the only solution. And so a succession of governors general simply disregarded orders, borrowing huge sums to wage wars on the subcontinent, always promising eventual profits—once their conquests were completed. "Our India prosperity is always in the future tense," lamented George Tierney, a president of the Board of Control.

Another source of the company's difficulties was its shipping arrangements. To avoid the expense of maintaining its own shipyard, the company had been hiring vessels from outside owners since the mid-1600s. And before these entrepreneurs would risk the money to build and outfit such a single-purpose ship—by 1790 the cost of an Indiaman was about £40,000—they understandably insisted that the company promise to charter her for several voyages. From this arrangement evolved an unwritten agreement that a vessel was hired in perpetuity. If she wore out or was lost at sea, her owners had a right to replace her with a new ship that John Company was obliged to charter in her stead—a right that came to be called a "hereditary bottom."

Sails billowing, seven Indiamen ride majestically through the South China Sea in this painting by W. J. Huggins, once an East India Company seaman. Despite sailing in such convoys, the British lost 1.4 million tons of shipping to the French during the Napoleonic Wars.

The hereditary-bottom system effectively restricted the ownership of Indiamen to a closed circle of immensely wealthy capitalists. "They build ships on what terms they please, and exact the most exorbitant freightage, to the incredible loss of the East India Company," complained one critic. Each ship had a managing owner, known as the ship's husband, and several other shareholders. Rather than compete against one another, the shipowners in this closed circle colluded in a Committee of Managing Owners, which virtually dictated freight rates to the company—a price-fixing scheme that resulted in overcharges of at least £150,000 each year, according to one estimate. The Honourable East India Company's rules precluded the shipowners from actually serving as directors, but through a complex of interlocking financial relationships the fortunes of many leading company shareholders and officers were linked to those of the owners. East India House was virtually helpless against this cabal, referred to as the shipping interest.

In 1786 the potency of this cartel was tested during a dispute over the proper size of the company's ships. The shipping interest championed the cause of a new class of 1,200-ton ships for the booming China tea trade, ostensibly so the company could get lower freight rates. The large ships would cost less per ton to build than did 800-ton vessels and would require only slightly larger crews, the shipowners argued, yet they could stow nearly twice as much cargo. In addition, such formidable ships, said one partisan, "will not only be capable of defending themselves, but the settlements of the Company in India"—a vital duty that was poorly served by the Royal Navy's small East Indies squadron.

Opponents of the scheme—mostly aspiring shipowners who were frozen out of the shipping cartel—conceded that bigger vessels might offer lower rates. But they held that a 1,200-ton ship could not adequately defend herself unless she was, in the words of former company chairman Nathaniel Smith, "properly manned, her guns all mounted, and the middle deck sufficiently cleared either from goods or stores"—strictures that were patently absurd aboard Indiamen, which ordinarily sailed so shorthanded that the crew could barely work the ship, and with cannon dismounted and gun carriages buried under tons of cargo.

Left unsaid in this debate was the real reason for the cartel's espousal of the larger size: The owners figured that the huge cost of a 1,200-ton ship would discourage competition from new investors. The strenuous opposition they met suggested that this cynical calculation was right.

To settle the controversy, the Court of Directors commissioned the *Nottingham* as a test case. But the influence of the shipping interest on company directors was so powerful that the putative experiment was quickly transformed into a full-blown policy. No sooner had the *Nottingham* set off on her maiden voyage than the company contracted for three more 1,200-ton ships. When the *Nottingham* returned to London—having met no adversity en route—the Court of Directors approved a building program that gave 28 new 1,200-ton ships to the China tea routes. Vessels of 800 tons were retained for the dwindling Indian trade only because 1,200-ton ships could not navigate the shallow Indian rivers.

The foresight of the shipping interest was amply demonstrated in 1796, when a rising clamor in Parliament finally forced the company to abolish the hereditary-bottom system and solicit competitive bids for all new ships. A few well-heeled newcomers shouldered their way into the shipowners' clique; but the cartel remained intact, and the company continued to be gouged.

For all their greed, however, the shipowners seldom skimped on the construction of Indiamen. Simple self-interest was partly responsible for the quality of the vessels: Badly built ships might founder and ruin their owners. But cheating would have been difficult even if the owners had been so inclined, since the company's shipping contracts prudently specified every detail of shipbuilding, from the seasoning of timbers to the workmanship of the riggers. A swarm of 55 company surveyors made sure that the specifications were followed to the letter.

Perhaps the single most important reason for the excellence of the East India Company ships was the technical genius of a man named Gabriel Snodgrass, the company's chief surveyor from 1758 until 1797. In his youth Snodgrass had worked as a shipwright in the company's Calcutta repair yards, and when he attained his chief surveyor's position he insisted that English workmen emulate several sophisticated Indian shipbuilding techniques. The traditional butt joint between hull planks was replaced by a stronger, interlocking rabbet joint. The ships were given watertight bulkheads to contain leaks in the hold. And ships were refitted by applying new wooden hull sheathing over the old—a simpler, stronger method than laboriously removing the old sheathing. To remedy a severe shortage of shipbuilding timber—particularly the crooked, or compass, timbers needed for knees—Snodgrass introduced iron throughout the ship, in knees, standards, breasthooks and crutches, until by the turn of the century a new Indiaman contained nearly 100 tons of wrought iron.

Overshadowing all of these innovations were the striking changes Snodgrass proposed in the shape of the ships themselves. Like all other 18th Century European ships, an Indiaman had a traditional tumble-home topside, one that curved sharply inward above the water line, bringing her guns closer to the ship's center line and—in theory at least—improving her stability. Snodgrass was among the first to realize that the tumble-home contours actually encouraged heeling. Drawing on his experience with vertical-sided Bengal rice ships, he argued that straight topsides would make an Indiaman stiffer when heeled, give better support to the masts by increasing the spread of the shrouds and create additional room belowdecks.

Just as important, Snodgrass rejected the prevalent deep-waisted ship design, with poop and forecastle rising above the main deck, which formed a kind of well between them. When a heavy sea crashed amidships, the load of swirling water trapped in the deep waist often threatened to capsize the vessel. Snodgrass introduced flush, well-cambered decks that ran the length of the ship and shed water easily.

Toward the end of his career Snodgrass proudly asserted that "the East India Company's Ships, as now constructed, are the finest and safest Ships in Europe." If all of the shipowners and builders had adhered to Snodgrass' strictures, this boast might well have been true. But many of them stodgily resisted radical changes in ship design—until Snodgrass was vindicated by tragedy. During a series of vicious storms in the winters of 1808 and 1809, 13 Indiamen were lost at sea, among them 10 homebound ships carrying cargo worth one million pounds.

The stunned Court of Directors ordered a thorough inquiry and soon established that all of the lost vessels were deep-waisted. Captain George Millet, a respected mariner who advised the directors, compared the logbooks of two ships that had survived the same storm, the deep-waisted *Huddart* and the flush-decked *Sovereign*. "The *Sovereign* weathered the gale with ease," Millet reported, while the *Huddart* came within a whisker of sinking. When the *Huddart* first shipped a wave she heeled onto her starboard beam-ends and stuck there, righting only after her crew cut away the starboard guns. Another sea heeled her dangerously to port; and although the crew threw overboard "what guns could be gotten at," she continued to wallow helplessly until the storm abated.

Millet concluded with a scathing indictment of deep-waisted ships and, by implication, of the company: "These were a very defective class of ships, over built aloft, and too deep below for their breadth, defects acknowledged by every builder, and felt by every experienced commander. The conclusion is clear, that the deep-waisted ships, when laden, are but ill calculated to encounter gales of wind."

T. S. Raffles: prophetic architect of an island empire

Most of the legions of British men who served the interests of the East India Company as clerks, merchants, seamen, soldiers and governors were fated to everlasting anonymity. But here and there one individual towered above the rest and made history in his own right. Such a man was Sir Thomas Stamford Raffles, a farsighted maverick who gave England one of its richest prizes in the East: the island of Singapore, athwart the sea route from India to China.

Thomas Raffles joined the East India Company as a 14-year-old clerk in 1795 and spent the next decade and a half rising through a series of routine clerical posts in London and the East. From the outset he proved himself anything but a routine servant. On his first foreign assignment, to an outpost on the Malay Peninsula, he took the enterprising step of studying the Malay language on the passage out and was able to speak it well when he arrived. A few years later he persuaded the British authorities in the area to seize Java from the Dutch, who were then under Napoleon's heel in Europe. Raffles, just 30 years old, was made governor.

He exulted in the task now before him. "I am here alone," he wrote, "without any advice, in a new country, with a large native population of six or seven millions of people." He swiftly instituted reforms that won him the profound loyalty of the local princes; where the Dutch had determined what crops the Javanese might grow and had fixed the prices at which they might sell, Raffles allowed them to grow what they pleased and sell on the open market. At the same time, he regaled company officials with pronouncements on the strategic importance of the Malay Peninsula.

Despite attacks of jaundice, he worked an 18-hour day, and it was said that he regularly dictated two letters at once, while penning a third himself. In 1815 he boasted: "I think that my Empire shall soon extend its branches through the Eastern Islands, and in the end become supreme."

He was somewhat premature. The same zeal for reform that won him devotees among the islanders earned him enemies at home; company officials were too preoccupied with India to heed his dream of dominion in the Indies, and were only too glad, in fact, to cede Java back to the Dutch when Napoleon met his downfall in 1815. Raffles then returned to London, where the company directors dallied for the next two years over a reassignment.

When at length they gave him a new post in 1817, it was the governorship of Bencoolen on the west coast of Sumatra, a region so remote that his superiors presumably believed he would be effectively silenced. Raffles himself said the place was "without exception the most wretched I ever beheld." But to that thought he cheerfully added another: "We will try and make it better"—and promptly set about

T. S. Raffles projects the concern that made a Malay recall fondly: "He listened with attention when people spoke to him."

repeating the reforms he had earlier instituted on Java.

All around him, Raffles saw that the Dutch had reasserted themselves more powerfully than ever, and he persisted in importuning East India Company authorities for a proper port of call and naval base on the route between India and China. The island of Singapore—then a mere mangrove swamp inhabited by a few hundred fishermen—was his favorite candidate. It was strategically located right at the tip of the Malay Peninsula, where the Strait of Malacca connects the Indian Ocean with the South China Sea. In 1819, having won the support of the Governor General of India, he negotiated with a local prince for the right to build a factory on the island. Within three years, he had converted Singapore into a thriving port, which he fondly called "my political child."

Raffles had only five years to nurture his progeny. In 1824 he returned again to London, this time plagued with severe headaches and other ailments. By his own account he was "a little old man, all yellow and shriveled." The headaches may have been symptoms of a brain tumor; he died suddenly on July 5, 1826, the day before his 45th birthday. But Singapore lived on and prospered. By midcentury it was doing a yearly trade of five million pounds—and was proving, as Raffles had seen it must, a vital counterpoise to the Dutch East Indies.

The shipping interest's boasts equating a 1,200-ton Indiaman with a ship of the line went untested during the decade of peace that followed the American Revolution. The armament of the smallest Indiaman—generally sixteen 12-pound carronades—was sufficient to deter Malay pirates and all but the most audacious privateers. But in 1793 the infant French republic declared war on England, initiating 22 years of nearly uninterrupted hostilities that could only exacerbate the company's fiscal frailty. The Royal Navy routinely escorted convoys of Indiamen to and from St. Helena, but beyond that Atlantic island the merchantmen usually were on their own, tempting targets for French warships.

The French Navy was still a formidable foe, even after the excesses of the 1789 Revolution had shattered its officer corps and allowed its ships to fall into disrepair. A ponderous East Indiaman was no match for a 20-gun French corvette, much less for a 40-gun frigate. Although the 1,200-ton Indiamen usually were fitted with ports for at least 50 guns, they ordinarily mounted only 30, to leave sufficient room for cargo. Moreover, the crews of Indiamen were seldom large enough to man even the reduced array of guns, particularly on the return voyages. A ship that sailed from London with a 130-man crew ordinarily would lose about 20 men to tropical diseases, and another 20 or so would jump ship in India to seek their fortunes ashore. Still others were taken by government policy: Navy press smacks (small sailing tenders) roamed the Channel, the Thames estuary and Oriental harbors as well, taking the best men from merchant vessels to replenish the crews of His Majesty's ships.

When a press smack approached, sailors aboard an Indiaman resorted to desperate, sometimes comical, ploys to avoid conscription. A passenger on a Bengal-bound vessel reported that "every sailor writhed his limbs and features into the most ludicrous distortions; some limped, some stooped, and all did their utmost to appear decrepit and unfit for service"—but he added that six of the topmen were taken just the same.

More often the crew simply hid in the pitch-black hold—a practice that proved nearly disastrous for one Indiaman in 1802. When the crew of the Lord Eldon saw a three-masted ship loom out of a pea-soup fog off the Isle of Wight, they immediately assumed that it was a Navy vessel and fled belowdecks. The intruder proceeded to crash into the Indiaman, however, and a shocked Captain Jasper Swete stepped out of his comfortable cuddy to find a French privateer grappled alongside, none of his own men in sight and cutlass-wielding brigands swarming over his deck. Bellowing for his crew to repel boarders, he seized his sword and decapitated a Frenchman who had seized the Lord Eldon's helm. Then, as his startled men poured from the hold, he led them in a short, bloody melee, driving the privateers over the side.

The Navy press in Indian seas was even hotter than at home. A 1,200-ton Indiaman visiting the East often lost its 40 best seamen to the Royal Navy's East Indies squadron. They usually were conscripted for a three-year term that, in the pestilential climate of the Indian Ocean, was tantamount to a death sentence. Sailors back in England so feared service in the East Indies squadron that most of them shunned the company's generous wartime wages rather than risk impressment.

The company coped with the deficiency of British sailors by signing on foreigners. One passenger aboard an Indiaman described "a strange motley crew, consisting of natives of almost every nation of Europe, besides Americans and Chinese. Certainly we had not more than 10 English seamen on board."

Chinese sailors and Indian seamen, called lascars, made up nearly two thirds of the crews of some homebound Indiamen. These sober, obedient, hard-working men were treated little better than slaves. They were paid only 10 rupees a month—half of a British seaman's wage—and were fed cheaply on a diet of rice. And they died by the dozens in the squalid East Indiamen. Accustomed to a temperate climate, the Asians were "unable to bear the cold, and utterly incapable of the vigorous exertion and rapid movements necessary in the boisterous seas of Europe," the commander of an Indiaman wrote. In battle the Asian seamen were notoriously unreliable: One captain reported that they "could not by any exertion of the officers be kept to their quarters, deserting as fast as they were brought back."

Despite their puny armament and sorry crews, the Indiamen did possess one advantage in wartime: They looked very much like British warships, even at close quarters. The lines and rigging of a 1,200-ton East Indiaman virtually matched those of a 74-gun ship, and an 800-ton vessel could easily pass for a frigate. The East India fleet made the most of this happy resemblance. The company's captains realized that fleeing from a strange sail would only advertise their weakness, so they often relied instead on a bold, calculated bluff: Acting like pugnacious Royal Navy captains, they steered straight toward the enemy—an intimidating tactic that also concealed an Indiaman's feeble broadside.

One of the first captains to test this daring ruse was Charles Lennox of the 1,180-ton *Woodford*. While leading a convoy of six Indiamen home from Canton in January 1797, he was surprised by a squadron of six French frigates in the Indian Ocean off Java. Lennox quickly hoisted to his mizzen peak the blue flag of a British rear admiral and signaled the other East Indiamen to display the pennants and ensigns of the Royal Navy. Then he cheekily dispatched two vessels to reconnoiter the enemy. When the Indiamen raced toward the French frigate *Cybèle*, her captain hastened to rejoin his squadron and frantically signaled, "The enemy force is superior."

French Rear Admiral Marquis de Sercey quickly withdrew, crowding on so much sail that one of his frigates snapped her main-topmast. Although Sercey, an experienced, feisty commander, thought it strange that the British did not continue the chase, the *Cybèle*'s captain assured him that the enemy squadron consisted of two ships of the line and four frigates. The credulous admiral later reported that he had narrowly eluded British Rear Admiral Peter Rainier and his East Indies squadron. Only when he learned that Rainier had been nowhere in the vicinity did he realize the mortifying truth: He had been duped by a convoy of half-manned Indiamen.

On August 4, 1800, Captain Henry Meriton of the Indiaman *Exeter* fooled the French with a still more outrageous masquerade. Ten weeks after leaving London for Canton, the *Exeter*'s 10-ship convoy, escorted by the 64-gun H.M.S. *Belliqueux*, sighted three French frigates shortly after dawn off the coast of Brazil. The French squadron steered toward the convoy, hoping to bag at least one prize; but by noon, when the distance had closed enough to reveal the Indiamen's two tiers of gunports, the dismayed French scattered.

Royal Navy Captain Rowley Bulteel of the *Belliqueux* dispatched the four 1,200-ton Indiamen in his convoy to chase two of the French frigates while he pursued the fleeing flagship *Concorde*. The *Exeter* and the *Bombay Castle* went after the 36-gun *Medée*, while the *Coutts* and the *Neptune* chased the 36-gun *Franchise*. At 5:30 p.m. the *Belliqueux* captured the *Concorde* without a fight. A little later the frigate *Franchise* jettisoned her boats and some of her guns and anchors and, thus lightened, outran her pursuers. Meanwhile the *Exeter* and the *Medée* raced on into the darkness, with the slower *Bombay Castle* lagging miles behind. Midnight found the 30-gun *Exeter*, with a crew of only 130 men, alone and closing quickly on the *Medée*, with 36 guns and 315 men.

Undaunted, Captain Meriton ordered all 27 of the *Exeter's* port gunports, many of them empty or unmanned, opened and bright lanterns placed behind them, lighting his ship like a fearsome, leering jack-o'-lantern. Then he ran alongside the *Medée* and, in stentorian tones, ordered her to surrender. The French captain, imagining himself under the guns of a British warship, instantly complied, hauling down his flag. As he climbed onto the *Exeter's* quarter-deck to surrender his sword, the Frenchman stared in disbelief at the tiny 18-pound carronades there and asked what ship he had surrendered to. "To a merchantman," Meriton replied. The chagrined Frenchman, seeking to redeem his honor, pleaded to return with his crew to the *Medée* and proceed with a proper battle—a request that Meriton, not unreasonably, declined.

In 1804 the company's unescorted China fleet—an awesome prize laden with eight million pounds' worth of tea, silk and porcelain—trumped all of these exploits. The fleet, under the command of Nathaniel Dance, sailed from Canton on January 31—a stirring spectacle to any seafaring soul. In unison, the crews of the newly painted Indiamen manned the creaking capstans to weigh anchor, the sailors' rhythmic chanteys echoing around the placid Chinese harbor; then one after another the ships sheeted home their sails in a thunder of shivering canvas and heeled before the northeast monsoon. The sixteen 1,200-ton Indiamen in the fleet dwarfed the 11 India-bound country-trade vessels that joined them for the first leg of the voyage.

Exactly two weeks later, as the fleet approached the Strait of Malacca just after daybreak, the 1,200-ton *Royal George* signaled Commodore Dance's flagship *Earl Camden* that she had sighted a number of strange sails hull down to windward, off the island of Pulo Aur. The sails represented an imposing French squadron: the 74-gun *Marengo*, the 40-gun frigate *Belle Poule*, the 36-gun frigate *Sémillante*, the 22-gun corvette *Berceau* and a 16-gun brig. French Rear Admiral Charles Durand-Linois, forewarned of the opulent British convoy by a spy in Canton, had been lying in wait at the mouth of the strait, and now the English ships were within his grasp. He slowly closed on the plodding convoy, scanning it by telescope to gauge its strength.

Dance, a shrewd and experienced leader, quickly formed the India-

Nathaniel Dance, commodore of the British East India Company's China fleet when it outbluffed French warships off the Malay Peninsula in 1804, stands by a table laden with charts of the sort he used during a lifetime at sea. He served the company for 28 years before rising to the rank of captain, then commanded Indiamen for another 17 years.

*Attacked by East Indiamen masquerading as warships (right),
a French fleet under Admiral Charles Linois flees from the Strait
of Malacca in 1804. "Tell Linois," fumed Napoleon to his
Minister of Marine, "that he has shown want of courage of mind."*

men in close line of battle, all the while maintaining his course under easy sail. He ordered the three leading Indiamen to fly the Royal Navy's blue ensign rather than the company's striped red-and-white flag. The precise formation and apparent unconcern of the British fleet worried Linois. He had been led to expect a 24-ship convoy, but now he counted 27 vessels. Suspecting that the three extra ships might be Royal Navy warships, he did not attack immediately. Instead he edged toward the convoy's stragglers. "At near sun set they were close up with our rear, and I was in momentary expectation of an attack there," Dance reported later, "but at the close of day we perceived them haul to windward."

As darkness came on, both fleets snugged down—but not to sleep. Through the hot, sticky night the British crews stood at quarters, barefoot on the sanded decks, stripped to the waist and glistening with sweat, peering out through the gunports toward their unseen adversary. Nothing disturbed their vigil. Linois too was watching closely, seeking clues to the ships' identity. "If the bold front put on by the enemy in the daytime had been a ruse to conceal his weakness, he would have profited by the darkness to endeavour to conceal his escape," the French admiral later wrote; "in that case I should have taken advantage of his maneuvers. But I soon became convinced that this security was not feigned; three of his ships constantly kept their lights up, and the fleet continued to lie to in order of battle throughout the night."

At dawn the British could see the French squadron about three miles to windward. Dance defiantly hoisted his colors; the French followed suit but continued to stand off, and Dance cautiously resumed his course. The French immediately made sail, again edging ominously toward the stragglers.

Finally, at 1 o'clock, Linois decided to attack, cracking on sail to slash through the convoy's rear and cut it off from the supposed escort. Dance immediately played his final card, signaling the Indiamen to tack in succession and double back on Linois—first the *Royal George*, then the *Ganges*, Dance's *Earl Camden*, and the others in turn. This was a desperate gamble: The undermanned Indiamen, always notorious for their sloppy seamanship and undisciplined captains, now were required to crisply execute a difficult naval maneuver and bear resolutely toward an overpowering enemy.

One by one the great Indiamen reversed course, bracing their yards and running toward the French squadron in perfect line, topgallant sails flying. The French hastily formed a line of battle and, as the Indiamen closed the range, began a fearsome barrage on the *Royal George*, slicing her rigging to ribbons and tearing enormous rents in her sails; five minutes later the *Ganges* was engaged, followed at 10-minute intervals by the *Earl Camden*, the *Warley* and the *Alfred*. As each ship entered the billowing cloud of acrid yellow gun smoke that spread over the sea, her world suddenly narrowed: On the cramped gun deck the sailors heaving at the gun tackles were deafened by the thunder of their own cannon and could barely see the outline of their target.

At 2 p.m., 45 minutes after the fighting had begun, the French gunfire ceased. As the smoke began to clear, Dance saw the French bearing off under a full press of sail. Admiral Linois, certain that he was engaging a superior force of British warships and oblivious to the paltry weight of the fire from the Indiamen's 18-pound cannon, had had enough.

As the guns cooled, Dance impertinently capped the hoax by signaling a general chase. For two hours the 16 half-manned Indiamen pursued the unnerved French admiral across the South China Sea, until at 4 p.m. Dance—"fearing a longer pursuit would carry us too far from the mouth of the Streights, and considering the immense property at stake"—hoisted the recall signal. At 8 p.m. the exultant fleet anchored at the mouth of the strait, ready for the uneventful remainder of the voyage. The Indiamen's losses had been negligible: The *Royal George* had one man killed and one wounded, and suffered considerable damage to her hull and rigging, but the other ships were virtually unscathed—a reflection on the marksmanship of the French. "The fire of the enemy seemed to be ill directed, his shot either falling short or passing over us," Dance noted dryly. The French suffered some cut-up rigging, but not a man was injured.

When Dance reached London on August 14, he was given a hero's welcome. King George III received him at court and knighted him, and society hostesses feted him for months. He became a rich man to boot. The Honourable East India Company gratefully awarded him a pension of £500 per annum, and the Bombay Insurance Society presented him with £5,000. In addition, the company appropriated £50,000 for the officers and men of the 16 ships—2,000 guineas for Dance; 1,000 for Captain John F. Timins of the *Royal George*, which had borne the brunt of the action; and proportionately smaller amounts for the rest, ranging down to six guineas for an ordinary seaman.

Although the convoy system served the company well, it was far from foolproof. Extremes of weather—both storms and dead calms—might hopelessly scatter a convoy, leaving its ships to proceed alone to the next scheduled rendezvous. And each year a few Indiamen sailed without convoy. Some the company dispatched singly, taking the risk in order to expedite special cargoes; some were detained in India for repairs; and a few were under the command of corrupt captains who deliberately missed sailing dates to pursue their lucrative private trade in the East. If unlucky enough to be sighted by a French cruiser, these solitary ships were usually easy prey. An exception was the 1,200-ton *Warren Hastings:* The epic battle she fought alone against the French became a legend in the company's fleet.

On the morning of June 21, 1806, the *Warren Hastings* was off Madagascar, driving west by south toward the Cape of Good Hope before a stiff northeasterly wind. Her voyage so far had been relatively uneventful. She had left Canton with a four-ship convoy 11 weeks before, but had lost sight of her consorts during a storm and had sailed on alone. Her manpower and armament were none too impressive. A Royal Navy ship had pressed 18 of her best seamen, leaving a mostly foreign crew of 138. To create additional storage space, four of her main-deck gunports had been calked shut and their guns stowed in the hold, along with four 18-pound carronades from the upper deck. This left 36 mounted guns.

At 7:30 a.m. her masthead lookout descried a sail on the lee bow, to the

The white raja of Sarawak

One of the unlikeliest figures ever to leave his mark on the East was Sir James Brooke, who was so addicted to romantic daydreaming when he was a youth that his family despaired of his ever amounting to anything. True to expectations, he served without distinction in an Army commissary ("a post for which he was totally unfitted," wrote a friend), then idled away whole years fox hunting or traveling. In 1839 his wanderings brought him to the little-known island of Borneo, and there he found adventure and glory beyond his wildest dreams.

The island's northern province of Sarawak was at the time embroiled in war between a feeble Muslim Sultan and rebellious Dyak tribesmen. Brooke plunged into the fray, using his military knowledge to organize the Sultan's motley forces and put down the insurrection. As a reward, the Sultan made him ruler of the province.

He proved a masterful sovereign. In settling his subjects' disputes, he always respected tribal customs, and soon other Borneans began traveling to Sarawak to seek his counsel. "The whole world had heard," one of them recalled, "that the son of Europe was the friend of the Dyak."

Along with peace came prosperity; the people of Sarawak took up trading in rice, antimony and opium with Singapore and China. So secure was Brooke's government that after he died in 1868 his 28,000-square-mile dominion passed to a nephew, and it remained a family possession until a third-generation Brooke ceded it to the British Crown after World War II.

James Brooke, aged 44 in this portrayal, affects the romantic dishevelment of a gentleman-adventurer.

A two-masted vessel under Brooke's command blasts two Malay proas in 1843, opening a six-year campaign to rid his coast of piracy.

southwest. Captain Thomas Larkins held his course, bringing the stranger into clearer view. She flew no colors, but was in fact the French 46-gun frigate *Piémontaise*, Captain Jacques Epron commanding, with a crew of 385 and an uncommonly heavy weight of ordnance. On her main deck she carried 28 long 18-pounders; on her quarter-deck and forecastle she had twelve 36-pound carronades, two long 8-pounders and four long 9-pounders; and on her gunwales and in her tops she mounted a veritable arsenal of swivel guns.

At 9 o'clock the *Piémontaise* came about and headed toward the *Warren Hastings*, as if to speak with her; 30 minutes later she added topgallant sails and fore- and main-topmast studding sails. At 10 o'clock the frigate, still about 10 miles away, hoisted the British Navy's blue ensign and pennants. Larkins, wary of the ship's speedy approach, replied by hoisting the company flag—but with it he flew the Admiralty's private signal, a recognition code used to identify British ships. The *Piémontaise* failed to answer. The *Warren Hastings* held course until 11 o'clock, but as the Frenchman approached, Larkins prudently shortened sail and cleared for action.

Just after noon the *Piémontaise* came within a mile to leeward of the Indiaman and replaced the British ensign with the French tricolor. Next, Captain Epron closed until he was only 400 yards from the Indiaman's port quarter.

At last the frigate opened fire, loosing a 15-minute series of broadsides, while the British crew hotly returned the fire. The Frenchman then pulled a mile and a half ahead, out of range. Considering the Indiaman's handicap—her 18-gun broadside totaled only 312 pounds, compared with 23 guns and 494 pounds for the *Piémontaise*—she had not fared badly in this exchange, suffering only some cut rigging.

The *Piémontaise* quickly came about and within an hour passed close to leeward again, pumping broadsides into the Indiaman's hull and rigging. In a hail of jagged oak slivers, several of the *Warren Hastings'* crew were killed and her top-hamper was grievously damaged. The foremast was nearly shot through, the fore shrouds were sliced to ribbons, many of the stays were cut and the ensign was shot away. Unable to maneuver, Larkins held his course; one sailor scampered to the masthead and nailed up another ensign, while others hastily patched the rigging. Meanwhile, the *Piémontaise* tacked neatly and loosed a third flurry of broadsides at the shattered port side of the *Warren Hastings*, crippling the foremast beyond repair.

Another hour later, on her fourth pass, the frigate shredded virtually all of the remaining rigging on the *Warren Hastings*, splintered her mainmast and knocked two of the quarter-deck carronades off their carriages. At this point there was no hope left. The *Warren Hastings* had lost five men killed and five wounded; the main-topsail, the only canvas still flying, was precariously straining the damaged mainmast; and the vessel was wallowing helplessly in the heavy seas. But still the Indiaman returned ragged, defiant broadsides at the frigate, killing seven Frenchmen and injuring five.

At 4:30 p.m. the *Piémontaise* closed for the kill. Captain Epron set his ship alongside his opponent's port quarter and poured in a relentless,

*The British East Indiaman Warren
Hastings (left), bested in an epic fight with
the French frigate Piémontaise
off Madagascar on June 21, 1806, waits
forlornly as the victor's crewmen row
through a tossing sea to seize their prize.*

devastating fire. One 18-pound ball crashed into the cockpit, smashing the surgeon's instruments in the middle of an amputation; another hurtled through the counter and set the gun deck aflame, driving the remaining gun crews topside. On deck the spanker boom was smashed to bits, and the steering tackle failed, immobilizing the rudder. Finally a 36-pound ball struck the mizzenmast, snapping it like a matchstick, toppling it forward and disabling every remaining upper-deck gun.

While the French gunners paused, Captain Larkins surveyed his ship—now a shattered, flame-licked hulk, with seven men dead and 13 wounded—and reluctantly ordered his boatswain to strike the flag. But the bloodshed did not end there. As the rudderless *Warren Hastings* drifted in the plunging seas, the French frigate bore up to avoid a collision—and in the process accidentally filled her main-topsail, which quickly carried her into the Indiaman's port bow with a shivering crash that locked the ships together. Immediately a boarding party of Frenchmen armed with cutlasses, drunk as lords and gibbering with rage, clambered onto the Indiaman, screaming that she had rammed their ship.

Their vengeance was bloody indeed. They brutalized the stalwart Captain Larkins, dragging him around the deck of his disfigured ship; then the frigate's first lieutenant stabbed him in the side with a poniard. The furious lieutenant next ordered Larkins, who was spurting blood

and near collapse, to jump across to the frigate's deck, and would have
driven him into the sea if another French officer had not intervened. The
crazed boarders stabbed four other officers and pillaged the wrecked
Indiaman before Captain Epron managed to restore order, attend to the
survivors and take his prize in tow.

After recovering from their wounds at Mauritius, Captain Larkins
and his crew were released and reached London aboard a neutral vessel
in late November, 1806. They found that their heroic defense had become a cause célèbre. The Court of Directors acquitted Larkins of "all
imputations of neglect," awarding him 500 guineas and voting a £2,000
gratuity to be shared among the crew; and British newspapers in London
and Calcutta excoriated the dastardly French. But all of these encomi-
ums did not recompense Larkins for his monetary losses, both from
captured private trade goods and from the cost of repatriating the ship's
company. The directors rejected his request for financial relief and also
denied his appeal to the company's benevolent fund for seamen—a fund
that more than once had supplied relief to needy directors.

As the years passed the French continued to do damage to the company
in a variety of ways. In India, French agents fomented a series of upris-
ings against the British, forcing the company to make military expenditures it could ill afford. Worse, the Napoleonic Wars, lasting until 1815,
virtually eliminated the lucrative Continental market for Indian goods
and at the same time allowed foreign ships and merchants, who as neu-
trals did not have to pay the same exorbitant wartime insurance rates
that were levied on British vessels, to undercut company prices and
invade its markets at home and abroad.

To be sure, there were some bright spots in the company's financial
picture. The tea monopoly continued to flourish, turning a clear profit of
one million pounds each year. And in one respect protracted war actually helped the company: It created a constant demand for Indian saltpeter, a vital component of gunpowder. On the strength of these few
successes, the company chose to affect a public pose of supreme confidence. In April 1800 the directors formally dedicated what was called
the new East India House, a magisterial structure that was deemed better
suited to John Company's eminence than the unassuming four-story
building that had served as India House since 1729.

The new edifice had an enormous neoclassical Portland-stone front
200 feet long and 60 feet high, with a center portico dominated by six
fluted Ionic columns. Surmounting the portico was a sculpted pediment
with an extravagant allegory: It depicted a robed woman, representing
Asia, pouring out her treasures at the feet of Britannia, while Mercury
(symbolizing commerce) introduced the two. Above these figures an
effigy of King George III—dressed in Roman costume and holding his
sword like a cane in his left hand—defended the commerce of the East.
But the most noteworthy characteristic of the new building was that it
was not a new building at all: It was, literally, a mere façade. Behind it
nestled the same old four-story edifice with its hodgepodge of offices,
meeting rooms, salesroom and storage spaces.

The imposing front of East India House masked the ominous truth:

An English bumbler's progress in the mysterious East

As the British East India Company entered its third century, thousands of Englishmen sailed forth to its Indian empire each year, some to seek their fortunes as business agents for the great enterprise, others to serve in the army scattered across the dusty distances of the subcontinent. Almost to a man, they were altered by the experience—often in ways that their countrymen back home found exceedingly droll.

A few acquired prodigious wealth and equally prodigious egos; they came to be known as nabobs, after the Indian term for "princeling." Others developed a permanent taste for such decidedly un-English sustenance as spiced meats, chutney, and an Indian punch brewed from wine, rose water and citron juice. The process of adjusting to this alien land naturally had its bumpy moments, and veterans of Indian service took considerable delight in the gaffes of newcomers, whom they called "griffins."

In 1828 connoisseurs of the Indian scene had their collective funny bone tickled by the appearance of a little book entitled *Tom Raw, the Griffin*, "a burlesque poem in twelve cantos." The poem was attributed to a transparently pseudonymous Mr. Quilldrive, and the 25 satirical engravings accompanying it to an unnamed artist. Actually, both artist and author were the same person: Sir Charles D'Oyly, the seventh Baronet of Shottisham, who spent more than 40 years in India serving in various posts from court clerk to customs collector for the opium trade.

Sir Charles's poem, written in mock-heroic style and running to more than 6,000 lines, recounts the career of Tom Raw from the time of his appointment as a cadet in the East India Company army at

"... Fort William,
A well-constructed fort with nought to do
But to receive new regiments and grill 'em,
(If they arrive in May or June—to kill 'em),"

through a variety of adventures in various locales of the Indian subcontinent.

A gently satiric tone prevails throughout. Tom, whose parents have secured the cadetship to get him out of the crowded family nest, is the quintessential bumbler, muddling his way through any number of ludicrous predicaments and emerging triumphant in spite of himself. British readers loved him—partly for his pratfalls, and also because his saga contained a wealth of accurate information about the far-off country that had become so bound up with their position in the world.

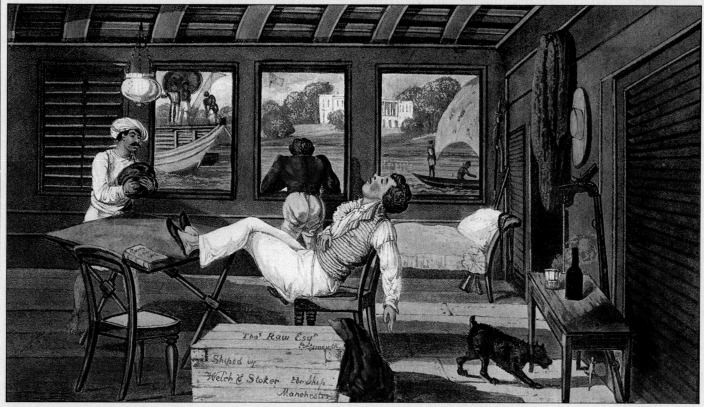

Oblivious to the passing scenery, cadet Tom Raw naps in the cabin of a riverboat as he sets forth on his first assignment to the Indian hinterland.

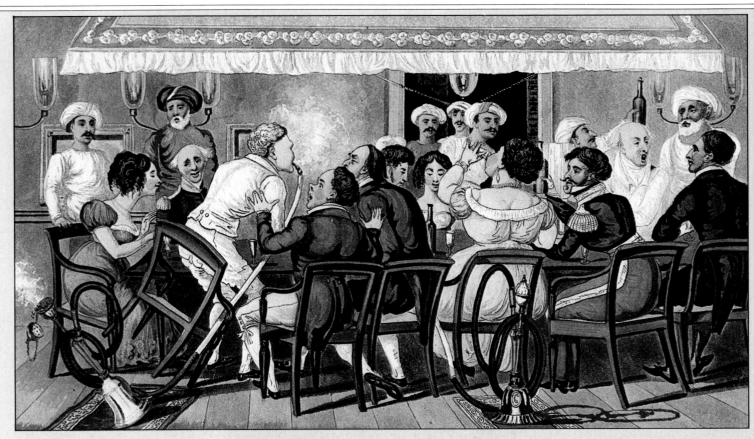

During a dinner party in Calcutta, Tom flings up his hands in dismay at the hectic, odoriferous proceedings. The two officials crowding him on either side are puffing on hookahs, serpentine pipes that draw smoke through scented water.

At the home of a rich Hindu, Tom strikes an insouciant pose as he studies two live dancing girls and a sculpture portraying the multiarmed Durga, Hindu goddess of war, in whose honor the dance was performed. Some affluent Englishmen adopted the Indian custom of keeping dancing girls in their homes.

Sent upcountry on a new assignment, Tom hangs on for dear life as the rattan floor of his palanquin gives way and —in the poem's words—drops him "stern foremost." Following the lead of wealthy Indians, Europeans commonly traveled in these man-powered vehicles.

Invited on a tiger hunt—the sport of rajahs—Tom unceremoniously evacuates his riding car as a Bengal tiger claws its way up the elephant's side. Only a timely shot from the gun of his friend behind saves Tom from the clutches of the cat.

Tom meets the commander of his new regiment, a crusty soldier who has taken up smoking a hookah and dressing during the day in Indian pajamas. In the background, the commander's daughter surveys the new arrival with interest.

Wounded in the thigh during his first encounter with Indian rebels, Tom sits out the battle. This incident brought the tale of Tom Raw to a happy ending: Taking his wound as proof of military prowess, the army rewarded Tom with a promotion and a yearly pension of £100—assuring a life of ease in India.

John Company was sinking inexorably into a morass of debt. Even by the company's own optimistic estimates, it owed £14.5 million by 1800 and more than £26 million by 1807. Despite annual projections of an imminent profit, it was losing almost four million pounds a year by 1812. The company sought to repay the debts by expanding commerce between Britain and India, but the growth of the British Industrial Revolution thwarted that attempt and actually aggravated the company's plight. With the advent of spinning jennies and power looms, British textile manufacturers could sell cotton cloth at a lower price than the company charged for its hand-woven Indian textiles. A single Lancashire factory worker could spin as much yarn as 40 Indians could, and the machine-made fabrics were indistinguishable from handmade Indian muslins and calicoes. By 1808 the company's sales had suffered so badly from domestic competition that its London warehouses held £7,148,000 worth of unsold Indian merchandise.

Strangely, this desperate situation aroused little alarm among the Court of Directors and the company's 1,800 shareholders. Even as its debts soared, the company continued to pay the statutory maximum dividend of 10½ per cent per year on its shares. The reason for such fiscal recklessness was simple: While the company withered, its directors and shareholders were waxing ever richer. Nor were self-serving dividends the only way the directors wrung wealth from their positions. The 24 directors took turns appointing clerks, cadets, surgeons and chaplains for the company's Indian service and collecting the patronage fees the appointees paid for their positions—payments that totaled more than £10,000 a year for each director. In addition, most directors maintained lucrative, illicit connections with the company's business partners, not least the shipping interest. "There is a numerous body of proprietors whose great object is to serve THEMSELVES," fumed James Fiott, a crusading shareholder who vainly attacked the system. "However the company may decline, they are sure of prosperity; and, in some cases, in exact proportion to that decline."

The company's financial straits provided a heaven-sent opportunity for the provincial British merchants and shipowners who long had fought to enter the India trade. As the company's charter came up for renewal in 1813, merchants and manufacturers from Glasgow, Bristol, Liverpool, Edinburgh, Manchester, Birmingham and Exeter descended on London, lobbying the government to open the India trade to all comers. As evidence of the company's ineptitude they cited its burgeoning debt and its bungled attempts to develop commerce with India.

The Court of Directors resisted with all its strength, forcing a showdown in Parliament. But the tide was turning against John Company. In July 1813 the House of Commons voted to let the company keep its China monopoly and the civil government of India, but it opened Indian trade to all vessels over 350 tons. "I had no idea we stood on such weak ground," said Sweny Toone, a veteran company director. "If an additional article was proposed to cut off the heads of two or more of the Directors, the House would have voted it by a very great majority."

Rivals on the routes to the Orient produced one unanticipated effect: The normally stately Indiamen and their overcautious captains surprised everyone with the speedy passages they made when faced with competition. Previously, the company's ships had been a poor school for seamanship: They rode under leisurely sail, heaved to at the first sign of a blow and took in royals and topgallant sails at night. There were no bonuses for a captain who crowded on sail; if anything, shipowners would censure him for the unnecessary wear and tear. The company's ships were so slow that news of the stunning British victory at Waterloo reached Calcutta via New York, aboard an American ship.

The spur of competition changed all that, because markets could be lost by dawdling at sea. Private British vessels raced company ships to India, and American interlopers began to challenge the tea monopoly in China. In 1817 a lone American merchantman astonished London shipowners by sailing from Canton to England in just 108 days, half an Indiaman's normal run. The Indiamen rose to the occasion, and only a few months later the company's entire China fleet of 13 heavily laden Indiamen covered the same distance in 109 days—a coup one proud London newspaper hailed as "a triumph of mercantile navigation, of which there is no record of an equal exertion."

But despite their new-found speed, John Company's ships turned out to be poorly suited to the cut and thrust of competition. The Indiamen had become obsolete. They cost nearly twice as much to build as did an ordinary merchantman and required twice as many seamen. As a stable peace descended on Europe and piracy waned in the face of improved naval protection along the Eastern routes, their gun decks became a colossal waste of space. So while private merchants, untrammeled by the exorbitant freights aboard Indiamen and the company's complacent bureaucracy, developed profitable Indian commerce—exporting cotton cloth, copper, iron, tin and lead, and importing Indian silk, indigo, raw cotton, saltpeter, sugar and rice—John Company quietly abandoned the Indian trade altogether. After 1826 company vessels concentrated entirely on the China tea trade and on carrying British men and matériel to the company's 40,000-man Anglo-Indian establishment.

The sailing Indiamen did not survive long as passenger liners, however. In 1824 the merchants of Calcutta had offered a lac of rupees—the equivalent of £10,500—to the first steamship that sailed between England and Bengal in less than 70 days. And on August 16, 1825, Captain James Henry Johnston took up the challenge, departing from London aboard the side-wheel steamship *Enterprise*. Clanking, wheezing and belching a great cloud of sooty black smoke, this ungainly 470-ton vessel seemed better suited to a sheltered lake than to the open ocean. With 120 nominal horsepower, she could do no better than nine knots. But the doughty *Enterprise* was eminently reliable. After 113 days—10 of them at coaling stations—she steamed into Calcutta, the first vessel to complete the voyage primarily under steam. And although Captain Johnston had failed to make the journey within the stipulated time, the merchants graciously awarded him £10,000 in recognition of his services in the cause of steam navigation.

Steamships like the *Enterprise* did not compete directly with sail-powered Indiamen until 1842, when the Peninsular and Oriental Line inaugurated monthly service around the Cape of Good Hope. But beginning in 1827 the company used steamships in a combination sea-and-overland service to India. Passengers took a steam vessel from Marseilles to Alexandria, traveled by canal and Nile riverboat to Cairo, then endured a bone-shaking 60-hour ride in a horse-drawn carriage across the desert to Suez. There they boarded a steamship that traversed the windless reaches of the Red Sea and crossed the Indian Ocean to Bombay. This complicated itinerary reduced the journey to as little as 61 days, nearly three months less than an Indiaman's usual voyage. Baggage was hauled overland by camel, and soon the route was so popular that 3,000 beasts were needed for each steamer's lading. The only passengers left aboard the Indiamen were the King's troops, who had no choice.

Steamships moved company personnel more quickly than Indiamen could, but they did not improve the organization's economic health. By 1833 the company's finances were in almost total chaos; its debts had mounted to nearly £40 million and would have soared even higher without the annual one million pounds' profit on Chinese tea. And when the company's charter came up for renewal in that year, the loss of the China monopoly was a foregone conclusion.

The British public and the government finally had lost patience with the coddled company. They felt, with considerable justice, that provincial merchants had been unfairly excluded from the China trade and that the company had greedily inflated the price of tea. The directors half-heartedly fought to retain the monopoly, but privately they had conceded defeat. In June 1833 Parliament ordered John Company to cease trading altogether. In exchange, the government provided a handsome reparation, guaranteeing that for the next 40 years shareholders would receive a 10½ per cent dividend—some £630,000 a year. The company would continue to function only as the government of India.

The Honourable East India Company retained civil and military authority over India mainly because no one in Parliament could decide how to replace it. Thomas B. Macaulay, a member of the Board of Control and later a famous Whig historian, admitted in Parliament: "It is strange, very strange, that a joint stock company of traders should be entrusted with the sovereignty of a large population. But what constitution can we give to our Indian Empire which shall not be strange? That Empire is itself the strangest of all political anomalies." So a succession of well-meaning governors general continued to negotiate the same tenuous alliances with Indian rulers, to fight the same interminable wars and to incur the same unending debts as their predecessors had since Robert Clive's day. And as always, controlling India was an anxious, nerve-racking business. Like a circus tiger, the populace of India was trained but scarcely tamed.

The end came in 1857 with the suddenness of a thunderbolt. The sepoys, Indian soldiers employed by the company, had chafed for years at Western encroachments on Indian culture and religion. Now the British began equipping them with the new Enfield rifle, which used cartridges that—at least according to a rumor that raced through the sepoy barracks—had been greased with beef fat, a forbidden substance that would forever defile any Hindu who touched it. When a callous British general at Meerut, 40 miles from Delhi, imprisoned 85 sepoys who had

The British steamship Enterprise, pictured here flying her auxiliary sails, enters the Madras roadstead in 1825. As the first ship to make the passage from London under steam, she marked the beginning of the end for Indiamen; within two years, 80 steamers would follow her into the Eastern trade routes.

refused to touch the cartridges, his three Indian regiments mutinied, massacring every European they could find.

The mutiny flashed through Bengal like wildfire. (The term "mutiny" actually is a time-honored British misnomer; the conflict, while spontaneous, was an all-out war, the most general and vicious struggle Britain had ever faced in India.) The East India Company lost the cities of Delhi, Cawnpore, Lucknow and Jhansi, and the company's employees in better-protected posts were obliged to wait in helpless terror for seven months until 16,000 Royal Army troops arrived to put down the rebellion. Even then, the war raged on for more than a year. Before the slaughter ended, 11,000 Europeans and untold thousands of Indians had died, and both sides had committed grisly atrocities that would sear the memory of generations to come.

The shocked British public immediately seized on the predictable, convenient and largely deserving scapegoat: the Honourable East India Company, with its faded, antique aura of privilege and ineptitude. On August 2, 1858, Queen Victoria signed the Government of India Act, a bill that abolished the East India Company and vested its possessions and powers in the Crown—which also assumed John Company's debt, by now a staggering £100 million.

On September 1 the company's directors assembled in their ornate room for the last time and issued an eloquent if self-serving farewell: "Let Her Majesty appreciate the gift—let her take the vast country and the teeming millions of India under her direct control; but let her not forget the great corporation from which she has received them."

By that time John Company's once-proud fleet was only a memory. Even before Parliament voted in 1833 to stop the company from trading, the Court of Directors had anticipated the inevitable and had ceased ordering new ships. Between 1830 and 1834 the owners in the cartel had sold virtually all of their Indiamen. Most were well-worn ships that had completed several voyages, and one third of them went straight to the ship breakers' yard. Even as scrap they fetched good prices, because of their excellent timber and fittings: £7,200 for the *Waterloo*, £4,100 for the *Atlas*, £5,750 for the *Canning*, £6,600 for the *General Harris*, £5,900 for the *London*.

Indiamen with some years of service left in them were purchased at bargain prices by Parsi merchants in India, by their own captains or occasionally by London shipping concerns. The *Earl of Balcarres* and the *Thames* each brought £10,700 and the *Buckinghamshire* went for £10,550, but the average price was about £7,900. None of these kettle-bottomed anachronisms returned to the East Indies trade, which came to be dominated by fast, economical cargo vessels called Blackwall frigates, and later by even faster clipper ships. A few Indiamen briefly eked out an ignominious living carrying emigrants to Australia or working as tramp freighters. But by the 1850s the only ones still afloat were coaling barges or anchored ships that served as prisons. The country-trade ships of India, those rot-resistant teak simulacra of Indiamen, lasted considerably longer; the last one on record ended her days in the 1920s as a dismasted coal hulk at Gibraltar, plodding across the harbor behind a tugboat to replenish the bunkers of steamships.

Arriving home after the suppression of the Indian Mutiny of 1857, a British soldier shows a welcoming crowd the medal he earned for bravery, and two seamen help a wounded sergeant ashore. After the rebellion, two thirds of the East India Company's 15,000 troops returned to Britain, many of them grown rich on plunder.

Bibliography

Boxer, C. R.:
The Dutch Seaborne Empire: 1600-1800. Alfred A. Knopf, 1965.
The Portuguese Seaborne Empire: 1415-1825. Alfred A. Knopf, 1969.

Burnell, Arthur C. and P. A. Tiele, eds., The Voyage of John Huyghen van Linschoten to the East Indies. London: Hakluyt Society, 1885.

Chadhuri, K. N.:
The English East India Company 1600-1640. London: Frank Cass, 1965.
The Trading World of Asia and the East India Company 1660-1760. Cambridge: Cambridge University Press, 1978.

Chatterton, E. Keble:
The Mercantile Marine. London: William Heinemann, 1923.
The Old East Indiamen. London: T. Werner Laurie, 1953.

Crowhurst, Patrick, The Defence of British Trade 1689-1815. Kent: William Dawson & Sons, 1977.

Davis, Ralph, The Rise of the English Shipping Industry in the Seventeenth and Eighteenth Centuries. Newton Abbot: David & Charles, 1962.

Forrest, Sir George, Life of Clive. London: Cassell, 1918.

Foster, Sir William:
The English Factories in India, 1618-1621. Oxford: Clarendon Press, 1906.
England's Quest of Eastern Trade. London: A. C. Black, 1933.

Foster, Sir William, ed., The Voyage of Thomas Best to the East Indies, 1612-1614. London: Hakluyt Society, 1934.

Fryke, Christopher and Christopher Schweitzer, Voyages to the East Indies. London: Cassell, 1929.

Furber, Holden, John Company at Work: A Study of European Expansion in India in the Late Eighteenth Century. Octagon Books, 1970.

Gascoigne, Bamber, The Great Moghuls. Harper & Row, 1971.

Grey, Charles, The Merchant Venturers of London. London: H.F.&G. Witherby, 1932.

Hakluyt Society, The, The Voyages of Sir James Lancaster to Brazil and the East Indies 1591-1603. London: 1940.

Hannay, David, The Great Chartered Companies. London: Williams & Norgate, 1926.

Hickey, William, Memoirs of William Hickey (Alfred Spencer, ed.). London: Hurst & Blackett, 1925.

James, William, The Naval History of Great Britain. London: Richard Bentley & Son, 1886.

Ketting, Herman, Prins Willem. Haarlem: De Boer Maritiem, 1979.

Lacey, Robert, Sir Walter Raleigh. London: Weidenfeld & Nicholson, 1973.

Lubbock, Basil, The Blackwall Frigates. Glasgow: Brown, Son & Ferguson, 1973.

Lubbock, Basil, ed., Barlow's Journal of His Life at Sea in King's Ships, East & West Indiamen & Other Merchantmen from 1659 to 1703. London: Hurst & Blackett, 1934.

Marsden, Peter, The Wreck of the Amsterdam. Stein and Day, 1975.

Morse, Hosea B., The Chronicles of the East India Company Trading to China. Harvard University Press, 1926.

Mottram, R. H., Traders' Dream: The Romance of the East India Company. D. Appleton-Century, 1939.

Nugent, Maria, Lady Nugent's Journal: Jamaica One Hundred and Thirty-Eight Years Ago (Frank Cundall, ed.). London: West India Committee, 1939.

Parkinson, C. Northcote, Trade in the Eastern Seas 1793-1813. Cambridge: Cambridge University Press, 1937.

Parr, Charles McKew, Jan van Linschoten: The Dutch Marco Polo. Thomas Y. Crowell, 1964.

Parry, John H., Trade and Dominion. London: Weidenfeld & Nicholson, 1971.

Philips, C. H., The East India Company, 1784-1834. Barnes & Noble, 1961.

Ramsay, G. D., English Overseas Trade during the Centuries of Emergence. London: Macmillan, 1957.

Ukers, William H., All about Tea. Tea & Coffee Trade Journal, 1935.

Wilbur, Marguerite Eyer, The East India Company and the British Empire in the Far East. Russell & Russell, 1970.

Acknowledgments

The index for this book was prepared by Gale Linck Partoyan. The editors wish to thank the following: Gerard J. A. Raven, consultant; John Batchelor, artist, and William Avery Baker, consultant (pages 125-127); Peter McGinn, artist (endpaper maps); Richard Schlecht, artist, and William Avery Baker, consultant (pages 112-119).

The editors also thank: In Australia: Fremantle—The Department of Maritime Archaeology, The Western Australian Museum. In Denmark: Copenhagen—Joan Hornby, Curator, Ethnographical Department, Danish National Museum; Ebba Waaben, Archivist, National Archives. In France: Paris—Edwige Archier, Curator, François Avril, Curator, Henriette Ozanne, Curator, Bibliothèque Nationale; Commissaire Général Pierre Jullien; Marie-Hélène Babelon, Mobilier National; Intendant Jean de LaSalle, Curator, Lieutenant Colonel Marc Neuville, Curator, Colonel Paul Willing, Curator, Musée de l'Armée; Henri Marchal, Curator, Sophie Amet, Researcher, Musée des Arts Africains et Océaniens; Daniel Alcouffe, Curator, Musée du Louvre; Marcel Redouté, Curator, Hervé Cras, Director for Historical Studies, Marjolaine Mathikine, Librarian, Denise Chaussegroux, Researcher, Musée de la Marine; Lorient—André Garrigues, Curator, Musée de Lorient; Saint-Malo—Dan Lailler, Curator, Musée de Saint-Malo; Colonel Hervé de Torquat; Vincennes—Marie-Annick Hepp, Curator, Service Historique de l'Armée de Terre. In Hong Kong: Kowloon—Monique McClellan, Editor, Heinemann Educational Books. In Japan: Tokyo—Tadao Takamizawa, Director, Takamizawa Institute; Kobe—Kobe Municipal Museum of Nanban Art; Osaka—Yoshiro Kitamura, Nanban Bunkakan. In the Netherlands: Amsterdam—Amsterdams Historisch Museum; Gemeentelijke Archiefdienst; Kweekschool Voor de Zeevaart; Herman Ketting, Restorer, Department of Dutch History, Rijksmuseum; Rijksmuseum Nederlands Scheepvaart Museum; The Hague—Koninklijk Huisarchief; Algemeen Rijksarchief; Martin de Vries, Photographer; Hoorn—Westfries Museum; Leyden—Bibliotheek Rijksuniversiteit; Stedelijk Museum de Lakenhal; Rotterdam—Maritiem Museum Prins Hendrik; Museum Boymans-Van Beuningen; Atlas Van Stolk. In Portugal: Lisbon—Alexandre Marques Pereira, Librarian, Library Staff, Sociedade de Geografia de Lisboa. In Sweden: Bålsta—Karin Skeri, Curator, Skoklosters Slott. In the United Kingdom: London—A.V.B. Norman, Howard Blackmore, Guy Wilson, The Armouries, H. M. Tower of London; British Broadcasting Corporation; A. C. Robinson, Lance Pordes, Department of Western Manuscripts, British Library; Mildred Archer, Pauline Rohatgi, Ruth Allen, Department of Prints and Drawings, Anthony Farrington, Marine Records, Ian Baxter, John Sims, Records, India Office Library; London Library; Stephen Wood, Aubrey Bowden, Department of Uniforms, Marion Harding, Library, National Army Museum; E.H.H. Archibald, Roger Quarm, Elizabeth Tucker, Picture Department, John Munday, Rena Prentice, Weapons and Antiquities Department, David Lyon, Stephen Riley, Ships Department, Joan Moore, Photographic Sales Department, National Maritime Museum; Bertram Newbury, Parker Gallery; Society for Nautical Research; Dartmouth—Harbor Master; Hertford—Professor Charles R. Boxer; Kent—Richard Knight.

The editors also wish to thank: In the United States: Washington, D.C.—Philip

M. Nagao, Japanese Section/Oriental Division, Library of Congress; Annandale, Virginia—Caroline Sigrist; Bethesda, Maryland—Lucinda H. Keister, Prints and Photographs Librarian, History of Medicine Division, National Library of Medicine; Boston, Massachusetts—Boston Tea Party Ship and Museum; Carl L. Crossman, Colleene Fesko, Childs Gallery; Massachusetts Historical Society; Fairfax, Virginia—Inger Raymond; New Haven, Connecticut—Yale Center for British Art; New York, New York—Russell Burrows; Sheila Curl, Francis Mattson, Daniel Traister, Rare Book Division, Anna Lou Ashby, Spencer Collection, The New York Public Library; Salem, Massachusetts—A. Paul Winfisky, Keeper of Prints, Peabody Museum; San Francisco, California—Yoshiko Kakudo, Curator of Japanese Art, Asian Art Museum of San Francisco, The Avery Brundage Collection; Silver Spring, Maryland—Sigrid Block; Whitehall, Virginia—Susan Bryan.

Valuable sources of quotations were *The Voyage of John Huyghen van Linschoten to the East Indies*, edited by Arthur C. Burnell and P. A. Tiele, The Hakluyt Society, 1885; *The Voyages of Sir James Lancaster to Brazil and the East Indies 1591-1603* by The Hakluyt Society, 1940; and *Memoirs of William Hickey*, edited by Alfred Spencer, Hurst & Blackett, 1925.

Picture Credits

Credits from left to right are separated by semicolons, from top to bottom by dashes.

Cover: Derek Bayes, courtesy National Maritime Museum, London. Front and back endpapers: Drawing by Peter McGinn.
Page 3: Réunion des Musées Nationaux, courtesy Musée Guimet, Paris. 6, 7: Rijksmuseum, Amsterdam. 9: Estudio M. Novais, courtesy Biblioteca da Ajuda. 10, 11: Photo Bibliothèque Nationale, Paris. 14, 15: Library of Congress. 16: Courtesy of the Marquess of Salisbury. 17: Derek Bayes, courtesy Skinner's Hall, London. 19: Frank Lerner, courtesy Rare Book Division, The New York Public Library, Astor, Lenox and Tilden Foundations. 21: India Office Library, London. 22: Library of Congress. 24, 25: Frank Lerner, courtesy Rare Book Division, The New York Public Library, Astor, Lenox and Tilden Foundations. 26, 27: Photo Bibliothèque Nationale, Paris. 28, 29: Photo Bibliothèque Nationale, Paris (2)—Giraudon, courtesy Photo Bibliothèque Nationale, Paris. 30, 31: Photo Bibliothèque Nationale, Paris. 32, 33: Rare Book Division, The New York Public Library, Astor, Lenox and Tilden Foundations. 34, 35: Library of Congress. 37: Photo Bibliothèque Nationale, Paris. 39: Giraudon, courtesy Bibliothèque du Ministère des Armées, Paris. 40, 41: Rigsarkivet, Copenhagen—Det Nationalhistoriske Museum, Frederiksborg Slot, Copenhagen; Olof Ekberg, Skokloster Castle, Bålsta. 43: Rare Book Division, The New York Public Library, Astor, Lenox and Tilden Foundations. 44: Rijksmuseum, Amsterdam. 45: Westfries Museum, Hoorn. 46, 47: Collectie Kweekschool voor de Zeevaart, Amsterdam. 48, 49: Amsterdams Historisch Museum. 51: Marcello Vivarelli, courtesy Biblioteca Casanatense, Rome. 52, 53: By permission of the British Library, London (Ms. Sloane 197, f.155 v/156). 54: Library of Congress. 55: Mauro Pucciarelli, courtesy Museu da Marinha, Lisbon—Kobe Municipal Museum of Nanban Art, Japan. 56, 57: Collection of Kimiko and John Powers—Nanban Bunkakan, Osaka. 58: Eugene Fuller Memorial Collection, Seattle Art Museum—C. R. Boxer. 59: Rijksmuseum Nederlands Scheepvaart Museum, Amsterdam. 60, 61: National Maritime Museum, London. 62, 63: Gemeentelijke Archiefdienst, Amsterdam. 65: Rijksmuseum, Amsterdam. 66, 67: Martin de Vries, courtesy Rijksmuseum, Amsterdam. 68: Rijksmuseum, Amsterdam. 70: National Library of Medicine. 73: Amsterdams Historisch Museum. 75-77: Library of Congress. 78: Derek Bayes, courtesy National Maritime Museum, London. 80, 81: Rijksmuseum, Amsterdam. 82: Rijksmuseum Nederlands Scheepvaart Museum, Amsterdam. 84: Maritiem Museum Prins Hendrik, Rotterdam—Museum Boymansvan Beuningen, Rotterdam. 86, 87: Derek Bayes, courtesy National Maritime Museum, London. 88, 89: Nationalmuseet, Etnografisk Samling, Copenhagen. 90: Mark Sexton, courtesy Peabody Museum of Salem. 93: The Metropolitan Museum of Art, Rogers Fund, 1942. 94, 95: Nationalmuseet, Etnografisk Samling, Copenhagen. 96: Estudio M. Novais, courtesy A. Medeiros de Almeida, Lisbon—The Metropolitan Museum of Art, Winfield Foundation Gift, 1958; The Helena Woolworth McCann Collection. 97: The Metropolitan Museum of Art, Rogers Fund, 1916; The Metropolitan Museum of Art, Purchase, Winfield Foundation Gift, 1962, The Helena Woolworth McCann Collection—The Metropolitan Museum of Art, Purchase, Winfield Foundation Gift, 1967, The Helena Woolworth McCann Collection; The Metropolitan Museum of Art, Gift of the Winfield Foundation, 1951. 98: Ellis Herwig, courtesy Childs Gallery. 99: Mark Sexton, courtesy Peabody Museum of Salem. 100, 101: Rijksmuseum, Amsterdam. 103: Derek Bayes, courtesy National Maritime Museum, London. 105: Photo Bibliothèque Nationale, Paris; C.F.L.-Giraudon, courtesy Musée National des Châteaux de Versailles et de Trianon. 106, 107: Larry Burrows, courtesy India Office Library, London—Larry Burrows, courtesy National Army Museum, London. 108: BBC Hulton Picture Library, London. 109: By permission of the British Library, London (Add.Ms.19820.f.2.). 111: National Maritime Museum, London. 112-119: Drawings by Richard Schlecht. 120, 121: National Maritime Museum, London. 125-127: Drawings by John Batchelor. 129: Derek Bayes, courtesy National Maritime Museum, London. 131: Henry Groskinsky, courtesy Spencer Collection, The New York Public Library, Astor, Lenox and Tilden Foundations—Derek Bayes, courtesy National Maritime Museum, London. 132, 133: Henry Groskinsky, courtesy Spencer Collection, The New York Public Library, Astor, Lenox and Tilden Foundations. 137: Derek Bayes, courtesy of Captain A. Coxon, R.N. (Ret.). 138, 139: National Maritime Museum, London. 140: Dmitri Kessel, courtesy Commissaire Général Pierre Jullien, Paris—Dmitri Kessel, courtesy Musée de Saint-Malo. 142: Dmitri Kessel, courtesy Musée de Saint-Malo. 145: Derek Bayes, courtesy National Maritime Museum, London. 146, 147: Parker Gallery, London. 149: At the National Maritime Museum, London. 152: National Portrait Gallery, London. 155: National Maritime Museum, London. 156, 157: Derek Bayes, courtesy National Maritime Museum, London. 159: National Portrait Gallery, London—Derek Bayes, courtesy National Maritime Museum, London. 161: Derek Bayes, National Maritime Museum, London. 163-166: Library of Congress. 168, 169: National Maritime Museum, London. 171: Derek Bayes, courtesy Private Collection, London.

Index

Printed in Spain by Novograph, S.A., Madrid. Depósito Legal: M-32191-XXVIII